IMMIGRANTS ON THE LAND

Thomas H. Holloway

IMMIGRANTS ON THE LAND

Coffee and Society in São Paulo,

1886–1934

The University of North Carolina Press *Chapel Hill*

The Hull Memorial Publication Fund of Cornell
University provided a subvention to aid in the
publication of this work.

Library of Congress Cataloging in Publication Data

Holloway, Thomas H 1944–
  Immigrants on the land.

  Bibliography: p.
  Includes index.
  1. São Paulo, Brazil (State)—Emigration and
immigration. 2. Land settlement—Brazil—São
Paulo (State)—History. 3. Coffee trade—Brazil—
São Paulo (State)—History. I. Title.
JV7462.H64   301.32'9'816   79-24805
ISBN 0-8078-1430-X

for Judy

CONTENTS

ILLUSTRATIONS

(Photographs courtesy of the Secretaria de Agricultura de São Paulo, Instituto Agronômico do Estado, Campinas)

TABLES

FIGURES

PREFACE

Ten years ago when I began research on the Brazilian coffee economy and the price support scheme of 1906, I soon realized that much remained to be learned about the rural labor system that replaced slavery in São Paulo in the late 1880s. By the early twentieth century the planters considered that system something of a burden. One of the arguments officials advanced in advocating an abandonment of laissez faire in coffee marketing was that the immigrant laborers' preference for work in newly planted groves had induced planters to expand the area under cultivation, despite the relative depression in the world coffee market. The resulting overproduction, culminating with the bumper crop of 1906, led to large scale government intervention in the coffee market for the first time. Was it possible that ex-slavocrats and their children yielded to pressure from plantation laborers? I began the present study as an exploration of that question and others related to the post-slavery labor system as it developed in western São Paulo, the dynamic center of the world coffee industry of the time.

The broad outlines of immigration to southern Brazil in the late nineteenth and early twentieth centuries were available in the work of T. Lynn Smith, Preston James, and other scholars; the importance of coffee in the emergence of São Paulo's regional economy was clear from the work of Richard Graham, Florestan Fernandes, and Fernando Henrique Cardoso. The preponderance of immigrants in the urban labor force was evident from the growing number of studies of the urban working class. Warren Dean had examined the emergence of an immigrant bourgeoisie and its amalgamation with the native elite during the process of industrialization. But what of the coffee zone during the period of mass immigration? From the abolition of slavery in 1888 to the early 1930s coffee production in São Paulo grew tremendously, and during that period most coffee workers were first generation immigrants. Yet who these people were, why they came or were brought, how they found their way hundreds of kilometers into the coffee zone, what became of them there, and what effect they had on the agrarian society they entered—all of these questions had been treated only as fragmentary parts of studies focusing on other issues.

Some of the best of these treatments are the work of French writers, notably Pierre Denis and Amour Laliére in the first decade of the twentieth century,

and Pierre Monbeig and Pierre Deffontaines among the geographers who did
research in Brazil during the 1930s and 1940s. Of the studies by Italians,
the most complete is that by Vincenzo Grossi, but like the accounts of Denis
and Lalíere it dates from early in the period of mass immigration. The problem of periodization is also apparent in Michael Hall's pathbreaking dissertation research, completed as the present study was beginning. Hall brought
to light much information from the reports of Italian consuls, but he ended
his account in 1914, a terminal date that did not allow him to trace career
patterns of the many immigrants who entered from the late 1880s to the beginning of World War I. While the present project was in progress there
appeared Warren Dean's study of Rio Claro, a single county in western São
Paulo. His time period of 1820–1920 roughly parallels Stanley Stein's work
on the Paraiba valley, but it also puts the era of immigrant labor and frontier
expansion in the shadow of the slave system. In many ways slavery was a
prelude to the period studied in this book, and in western São Paulo 1920 was
near the midpoint of an era better bracketed by the decline of slavery on one
end and the Great Depression on the other. Furthermore, the view in the following pages is through a wide-angle rather than a close-up lens, for the
socioeconomic system of coffee and immigrant labor was regional rather
than local.

When I began research in Brazil I searched initially for quantitative sources
and considered their interpretive possibilities. I learned to appreciate the
pioneering use of historical statistics of São Paulo by Sérgio Milliet, José
Francisco de Camargo, and Samuel H. Lowrie. I discovered that, among
many other things, the Paulistas knew how many immigrants of each type
entered the port of Santos, and how many went to which counties in the coffee
zone. They also had a reasonably good idea of how many coffee trees were
in each county, and of the average productivity of the groves. These and other
statistical and descriptive sources on which this study is based attest to the
importance the Paulista elite attached to the coffee industry and immigrant
labor. The documentation is rich and varied, unequalled in other states or
at the national level during the Brazilian old republic. The preponderance of
official or semiofficial sources in this study is one result, and I have tried
to complement, diversify, and fill in the record by using information from
planters and their organizations, the press, travelers' accounts, and the
invaluable first-hand reports of the Italian consular service.

Early in my search for quantitative data I discovered that many first generation immigrants became the owner-operators of small and medium-sized
farms. Like the original suggestion that planters yielded to pressure from the
workers, this new finding seemed incompatible with standard assumptions
about exploitative labor systems in plantation societies and monopolistic
control of land resources in the hands of the native elite. I found the latter

assumption false in respect to this historical time and place, for there was more good land in the São Paulo plateau than anyone at the time knew what to do with. With an immigrant labor supply streaming into the port of Santos, moreover, the planters had little incentive to force native peasants off subsistence plots and into the coffee groves. I also found that the rural labor system under which immigrants worked was too varied and complex to yield to facile generalizations. There was misery, isolation, and exploitation, but there were also opportunities in the expanding and diversifying frontier economy. For the immigrant who managed to put together a nest egg, there were few barriers to upward mobility through the acquisition of land. Eventually I sampled several notarial archives of land transfer records to confirm the link between the possibility of some immigrant plantation workers accumulating savings and the subsequent emergence of a sizable proportion of immigrant farmers in the coffee zone.

Partly because of the nature of the historical record, this study has become both more and less than a history of immigrant labor in rural São Paulo. It is more in the sense that the book sets the development of the socioeconomic complex of which the immigrants were a part, and which they changed by their actions, in the broader context of the growth of the world economy. It is less in the sense that the perspective of the immigrants themselves rarely emerges. Their view is nearly always filtered, probably with some distortion, through an intermediary who interprets their comments and presumes to speak for them. Often the workers' attitudes and perceptions must be inferred from their actions, both individual and collective, which left traces in the records now available. Perhaps in the future, diaries, letters, and similar sources may come to light and give voice to the immigrants on the land. If that happens, I could ask for no better than that this book should stand as background and context.

This book could not have been written without the support of several institutions, the guidance and advice of many individuals, and the assistance of those who preserve the sources of historical research.

For financial support I am grateful to the Foreign Area Fellowship Program of the Social Science Research Council, the Brazilian Fulbright Commission, the University of Wisconsin, and at Cornell the Latin American Studies Program, the Department of History, and the College of Arts and Sciences.

Scholars who have helped along the way include José Francisco de Camargo, Edgard Carone, Peter Eisenberg, Peter Fry, Douglas Graham, Sérgio Buarque de Hollanda Filho, Joseph Kahl, Catherine LeGrand, Darrell Levi, Joseph Love, Barbara Lynch, Verena Martínez-Alier, Odilon Nogueira de Matos, Robert Mattoon, Carlos Guilherme Mota, Fernando Novais, Paulo Sérgio Pinheiro, Thomas Skidmore, Robert Slenes, and Peter Smith. Friends who have taught me more about Brazil than they are probably aware are Plínio and Marietta Sampaio, Fernando and Nilce Bueno, and Luis and Lenira Cerri.

Dona Luisa Herrmann and the library staff of the Instituto Agronômico in Campinas greatly facilitated my research in official records, reports, periodicals, and photographic collections. Dona Maria Luisa Pinto de Moura kindly gave me access to the library of the Centro de Ciências, Artes e Letras in Campinas. I also thank the library staffs of the Universidade Católica de Campinas, the Escola Superior de Agricultura "Luiz de Queiroz" in Piracicaba, the São Paulo State Archive, Biblioteca Municipal de São Paulo, Faculdade de Direito de São Paulo, Museu Paulista, Museu do Café in Ribeirão Preto, the University of Wisconsin, and Cornell University.

For the use of the photographs in this volume, all dating from about 1905, I wish to thank the Secretaria de Agricultura de São Paulo, Instituto Agronômico do Estado, Campinas.

I owe special thanks to the notaries of land transfer registry offices who took time from their busy schedules to hear my request, explain the organization of the invaluable records over which they preside, and make a place for me to work. They include Elvino Silva Filho in Campinas, João Foz Júnior in Ribeirão Preto, Clovis Vassimon in Sertãozinho, José Luiz Paul in Taquaritinga, and Osório Morato Filho in Rio Claro.

Leslie Wilson and Eric Clay were able research assistants, and Sally Kramer and Susan Greenberg were especially helpful in the final stages of editing and typing.

The contributions of these people and institutions were essential. I alone am responsible.

Ithaca, August 1979   Thomas H. Holloway

IMMIGRANTS ON THE LAND

1

SÃO PAULO IN
THE WORLD ECONOMY

The history of Brazil was profoundly altered during the late nineteenth century because a broad mass of the population in the United States and Europe
took up coffee drinking. From the 1880s to the onset of the Great Depression,
many people born outside Brazil changed their lives as they responded to
the demand for workers in the coffee fields of São Paulo. The conjuncture
of rising coffee consumption in northern Europe and North America, increased coffee production in Brazil, and the flow of working people from
southern Europe to São Paulo should be seen over the long term and in the
broadest perspective as a case of expansion on the periphery of the modern
world economy. Important themes of the story told in this book are the international coffee trade and the pattern of coffee production in southern Brazil,
the entrepreneurial and administrative activity of the native elite there, and
the actions of the foreign workers who migrated to rural São Paulo. These are
essential elements, but the underlying dynamic is in the system of capitalism
itself, a system that emerged in the four centuries before this story begins.
As both historical and thematic context for understanding the history of mass
immigration to the São Paulo coffee zone, it is useful to explore briefly
the legacy of Brazil's inclusion into the world economy.

Since it began to develop in its modern form with the expansion of Europe
in the sixteenth century, the world economy has been characterized by a
diversity of functions among the regions of the globe. The role of Latin
America in the division of labor was to supply raw materials—gold and silver
specie, other minerals, and agricultural products. Several related reasons—
involving land, labor, and political structures—explain why Latin America
came to serve this function. Underlying all of these is the immense and
varied natural endowment of the region.[1]

The Iberian conquests of the sixteenth century brought quantitative and
qualitative changes in the resources at Europe's disposal. Huge silver de-
posits, the exploitation of which became the reason for the Spanish colonial system, obviously broadened the resource base for Europe, for silver
was silver whether it originated in the Tyrol or in Peru. The expansion of
European control to tropical zones, for the first time on such a large scale,
brought a qualitative change in the resources. The lowlands of Latin America

had conditions of temperature, rainfall, and soil types that made possible the diversification of production and consumption patterns beyond the ecological limitations of Europe itself.

Except for a period in the eighteenth century when it was a major supplier of gold and diamonds, Brazil has been a source of tropical products that Europe could not obtain internally. Dyewood, cane sugar, cotton, rubber, cocoa, and coffee are the most important examples. The successive periods in which each of these products rose to prominence are the chronological units of Brazil's economic history. During the nineteenth century, Europe and North America entered a phase of technologically advanced industrialization in growing urban centers, accompanied by expansion of the middle-income groups and an eventual rise in the living standards of working people. These developments made possible a broadening of mass consumption patterns that led to an increased demand for coffee, a product previously consumed by the wealthy and cosmopolitan few. Southeastern Brazil, particularly the interior plateau of São Paulo, had conditions of topography, temperature, rainfall, and soils ideal for coffee cultivation. That natural endowment underlies the socioeconomic history of rural São Paulo.

Natural resources exist only as potential until people want to use them. The mountain of silver at Potosí lay for eons until Spaniards induced or coerced the native population to dig and carry the ore that contributed to the rise of modern capitalism. The Portuguese saw economic possibilities in the tropical soil of Brazil, but the barrier to its use was a shortage of manpower. Soon after the conquest, the already sparse native population of the lowlands was decimated by warfare, European diseases, and forced labor. The vast hinterland of the continent became the refuge of the surviving natives who fled from involuntary induction into the labor pool.

The solution was chattel slavery, the forced transfer of Africans to work the soil of the New World. Although modern slavery was first and always an economic institution, the political apparatus to maintain it and the social structure built on the master-slave dichotomy infused the history of Brazil.[2] In the nineteenth-century prelude to the expansion of coffee in western São Paulo, this institution was on the decline and was eventually abolished, but centuries of slavery had conditioned the attitudes toward work and working people that the Brazilian elite carried over into the new era. The subsequent importation of laborers from southern Europe and later other areas was motivated by the same goal as that of the sixteenth-century slaver: overcoming the shortage of manpower, so that the natural resources of tropical America could be used to respond to demand at the center of the world economy.[3]

The political structures of the Europe-centered economic system also affected Latin America's role and left a legacy for the São Paulo coffee boom. By the time Iberian control of Latin America was consolidated in the late sixteenth century, Spain and Portugal were already relegated to semi-peripheral status. As they became dependent on northern Europe for markets for their tropical products and for supplies of industrial goods, their continuing participation in the system depended on extraction of surplus from their colonies. Thus Spain and Portugal provided administrative and commercial services, to the ultimate benefit of the northern European nations involved and at the expense of their own autonomous development. They were left poor because they were rich, to paraphrase a perceptive contemporary analyst.[4] Despite their secondary position, the Iberian nations had a desperate stake in the stability of the system as it evolved. While they were able, then, Spain and Portugal used their political control of Latin America to perpetuate the region's peripheral role as supplier of primary products.

Over several centuries these political and economic forces forged the social structure Brazil was left with when Portuguese control was finally broken in the early nineteenth century. By that time a local, native-born elite had emerged that also owed its existence to the stability of the world economy and Brazil's peripheral role in it. The Brazilian elite took over direction of the new nation with the same goals as those of the Portuguese before. The increasingly superfluous Iberian middleman was eliminated, and ties of dependence between northern Europe and Brazil were made direct and explicit.[5] At the time political independence brought a redefinition of Brazil's position, the traditional export-oriented agricultural sector—and therefore the new nation's entire economy—was stagnating. In the ensuing decades coffee emerged as a new possibility. From the mid-nineteenth century onward coffee thus gave the native elite, heirs of the colonial regime, a new lease on their privileged position at the periphery of the world economy.

Coffee's profitability gave slavery a further lease on life, but it was a form of labor that could not survive mounting pressure from the core of the system, from Brazilian abolitionists, and from the slaves themselves through passive and active resistance to bondage.[6] The abolition of slavery in 1888 did not signal the end of Brazil's coffee industry. On the contrary, coffee production in São Paulo grew tremendously after abolition. That fact illustrates the Brazilian elite's adaptability and capacity for self-preservation. The new solution the Paulista coffee planters found to this recurrence of the manpower problem was to tap the surplus labor force of southern Europe, particularly Italy, but also Portugal and Spain.[7]

Thus the rising demand for coffee in Europe and North America, the possibility of increased production in Brazil, and mass migration from southern Europe to the coffee plantations converged in the 1880s to form a historical complex in rural São Paulo that lasted until the crisis of the 1930s shook its foundation. That complex—its components, workings, and broader effects—is the subject of this book. I will return to the general implications in the concluding chapter, but several more immediate aspects of São Paulo's ties to the world economy should be considered in this introduction. These include improvements in transport technology and the evolution of the all-important world coffee market.

Steamships and railroads—related technological advances of the nineteenth century—facilitated coffee expansion. Both originated in Europe and served its purposes along with those of the dependent elites in the periphery. The introduction, improvement, and proliferation of the transatlantic steam cargo vessel were stages in the continued technological and commercial hegemony of the North Atlantic axis—an absolute superiority in the oceans of the world achieved in the sixteenth century and never lost. Shipping was the life line, the umbilical cord, that made participation in the world economy possible for São Paulo. The ships took coffee to the indispensable markets, and they brought in workers from the southern European sources.

The land-based complement to transatlantic shipping was the railroad, tying the hinterland to the coast. The rails eventually pushed at the western frontier of settlement and made exploitation of the rich soils of the interior plateau economically feasible. One could hardly find a more graphic physical representation of São Paulo's ties to the world economy than its rail network, developed between 1867 and the 1880s. The 139 kilometers running from the port of Santos up the coastal escarpment, through the capital city and misty hills to the edge of the coffee-producing area, were built by British engineers, financed and controlled by British capitalists. Brazilians nicknamed this short and immensely profitable line *a Ingleza*, "the English one." Like the narrow end of a funnel it collected the coffee produced in the vast area spreading from its western terminus. The three major and many smaller railroads that fed into the English line comprised some two thousand kilometers of track by 1890. They were organized and financed by the Paulista coffee planters and their allies in local commerce and government, with British technology, British rails, and British rolling stock.[8]

The international coffee market was the context for São Paulo's participation in the world economy. The organization of the productive unit, the aggregate volume of production, and the changes in the price of coffee were important links in the system that developed piecemeal after the coffee plant was introduced into northern Brazil in the 1720s. In the ensuing century its cultivation spread south through the populated coastal regions as far as São Paulo, where the frost line stopped it at the Tropic of Capricorn. By the late 1830s coffee surpassed sugar as Brazil's most important single export crop.[9] During the first phase of coffee's dominance, roughly from 1830 to the 1870s, production was centered in the valley of the Paraiba River to the north and west of Rio de Janeiro, extending southwest into the province of São Paulo.[10] Secondary centers developed in the province of Espirito Santo and southern Minas Gerais, but those areas did not become as important as the Paraiba valley.

During this early period the economic and social matrix grew from rudimentary beginnings, borrowing from the organization of the sugar industry before. The basic unit of production was the plantation—the self-contained enclave, appendage of the European economy in tropical America. In its original conception in the sugar areas of northeastern Brazil, the plantation was a frontier institution, carved out of territory from which the New World natives had only recently been eliminated. In its later evolution, extending through the period of coffee expansion under slavery and on into the free labor era, the plantation retained this function as a mechanism for absorbing new areas. Unlike the semiisolated hacienda of highland Spanish America, the Brazilian fazenda had no purpose other than export-oriented agriculture. From the beginning it was a capitalistic enterprise, in the sense that its reason for existence was production for the market, at a profit. As such, it brought together factors of production in a way ideally suited for the purposes of the original European colonists and their eventual heirs among the Brazilian elite.[11]

Coffee got its start in the western plateau of São Paulo concurrently with its development in the Paraiba valley. By the 1840s and increasingly in the 1850s, local farmers and newcomers from neighboring Minas Gerais began to open plantations and ship coffee by mule train to the port of Santos. By the 1880s railroads had revolutionized transport and greatly expanded the area within easy access of the coast. Western São Paulo, previously a wild frontier area traversed by explorers, sparsely populated by native Indians and Brazilian farmers who produced foodstuffs, livestock, and some sugar, became the dynamic center of Brazil's coffee industry.[12] In sheer magnitude, the Paraiba valley era pales in comparison with developments in western São Paulo in succeeding decades.

While the São Paulo plateau grew in importance, the limited lands along the Paraiba River were becoming less productive as the trees there aged and the soil was increasingly exhausted. In 1850–54 annual coffee receipts in Rio de Janeiro averaged about two million bags, and by 1875–79 that figure had reached about three million bags. As illustrated in figure 1, the latter average was maintained through the 1930s. Rio would have declined as an export center had it not been for the development of new coffee areas in that part of Minas Gerais exporting through the Brazilian capital. As the total production in the region exporting through Rio de Janeiro stagnated, so did the production in other coffee areas of the world. Figure 1 shows that the total coffee exports of all countries outside Brazil fluctuated between about three and five million bags from 1880 to World War I.

By 1890 Santos was equal to Rio in the amount of coffee received from

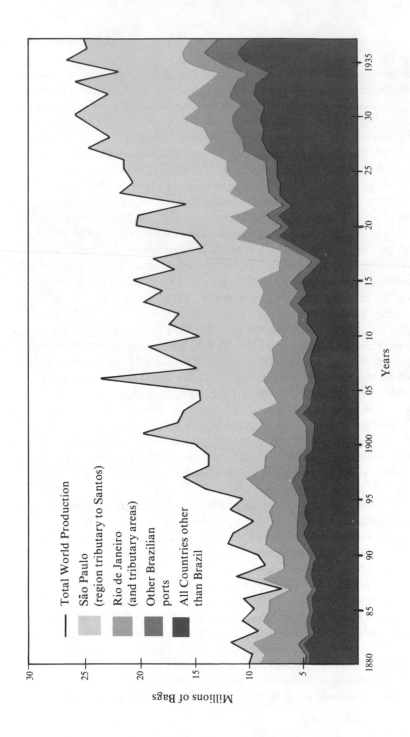

1. *World Coffee Production by Geographical Area, 1880–1937*

Total World Production

São Paulo
(region tributary to Santos)

Rio de Janeiro
(and tributary areas)

Other Brazilian
ports

All Countries other
than Brazil

Millions of Bags

Years

Loading coffee, Santos docks

the interior, and since 1894 Santos has been the single most important coffee
export center. The annual average of world coffee production shot up from
9.3 million bags in 1885–89 to 18 million bags in 1905–9. As can be seen
in figure 1, that increase took place entirely in the region exporting through
Santos. In percentage shares, the preponderance of Brazil and São Paulo is
equally impressive. For more than fifty years prior to 1935 Brazil consistently supplied more than half the world's coffee, and from the turn of the
century through World War I Brazil's share hovered around 75 percent.
The region exporting through Santos—that is, the interior plateau of São
Paulo alone—contributed an average of more than 50 percent of all the
world's coffee from 1900 to 1918. Although its proportional share of the
market subsequently fell as the production of circum-Caribbean nations
increased after World War I, São Paulo's absolute levels of production
remained high.

The period from the 1880s to the 1930s, then, was the time when western São Paulo predominated among the coffee-producing areas of the world, a period historically as well as geographically distinct from the earlier Paraiba valley era and separated from later developments by the hiatus of the Great Depression. During that time the factor that determined the general health of the coffee industry was the movement of prices in the world market. Coffee price levels had a direct and profound effect on most aspects of economic activity in São Paulo and an indirect but no less profound effect on the social and political development of the state. Figure 2 traces the movement of coffee prices from 1885 to 1933.

The milreis price shown in figure 2 is the yearly average for Santos grade seven or "good average," the standard by which the prices of other grades were fixed in this period. The equivalent price in current U.S. dollars is given to compensate for changes in the value of Brazilian currency in the international exchange market. The dollar price is thus an approximate indication of the gold or "hard currency" value of São Paulo coffee.

Prices rose rapidly after 1885, remaining at high levels until 1896. This was the boom era, with high profits and rates of expansion not equaled before or since. By 1898 Brazilian production had roughly doubled from the mid-1880s, and prices had fallen to about one-third the average of the early 1890s. This relative depression lasted more than a decade, as increases in Brazilian production brought a glut on the market. The brief upswing of 1910–12 resulted from the manipulations of coffee speculators in the European and North American wholesale markets, which were cut short by World War I.[13] The return of high levels of demand after the war coincided with a supply shortage resulting from a severe frost in 1918, bringing another price rise that continued erratically into the prosperous 1920s. But after compensating for the concurrent devaluation of the milreis, average prices in the 1920s only reached the levels of the early 1890s, and the planters' costs had risen considerably since the earlier boom. Finally, the onset of the Great Depression brought prices to the lowest levels in more than half a century.

The people who controlled São Paulo, as well as many of the people under control there, were very sensitive to the ups and downs illustrated in figure 2. The line shown, moreover, ignores the jagged details of monthly, weekly, and daily fluctuations carefully reported in newspapers of the period. More than stock market quotations in modern North America, coffee prices were *the* indicator of economic conditions. A slogan originating in the slave era and still heard among planters in the 1920s was *o café dá para tudo*, "coffee provides for everything." To appreciate such a statement is to understand the role of that superfluous brown beverage in the history of São Paulo and Brazil.

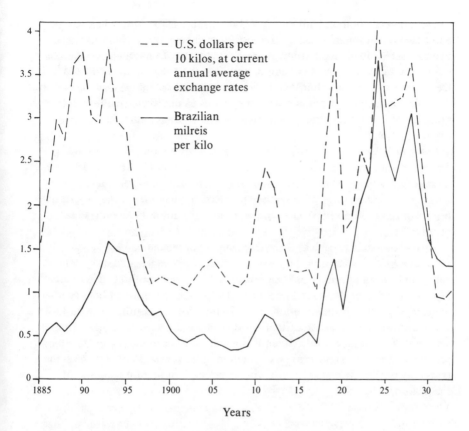

2. *Average Coffee Prices in Santos and U.S. Dollar Equivalents, 1885–1933*

Expansion of plantation agriculture based on immigrant labor calls to mind several themes in social history less sweeping than the growth of the world economy, but no less pertinent for understanding the absorption of São Paulo into that larger system.

One such theme is frontier expansion, the creation of a new society from old parts of disparate origins. There have been many cases of frontier expansion in modern history that involved increasing the resources available to the European economy, often at the expense of the previous occupants of the territory. But frontiers have been studied with other, more specific questions in mind. Some historians of the United States are still haunted by the ghost of Frederick Jackson Turner, rattling out revised hypotheses about safety valves for labor and the democratizing effects of free land.[14] For students of society concerned with such questions, the spread of coffee into western São Paulo provides a case for comparison.

One point of contrast with the stereotypes of the United States experience has already been hinted at: the institutional basis for frontier expansion in São Paulo was the plantation. Another subtheme of this book, then, is the coffee plantation as a socioeconomic unit. The way labor was organized in the plantation complex after the abolition of slavery defies easy labels, facile analysis, and quick comparison with systems of plantation agriculture in other places at other times. It must be understood on its own terms, in its specific historical context.

Entry into that plantation system was the lot of hundreds of thousands of families from outside Brazil. A third subtheme is the immigration and assimilation of those people into the rural environment. It will involve a discussion of the goals and policies of the native planters, a quantitative and descriptive profile of those working people who went to São Paulo, and a consideration of their fate.

Roughly speaking, each of these three subthemes is the subject of a chapter. Frontier expansion, immigration and assimilation, plantation labor systems—each can be seen as a unit and examined by itself, but the three also overlap as empirical and analytical components of the complex agrarian history of western São Paulo from abolition to the Depression. A familiarity with those components will help us understand the evolution of the more general agrarian structure during that period, which is the subject of two later chapters. In the conclusion I will return to an evaluation of this case of expansion on the periphery of the modern capitalist world system, and its implications for the history of Brazil.

2

THE COFFEE FRONTIER

The history of human activity in rural areas has a geographical basis. Climate, soil types, topographical features, distances, transport routes—all influence the chronology and pattern of settlement in frontier areas as well as the evolution of rural society in older zones. Because coffee is a demanding and delicate plant, natural factors have been especially important in the history of its production. Natural conditions in São Paulo and the technical requirements of coffee helped determine the way the plantation work force was organized, as well as overall levels of labor demand. Therefore, an understanding of the relationship between the rural development of São Paulo and the influx of immigrants requires some familiarity with the historical geography of the area. In order to understand why immigrants were brought in and what they did after arriving in São Paulo, it is important to know about the natural and technical determinants of rural labor market conditions.

The abundance of land and continued availability of virgin land on the western frontier was a fundamental element in São Paulo's agrarian history. I will qualify and elaborate on that statement in various ways in the following pages, beginning with a scheme of regional division. Such a breakdown provides reference points for discussing the complexity and diversity of the natural environment. It has long been common to divide São Paulo into distinct regions. The state is roughly equivalent in total area to Italy, half the size of France. Some coffee areas were already in decline by the start of the free labor era. Other large areas were never planted in coffee, and others were inaccessible until the advent of the railroads. Statewide generalizations can thus be misleading.

The most universally recognized division has been between the Paraiba valley, or "north" of the state, and the interior plateau, the "west." If the coastline ran north to south, such nomenclature would conform to true compass points. The São Paulo coast actually runs from northeast to southwest, however, and so the plateau that extends at a right angle to the coastline lies in reality more north than west from the capital city. It forms a hydrographic basin beginning at the coastal escarpment, at an altitude of about eight hundred meters, gently sloping toward the Rio Grande on the north and the Paraná River on the west, infrequently broken by bluffs and hills, to an altitude of about three hundred meters. The plateau is the economic hinterland of the city of São Paulo, and its coffee exports have always been funneled through the port of Santos. The area extending south and west from the capital city, comprising less than one-fourth of São Paulo's total area, has generally been ignored in informal regionalization schemes. Coffee does not grow well there, and the area remains relatively undeveloped to the present day.

In such a general division the regions are neither specific nor discrete. In order to make quantitative data on the socioeconomic history of São Paulo usable, a more formal scheme is required. Several general criteria were considered in determining the regional breakdown used throughout this book. First, regions should reflect the historical development of the state. Also, the divisions must be defined consistently over time, to permit the comparison of various types of data and to follow chronological change. The regions should be small enough to retain some degree of cohesion and differentiation from other regions. Separation into many small units, on the other hand, would render the plan confusing to all but specialists. More specific considerations were the development of the railroad network, predominant physical features and economic activities, and the patterns of institutional expansion into the frontier.

The establishment of municipio units—roughly analogous to counties in the United States—was the basic instrument of governmental penetration into the hinterland. At any given period in São Paulo's history up to the 1930s, towns known as the *bocas do sertão*, literally "mouths of the backlands," occupied the pioneer fringe of permanent settlement, functioning as staging areas for expeditions beyond the frontier. In the initial stages of occupation such border villages fell under the administrative jurisdiction of the nearest municipio center, located in the direction of the state capital. The territory of the older municipio included the smaller frontier settlement and all the territory beyond the pioneer fringe as well, often extending to the major rivers that form the northern and western boundaries of the state. As the frontier town grew in importance, it and the territory beyond would be *desmembrado*, "dismembered," from the older municipio. Often by that time another *boca do sertão* had already grown up on the new pioneer fringe. A few years or decades later the process would be repeated further west. Behind the frontier, as the population grew and the economy diversified, outlying towns would be set up as municipios separate from their older parent.

The pattern of institutional expansion along the frontier might be conceived of as the total growth of a political organism through the absorption of new territory—the addition of de facto to what had previously been only de jure control. The subdivision of older municipios is similarly analogous to increased internal complexity through cell division. By these two related processes the number of municipios in São Paulo grew from 46 in 1850 to

121 in 1886, to 206 by 1920 and 261 in 1934.[1] Within the time span of this study, 1886–1934, the number of municipios more than doubled. Of the 140 new units created in that period, 118 were in the western plateau. Such a statement is possible only in the context of a regionalization that defines the western plateau in terms of specific municipios. Keeping in mind that the regions discussed below are made up of discrete territorial units, we may turn to the division of São Paulo into historical zones.

Map 1 shows the outline of the zones used here; the most important towns, mountains, rivers, and railroads of São Paulo are shown in map 2. Zone 1, the Capital zone, consists of the city of São Paulo and its immediate environs. During the period covered in this study the city of São Paulo was the undisputed center of financial, commercial, and industrial activity of the state, as well as the political and administrative capital. Since its founding in the mid-sixteenth century it has been the center of land transport routes, and it became the crossroads of the state's railway network after the 1860s. The city was the initial destination of the mass of immigrants who entered the state from the 1880s onward and the distribution center for the labor force into the coffee zones of the west. As late as 1874 the municipio of the capital was second to Campinas in total population, 26,040 to 31,397. But by 1886 the capital had grown to 47,697, versus Campinas's 41,253. The population of the capital continued to grow much faster than any other city in the state, reaching just over one million inhabitants by 1934.[2]

The other municipios of zone 1 contain settlements dating from the colonial era that have been economically dependent on the capital. This zone is not well adapted to large-scale commercial agriculture, and coffee does poorly in the inferior soils and damp climate. Through the period of this study, small farms that supplied the growing needs of the city for truck, poultry, and dairy products predominated in the rural municipios around the capital. Increasingly since the 1920s the industrial installations of the capital have spread into the surrounding area. Zone 1 contained five municipios in 1886, grew to seven in 1920, and in 1934 still had seven. It now comprises most of the urban-industrial complex of greater São Paulo.

Zone 2, lying northeast of the capital, includes the Paraiba River valley, the hills of the coastal escarpment, and the coastline northeast of Santos. The first permanent settlements—a series of way stations on the trail from Rio de Janeiro to São Paulo—date from the seventeenth century; during the eighteenth century these towns became centers of gold transport from the interior of Minas Gerais. As agricultural development intensified in the nineteenth century, mule trains transported the valley's coffee harvest over the coastal hills to secondary ports, from where it was shipped to Rio de Janeiro for export. By the 1870s the construction of the railroad up into the Paraiba valley from Rio made direct shipment to the national capital feasible, and the towns

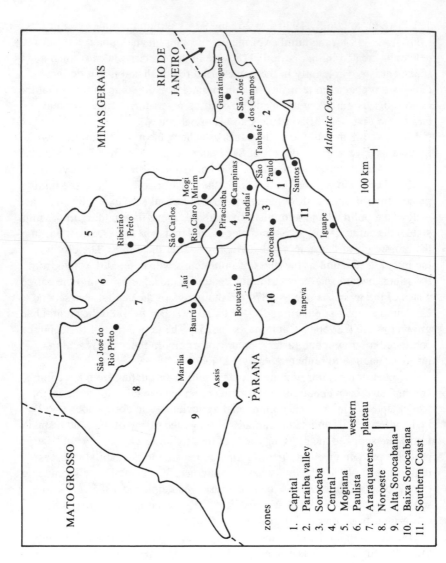

MATO GROSSO

MINAS GERAIS

RIO DE JANEIRO

Atlantic Ocean

100 km

Guaratinguetá
São José
dos Campos
Taubaté   2

Mogi
Mirim
Ribeirão
Prêto   5
São Carlos
Rio Claro
Piracicaba
Campinas
Jundiaí   4
São
Paulo   1
Santos

6

7

Jaú   Sorocaba   3

Botucatú   10

Baurú   Itapeva

São José do
Rio Prêto

Marília   8

Assis   9

PARANA

Iguape   11

zones
1. Capital
2. Paraiba valley
3. Sorocaba
4. Central ⎤
5. Mogiana ⎥ western
6. Paulista ⎥ plateau
7. Araraquarense ⎦
8. Noroeste
9. Alta Sorocabana
10. Baixa Sorocabana
11. Southern Coast

1. São Paulo: Regional Divisions

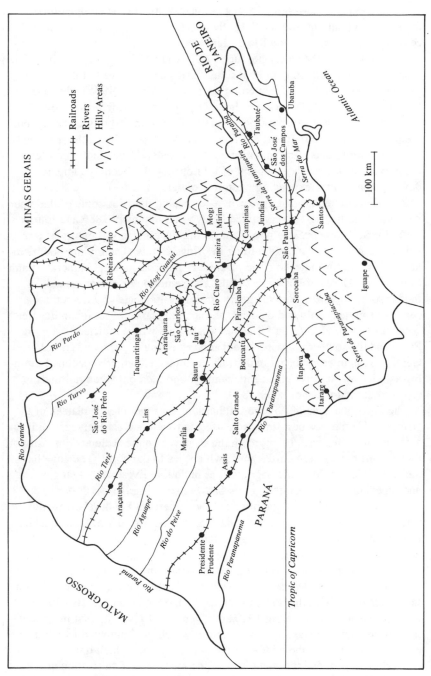

2. São Paulo: Physical Features, Major Towns, and Railroad Network, Circa 1930

along São Paulo's coast fell into stagnation. Even after the completion of the Rio–São Paulo railway in 1877, the production of the Paraiba valley continued to be exported via Rio de Janeiro.

In 1886 the Paraiba valley produced 21 percent of São Paulo's coffee, but it subsequently declined both in absolute terms and relative to the western plateau. It produced only 5 percent of the state's coffee in 1905 and had fallen to 2 percent by 1932. There were already thirty-three municipios in zone 2 in 1886, rising to thirty-seven by 1920 and just thirty-nine by 1934. Throughout the period of this study it was an economically depressed area that received very few immigrants. As a stagnant zone previously dependent on coffee, the Paraiba valley provides a point of reference with which to compare developments in the expanding western frontier.

Zone 3, centered around the town of Sorocaba, contains some of the older settlements in the state. It contained twelve municipios in 1886 and fourteen by 1934. Sorocaba became important during the eighteenth century as a result of the gold and diamond mining in Minas Gerais. The mining boom created a demand for mules to drive machinery and transport the mineral wealth to the coast. Herds of horses and mules ran semiwild on the grasslands of the far south of Brazil. Sorocaba was strategically located between these centers of mule supply and demand, and an abundance of forage in the area made it the natural location for annual trade fairs where muleteers from São Paulo and the southern provinces sold and traded mules to buyers from Minas Gerais.[3] This interprovincial mule traffic diminished with the decline in mining activity by the early nineteenth century, and died out when railroads replaced animal transport after 1870.

The Sorocaba zone lies on the southern edge of the interior plateau of the state, outside the area best suited to coffee cultivation. Relatively insignificant amounts of coffee have been grown there, never on the scale and intensity of the heart of the western coffee zone, which lies to the north. The zone has had a tradition of diversified agriculture, including livestock, sugar cane, and especially cotton. Cotton got its first boost during the Civil War in the United States, as the short supply from the American South raised world prices enough to make cotton a paying crop.[4] After World War I technical improvements combined with increased demand again brought a minor cotton boom in the Sorocaba zone. The soil and climate are well suited to cotton cultivation, and cotton continues to be important in the area.

Zone 4, the Central zone, was first settled in the late colonial period, contemporaneously with the Sorocaba area. By 1886 it contained sixteen municipios, rising to nineteen in 1920 and twenty in 1934. The first important agricultural activity was sugar production, which predominated from the late eighteenth century to the middle of the nineteenth, by which time coffee cultivation had spread through much of the area.[5] Sugar cultivation never died out completely, especially around Piracicaba in the western part of this zone, and today sugar is one of several crops that make up the diversified agricultural production of this part of the state. From the first years of permanent settlement Campinas has been the most important city of zone 4, lying in the center of a rich agricultural area and on natural land transport routes. During the period here under study, Campinas—where two of the major rail systems from the coffee zone, the Paulista and the Mogiana, converged— was second only to the state capital as a major transportation center. Sections of the Santos-Jundiai and Sorocabana networks and several smaller feeder lines completed the well-developed transport system of the Central zone.

In the chronological order of the advance of coffee cultivation, the Central zone came second after the Paraiba valley. Toward the middle of the nineteenth century new settlers, many from the previously developed areas of neighboring Minas Gerais, brought coffee from the upper Paraiba valley over the hills of the Mantiqueira range into the area around Campinas. In those early years transportation was one of the serious problems the coffee growers faced. Mule trains took three weeks to a month to get from Campinas through the Mantiqueira hills to São Paulo and then down the escarpment to Santos. It was a slow and expensive system, which limited the possibility of coffee expansion. Another problem was that of labor supply. In the new economic activity of coffee production, planters in the Central zone adopted the cultivation and processing techniques used in the Paraiba valley, with black slaves providing the muscle power. At mid-century, about the same time coffee was becoming important in the zone, the transatlantic slave traffic was effectively halted. This forced the planters to depend in large measure on interregional transfers of slaves within Brazil to supply their growing labor needs.[6]

Zone 5, the Mogiana, takes its name from the railroad that runs from Campinas north to the border of Minas Gerais, with numerous spurs and branch lines forming a network serving most of the zone. To the east the hills along the Minas Gerais border form the natural boundary of the São Paulo plateau. Coffee from the contiguous areas on the Minas side of the border has traditionally been exported from Santos via the Mogiana system, but the amounts have been small relative to both the total production of Minas Gerais and the total exports from Santos.[7]

The most important part of zone 5 for the history of coffee and immigration is around Ribeirão Preto, the center of a large concentration of the most ideal soil for coffee in the world. The first settlers came westward into the Mogiana zone from Minas Gerais in the late eighteenth century, but the agricultural development of the area had to await the solution of the transport problem. The five hundred kilometers separating Ribeirão Preto and Santos could not be economically bridged by mule train. The Mogiana railroad, organized and financed by planters in the area, began construction from Campinas in 1874 and reached Ribeirão Preto a decade later, setting the stage for the rapid expansion of the coffee groves.[8] One reflection of that boom was the proliferation of municipios in zone 5, increasing from twenty-one in 1886 to thirty-two in 1920 and thirty-nine by 1934.

The English company that built the railroad from Santos to Jundiai declined to extend its trunk line beyond the original 139 kilometers. A group of local planters and political leaders took it upon themselves to continue the development of the rail system further into the coffee zone. They formed the Companhia Paulista de Estradas de Ferro and began construction from Jundiai in 1868.[9] After reaching its initial objective of Campinas in 1872, the Paulista continued northwestward toward Rio Claro and continued to develop its trunk and feeder network into what became known as the Paulista, zone 6 in the territorial division used here. Prior to the expansion of coffee, this area was even more sparsely settled and less developed than the Mogiana, although Rio Claro, São Carlos, and other towns had been established there for some time. The Paulista zone contained ten municipios in 1886, twenty-one in 1920, and twenty-four in 1934.

The coffee boom of the late nineteenth century was concurrent in the Mogiana and the Paulista zones and affected both in similar ways. The economic activity that attracted rail lines into the coffee-producing areas developed most intensely in the interfluvial tablelands, rather than in the lowlands and river valleys, which generally had poorer soils, were poorly drained, and were more susceptible to frosts. Such a valley, that of the Mogi Guassú River, forms a natural buffer between the Mogiana and the Paulista zones. The two zones were parallel geographically, and from the 1870s on, their economic and demographic development was also roughly parallel. Together the Mogiana and Paulista zones form a third unit in the chronological advance of coffee in São Paulo.

By 1886 the Central, Mogiana, and Paulista were well-developed zones of coffee production. These three areas constitute the "old" west, the area most affected by the boom from the mid-1880s to 1896 and the ensuing relatively depressed conditions from 1897 to 1910. Only the Central zone was by the 1880s surrounded by population centers and had no pioneer fringe, in the sense of a border between settled territory and hinterland, and most of the land in the Paulista and Mogiana suitable for coffee had been explored and was at least sparsely settled. Further growth took place primarily through more complete use of land behind the pioneer fringe in these three zones.

One characteristic dividing the "old" west from the "new" west is once again related to the transportation network. Planters calculated that mule transport could be used economically within a radius of some two hundred kilometers from the current railhead.[10] Thus after 1867 coffee began to spread much further inland than had been practical in prerailroad times. The construction of rail lines into the Central, Mogiana, and Paulista zones came only after coffee was well established there. Railroads were built to exploit the commercial potential of areas that had previously depended on mule trains, rather than to open virgin territory. Beginning with the development of the Araraquarense zone, the chronological relationship began to change. While in zones 4, 5, and 6 coffee preceded rails, in zone 7 the two activities were more nearly concurrent.

The major railroads continued to develop feeder lines after the mid-1880s, but nearly a decade passed before a new trunk line into the west was begun. In 1895 the Araraquarense railroad began construction northwest from Araraquara. A prolonged period of low coffee prices began the following year, and the work progressed in fitful stages. The first train did not reach the goal of São José do Rio Preto until 1912. Rio Preto had been a *boca do sertão* for many years, and some coffee had been grown along the uplands between the Tieté and the Turvo rivers, but the Araraquarense zone was still largely virgin territory before the construction of the railroad. Around the turn of the century the Douradense railroad began construction of a secondary network extending west from São Carlos to serve the western part of zone 7. The Araraquarense zone lies intermediate in the chronology of coffee's advance between the "old" frontier areas of the Mogiana and the Paulista, and newer zones to the west. It contained only three municipios in 1886, but the number shot up to twenty-four in 1920 and thirty-six in 1934. The Araraquarense included areas of new development well into the 1920s and later.

The settlement and economic development of zone 8, the Noroeste, took place after the turn of the twentieth century and after the construction of the principal railroad into the region. In this case, rails definitely preceded coffee. In 1887 the small *boca do sertão* village of Baurú became the first town in the Noroeste zone to achieve separate municipio status. A branch of the Sorocabana railroad reached Baurú in 1905, but the territory to the west of the town remained largely unexplored. Prior to 1906, maps showed the vast expanse of São Paulo south of the Tieté River and west of Baurú as simply "lands inhabited by wild Indians" or "unexplored territory." Such maps reflect the limited state of knowledge in illustrating the locations of the major rivers of the area. The cartographers assumed that the Peixe and the Feio were either different names for the same river or that the two converged to form the Aguapeí before joining the Paraná River along the São Paulo–Mato Grosso border.[11]

In 1905 and 1906 the São Paulo Department of Agriculture sent survey parties into the region west of Baurú for the first time. The group that was to explore the Feio River had no sooner set out than it was attacked by Indians. The leader of the expedition and several others were wounded, and the party made a temporary retreat to the last fazenda on the frontier. After again entering the *sertão* the party was attacked on several other occasions and at times was forced to take up defensive positions. The major discovery of the expedition was that the river called the Feio at its headwaters was the same as that called the Aguapeí where it joined the Paraná. The survey party exploring the Peixe River also suffered an Indian attack. They discovered that the Peixe was not part of the Feio-Aguapeí system, but formed a separate river, which earlier explorers had called the Tigre where it joined the great Paraná.[12]

Through this virgin woodland and scrub forest, inhabited by the nomadic Coroado and Kaingang Indians, the Noroeste railroad was built. Construction began at Baurú in late 1905, continued along the tableland between the Tieté and the Aguapeí, and reached the Paraná River in 1910. This rapid penetration beyond the pioneer fringe of Brazilian settlement brought about the rapid and violent end of the Indians who had fought the earlier survey parties with some success. In the aftermath of this one-sided conflict, a writer in the journal of the Brazilian Rural Society noted that the "circumstances gave rise to many atrocities between whites and Coroados, and not the least to blame were the former, who many times acted in unjust and inhuman ways."[13] Following a recurrent pattern in frontier expansion, the native population was eliminated—this time for the sake of coffee.

The railroad opened the Noroeste to European settlement during a period of low coffee prices, production surpluses, and labor shortages. In an attempt to bring the excess production under control, the government of São Paulo had instituted a prohibitive tax on new coffee planting, technically in effect from 1903 to 1911. The availability of new lands was a powerful attraction, and some pioneering planters opened groves in the isolated Noroeste without paying the tax. But the initial spurt of agricultural development of zone 8 came in the 1911–14 period when the expiration of the law restricting planting coincided with a general improvement of the coffee market. The first new municipios in the Noroeste after the establishment of the Baurú in 1887 were carved out of the latter's western territory beginning in 1913, and by 1920 there were still only six municipios in zone 8. Poor economic conditions during World War I again held back expansion, but in the 1920s there was considerable economic and demographic growth in the Noroeste, with such cities as Lins, Penapolis, and Araçatuba becoming important coffee centers.

A branch of the Paulista railroad reached Baurú in 1910, and during the 1920s the Paulista company began construction of the last major trunk line into the west of São Paulo. This railroad, known as the Alta Paulista, begins at Baurú and follows a parallel route south of the Noroeste, along the uplands between the Aguapeí and the Peixe rivers. The Alta Paulista had reached only as far as Marília when the Depression forced a delay in railroad construction and agricultural expansion in the frontier.[14] By 1934 there were twenty municipios in zone 8.

The last area of the western plateau that remains to be discussed is the Alta Sorocabana. The eastern edge of zone 9, from the municipio of Tieté to Botucatú and São Manuel, forms part of the zone of nineteenth-century settlement. The Sorocabana was constructed as far as Botucatú by 1886, at which time there were ten municipios in zone 9, and that area participated to some degree in the ensuing coffee boom. It was not nearly as important as the Mogiana and the Paulista, however, and the Sorocabana railroad had recurrent financial problems. Not until the second and third decades of the twentieth century did the Sorocabana network rival the Mogiana or the Paulista lines in transporting coffee. Around the turn of the century, concurrently with the drive north to Baurú, the Sorocabana began to extend its tracks to the west. By 1909 it reached Salto Grande on the Paranapanema River, and stopped at the banks of the Paraná in 1922. This rail line and the region it served became known as the Alta, or "Upper," Sorocabana, to distinguish it from the other branches of the Sorocabana system. Built through an area where coffee had not yet penetrated to a great degree, it was in part a speculative venture aimed at opening new lands to commercial agricultural development. There were twenty-nine municipios in the Alta Sorocabana by 1920 and thirty-nine in 1934.

A few isolated settlements existed in the western reaches of zone 9 prior to the coming of the railroad, where pioneers from Minas Gerais had taken up livestock raising and subsistence farming. One such town was Campos Novos do Paranapanema, an outpost of European settlement that could not quite be called civilization. Campos Novos might have been a logical goal in the extension of the Sorocabana, but the final route bypassed the town by a wide margin. During the prosperous 1920s towns such as Assis and Presidente Prudente grew up along the railroad through territory where only a decade earlier Indians had hunted tapir in the trackless woodlands. Campos Novos fell into stagnation and never recovered.[15]

The pioneer zones of the Noroeste and the Alta Sorocabana are similar in many ways, and together they form the "new" west. Whereas in the older areas coffee attracted railroads, the process was reversed in zones 8 and 9. There the construction of rail lines made subsequent agricultural expansion possible. In the older zones the high point of the coffee economy had definitely passed by 1930. In the Noroeste and Alta Sorocabana zones the economic problems of the Great Depression forced a temporary pause in further development, but it was a slowing down of the high rate of expansion of the 1920s rather than stagnation or absolute decline. Large areas of zones 8 and 9 could be considered frontier areas in the present day, with low population density and underexploited agricultural potential.

Zones 4 through 9 of this division comprise most of the state economically tributary to the port of Santos. Throughout this study it should be understood that the term "western plateau" refers to the territory encompassed by zones 4 through 9. Quantitative statements about a given zone refer to the entire territory of the zone in question, as composed of specific municipio units.

Natural conditions in western São Paulo are excellent for coffee. A layer of diabase lava that once covered much of the area has decomposed into a porous loam rich in the iron and potash coffee plants need. In a few areas of highest concentration such soil takes on a purplish cast. This is the *terra roxa* for which São Paulo is famous among coffee regions of the world. Only about two percent of the plateau is covered with true *terra roxa*, however. A much larger area has red soils called *massapé* and *salmourão*, which are nearly as good. Plantations spread across many types of soil, from ''purple earth'' to inferior sandy areas known as *terra branca*, ''white earth,'' and even in such infertile land the climate is favorable for coffee.

Situated just within the southern tropic belt, the area is on the northern edge of the frost line, but is far enough away from the equator to escape the most intense tropical heat. Killing frosts are thus infrequent, yet the average temperatures are not so high as to require a cover of shade trees. In São Paulo shade has been used only for delicate seedlings. The average annual rainfall of one to two hundred centimeters is ample but not excessive, and it occurs in a yearly cycle that leaves a dry season during the harvest period from June through August. The characteristic rolling terrain provides good drainage, yet there are few areas with slopes so steep that coffee planting is impossible. Coffee planted over the tops of the ridges usually escapes the freezing temperatures that occur at times in the valley bottoms. This pattern of selective planting left large areas of valleys and lowlands available for subsistence crops and pasture for livestock, interspersed throughout the western plateau.[16]

Zone 10 is called the Baixa, or ''Lower,'' Sorocabana after the railroad branch built through the area between 1900 and 1910 to connect the southern Brazilian states with São Paulo and points north. The Baixa Sorocabana lies south of the area climatically suitable for coffee, and it has never produced significant amounts of the product. This zone has poor soils and hilly terrain, appropriate for limited food production and livestock grazing. This large and chronically stagnant area of southwestern São Paulo serves as a point of comparison to help measure the development of other zones.

Zone 11 includes Santos and the coastal lowlands to the southwest of the port. In contrast to the cool and humid climate of the city of São Paulo and the temperate and drier weather of the interior plateau, Santos and the lowlands have suffered from the constant heat and humidity of the tropics relieved only by occasional sea breezes. Around the turn of the century a project to channelize the city's natural drainage system and adjacent swamps greatly reduced the problems of yellow fever and malaria, but commerce and finance continued to be centered mainly in the more pleasant surroundings of the capital. The business of Santos was shipping—the physical task of transferring millions of bags of coffee annually from railroad car to warehouse and waiting steamer. Of the imports that came off the ships and went up to the plateau, not the least important was manpower. Santos was the port of entry for the mass of European immigrants bound for the coffee groves.

Northeast of Santos the escarpment plunges almost directly into the sea. But to the southwest the coastal plain widens to form a tropical lowland appropriate for rice and other products adapted to the warm and humid climate. Some of the settlements along the coast were first founded in the sixteenth century, but the agricultural development of the area, beyond the subsistence needs of local communities, had to await the increased demand for food products that accompanied the coffee boom. Topographical barriers and differences in climate and elevation separate the Santos lowlands from other parts of the state. If the rural areas of zone 11 have not been the center of a significant economic boom, they at least did not experience the continued stagnation characterizing the Baixa Sorocabana.

The regional division used here, like any other, is arbitrary to some degree. However, given the purposes of this study, the nature of the historical record, and the time span to be covered, it is more adequate and less arbitrary than others that have been proposed. It provides a way to define explicitly such less specific concepts as the Paraiba valley zone, the western plateau, and other informal terms that have been used to distinguish parts of São Paulo. Regionalization is thus a methodological device enabling us to use a body of quantitative data to help describe and analyze the coffee boom, the immigrant inflow, and the changing agrarian structure.[17]

One reason for emphasizing the regionwide aspects of this socioeconomic complex is that the people involved—the planters, their allies in municipal and state politics, immigrant workers—saw it as a regional system, rather than as restricted to constituent towns and subregions. Local loyalties and rivalries persisted, but the sense of community shared by the elite was regional rather than local. The immigrant workers, lacking long-standing ties of origin, tradition, or family to a specific plantation or municipio, soon developed an areawide understanding of the labor market. At several levels of the socioeconomic hierarchy, the regional sense was reinforced by the rapid and extensive interchange of both people and information.

Once the railroad network was in place, people could move from one point to any other in the settled area of the plateau, or to the state capital, in a day or less. Passenger movement on the Paulista and Mogiana networks provide an indication of the importance of the railroads as transportation routes for people as well as for coffee and other goods. In 1887 these two lines totaled 800 kilometers of track, and they carried 435,000 people, equal to about one-third of the total population of São Paulo in that year. By 1896 the Paulista and Mogiana had 1,726 kilometers of track and carried 2,632,000 people, more than the estimated 2,300,000 population of the state. In 1908, when they had 2,479 kilometers of track, the two railroads carried 2,711,000 people, compared to an estimated population for all São Paulo of some 3,000,000.[18]

These data for only a part of the state's rail network illustrate one of the pervasive social characteristics of western São Paulo in this era: the fluidity, the geographical movement, of the population.

Furthermore, the telegraph, which accompanied the railroads, enabled the planter and commercial elite to communicate rapidly over the distances separating the coffee frontier, the state capital, and the port of Santos. Local newspapers and word of mouth, from the general store to the Jockey Club, extended the web of communication. Coffee price changes, the opening of a new rail spur, a state government contract subsidizing more immigrants, frost damage in the Alta Sorocabana zone, a labor shortage in the Mogiana zone, the arrival of an immigrant ship—all became part of a body of knowledge common across the western plateau. A locally specific phenomenon—such as the exhaustion of good coffee land, the iron-fisted control of a municipal political boss, or the opening of a new area in a remote part of the frontier—had regional repercussions as well. The Central zone became old in the context of newer areas further west. Plantation wages on the frontier were high not only in the absolute sense of real income, but also relative to less favorable conditions in older zones.

Figure 3 illustrates the extent of coffee expansion in western São Paulo during the period under study, with the contribution of each zone in the plateau region. The unit of measurement is the coffee tree itself, which Paulistas normally grouped in aggregate units of one thousand trees. A change in the tree totals implies a directly proportional change in the land area planted in coffee, but in São Paulo the number of trees, rather than area, was the universal indicator of productive capacity.

Several aspects of figure 3 require comment. The most salient feature is that the total productive capacity of western São Paulo's coffee industry doubled from the mid-1880s to the early 1890s, doubled again by the turn of the century, and doubled yet again by the late 1920s. By the time the Great Depression hit, there were ten times as many trees in production as in 1886. While the overall increase was phenomenal, the rates of growth generally reflected the changing price levels in the world market. The first rapid rise took place during and immediately after the period of very high prices from 1886 to 1895. Growth rates slowed then for about a decade and rose sharply through the 1920s, when prices were again high. The lags of several years between high prices and increases in productive capacity were due to a biological feature of the coffee plant: four to six years passed between the planting of seedlings and the first crop. Thus expansion of the groves under favorable economic conditions showed up in increased production only several years later. The Paulista planters entered the periods of relatively low prices in the first decade of the twentieth century and in the 1930s with vast new areas that were planted in the preceding years.

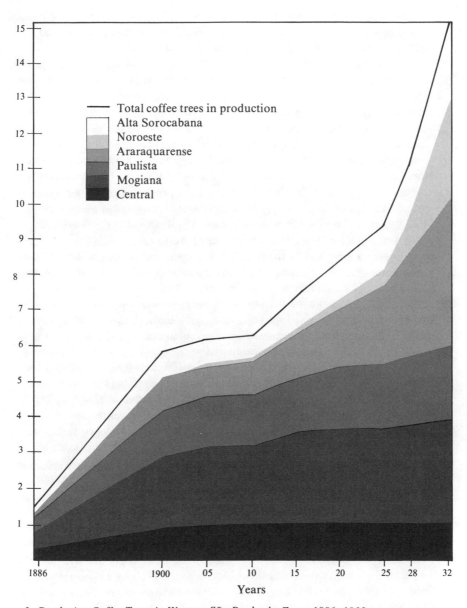

3. Producing Coffee Trees in Western São Paulo, by Zone, 1886–1932

A second general feature of figure 3 is that there was no absolute decline in the productive capacity of any zone, and all but the Central continued to expand. Before the widespread adoption of contour planting and chemical fertilizers after World War II, coffee land in Brazil would support only one life cycle of the trees, a period ranging from twenty to perhaps forty years. It was an axiom among planters that new groves were only viable in virgin woodlands, and not just any new land would do. Areas appropriate for coffee were identified by certain vegetation. *Peroba, pau d'alho, figueira branca,* and *jangada brava* were among the most sought-after types of trees, with other native plants indicating soil less favorable for coffee.[19] Over the long term, then, coffee planting was an inherently migratory activity, and the stability of productive capacity in the older zones reflects a process of planting previously unused land in coffee, as old groves declined and died out. Coffee moved into virgin land behind the pioneer fringe, and in all but the Central zone it moved further into the western frontier as well.

A survey carried out by the São Paulo Department of Agriculture in 1900 provides an early benchmark for examining the availability of land in western São Paulo. These data include the area planted in coffee during the post-abolition boom, and by definition they cover only the territory behind the pioneer fringe of coffee expansion. According to the 1900 survey, a total of 1,517,978 alqueires were claimed in coffee plantations in the western plateau, equal to 21 percent of the total area of the plateau region.[20] But just 282,686 alqueires were actually planted in coffee, equal to 19 percent of the land claimed in plantations and only 4 percent of the total area of the western plateau. In addition, the plantations reported a collective total of 362,715 alqueires of land held in reserve, appropriate for coffee cultivation but not yet used. In other words, in the land reported as held in private plantations in 1900 behind the pioneer fringe, there remained enough virgin territory to more than double the level of coffee production. In addition, the properties that cultivated coffee claimed 872,580 alqueires, or 57 percent of their area, as land not suitable for coffee.[21]

Brazilians have used the image of a green wave to characterize the penetration of coffee into western São Paulo in the late nineteenth and early twentieth centuries.[22] Such oceanic imagery requires considerable qualification. It was selective growth, localized along transport routes and in areas with the best soil types and climate. And while the increase was enormous in absolute terms and relative to its beginnings in the slave era, it was dwarfed by the expanse of land available. At no time have coffee fields covered as much as 15 percent of the surface area of São Paulo's western plateau. We shall return to the spotty and partial nature of the occupation of the land in chapter 5. For now there are technical aspects of the aggregate expansion shown in figure 3 that need to be considered. These technical requirements dictated labor needs, which in turn led to the mass importation of immigrant workers.

Just as figure 3 directly reflects changes in the total area planted and the relative shift through time from the "old" west to the "new" west, it also indirectly shows the changes in the work force required to produce the coffee of western São Paulo and its constituent zones. This is because labor requirements, from the abolition of slavery to the Great Depression, were directly proportional to the number of trees in production. Labor productivity was measured by the number of trees a worker could care for, rather than the amount of coffee produced. And since the technology of the coffee industry did not change significantly, neither did labor needs per unit of one thousand trees.

The methods of cultivation were essentially the same as those used when agriculture began several thousand years ago, adapted to the technical requirements of coffee. The basic instrument has always been the heavy hoe, or *enxada*, used to keep the groves free of weeds and grass by scraping the surface of the soil, taking care not to disturb the extensive root system of the coffee shrub. This operation was known as the *carpa* or the *limpeza* ("cleaning"). A more general term including weeding, clearing away dead twigs, replanting dead trees, and preparing the groves for harvest was the *trato* ("care"). Cultivation in western São Paulo was normally carried out five times during the yearly cycle. If the *carpa* was not performed regularly, young plants would not develop properly and older trees would become unproductive. Grass and weeds would soon take over the grove, robbing the soil of nutrients and water and crowding out the coffee root system. Inadequate care reduced yields, and if a grove were abandoned for as long as a year the damage might be beyond repair. The requirement that coffee groves be kept free of weeds was central to the problems of work organization and labor needs. As long as the hoe remained the standard implement, it meant that the labor requirements would remain high.

Attempts to replace the hoe began as early as the 1870s.[23] Around the turn of the twentieth century there was a flurry of well-publicized activity to introduce animal-drawn cultivators. Carlos Botelho, scion of one of the great landholding families of the Paulista zone and state secretary of agriculture from 1904 to 1908, had experimented with such implements on his own plantation in the 1890s. Among the many active policies the state carried out during his tenure was the promotion of mechanized farming. In 1904 a Department of Agriculture district inspector reported that some plantations were experimenting with a cultivator called the "Planet Junior." In 1907 the Deere and Mansur Company of Moline, Illinois, sent a representative to São Paulo to study the technical problems of coffee, and subsequently introduced the Deere Coffee Cultivator specifically designed for São Paulo conditions.

Several factories in São Paulo also manufactured weeding implements of various types.[24]

Several factors militated against such mechanization efforts. Advocates praised the animal-drawn cultivator as a technical improvement over the hoe, which they criticized as a primitive legacy of the slave era, but had to admit that the annual cost of care per tree was about the same with either method. The hoe, however, was tried and true, and many planters were skeptical of the technical superiority argument. Critics countered that the cultivator blades could not be controlled and would cut too deeply, damaging the delicate root system of the coffee plant. And in hilly areas the steep slopes made mechanical cultivation impossible.[25] Those in favor of mechanization admitted that even when cultivators could be used most effectively, in places where the terrain was reasonably level and the plants were not too close together, hoe workers would still have to pass through the groves to weed around the coffee stems themselves.

Much of the controversy over improved cultivation techniques was related to problems of labor supply and plantation work organization. Summing up the promechanization argument in 1902, Augusto Ramos pointed out that "each cultivator is worth four to six immigrants, and has the immense advantage of neither sending money home to Italy nor bleeding the treasury with transportation expenses."[26] One student of the problem calculated that under ideal conditions a man with a cultivator could weed one thousand coffee trees per day, compared to an average of two hundred per day with a hoe. Carlos Botelho claimed that one man, a mule, and a cultivator could do the work of five hoe workers, but admitted that the corresponding reduction in the labor pool of the plantation could result in a serious manpower shortage during the harvest, when entire families were needed.[27] Critics pointed out that with the old methods the number of workers necessary to cultivate the groves was usually sufficient to complete the harvest, when joined by the other members of their families. Speaking before the Brazilian Rural Society in 1921, a proponent of improved techniques expressed the problem in the following terms: "Needing numerous workers for the harvest, we keep them occupied the rest of the time with hoe work. But this . . . is not really an 'advantage.' It is more in the nature of a situation to which we submit ourselves, because otherwise we would not be able to harvest all the coffee, especially in a bumper crop year."[28]

When cultivators were used, it was impossible to plant corn and beans in the spaces between the coffee trees. But many planters offered interrow cropping privileges to attract workers, and mechanization would eliminate that incentive. Related to the need to attract manpower was worker resistance to mechanization on the justifiable grounds that it would reduce the number of plantation jobs. In discussing coffee labor problems in 1902, a Department of Agriculture inspector reported that due to pressure from the workers, the planters could "never attempt to introduce even one mechanized technique, under threat of a strike at harvest time."[29] A 1952 study of the São Paulo coffee plantation reported cultivation and harvest methods essentially the same as in the nineteenth century, with the hoe and the manual winnowing tray still the standard implements.[30] Despite the labor-saving potential of mechanization, animal-drawn cultivators were adopted only on a limited scale and under exceptional conditions in the São Paulo coffee industry, for the harvest manpower problem was never solved.

Like cultivation techniques, the methods used during the coffee harvest dated from the slave era. In the Colombian and Central American highlands the branches of coffee trees are loaded with blossoms, green fruit, and mature red berries simultaneously through much of the year, and each ripe berry must be carefully plucked off without disturbing those in earlier stages of development. In southern Brazil, in contrast, the noticeable climatic changes cause coffee to develop in distinct stages. From September through November the shrubs turn white with flowers. The intensity and duration of the blossoming gives a rough indication of how abundant or sparse the subsequent crop will be. By late May, in the groves that flowered earliest, most of the berries turn bright red and are ripe for picking. By the first part of August, maturation is normally complete; the berries that ripened in May shrivel and blacken as they dry on the trees.

Since the berries ripened at approximately the same time, the harvest needed to be carried out only once in any given grove. The pickers grasped each branch tightly near the center of the shrub and in one swift stroke stripped off all the berries. Whether the fruit was directed into a basket in front of the picker, onto cloths spread around the tree, or allowed to drop to the bare ground, the stripping action, known as the *derriça* or *apanha*, has always been the same. The berries were then gathered together on the *peneira* (a wicker or wire mesh tray) and tossed into the air to let the breeze carry away the leaves and twigs broken off in the stripping.

As with cultivation, there were efforts to modernize harvest techniques in western São Paulo. Most such innovations were related to the fact that if the berries were allowed to dry completely on the tree they would fall if the tree were struck or shaken. A report to the Paulista Society of Agriculture in 1908 described experiments with labor-saving techniques in which workers knocked the ripe berries from the trees with poles, carried away the debris, or *cisco*, with a wide-gauge rake, leaving the berries to be gathered together with a narrow-gauge rake. The success of the method, however, depended on three prerequisites most planters would find difficult to fulfill: the ground made smooth and clean by mechanical cultivation, the berries all completely dried, and the soil dampened by a recent rain. In the 1920s a similar method was widely publicized as the "natural harvest" (*colheita natural*).[31]

Augusto Ramos pointed out in 1923 that in spite of such "interesting and ingenious attempts, it has not been possible to solve the problem of mechanizing the coffee harvest."[32] The experiments to improve on the *derriça* may have been technically possible under ideal conditions, but it was not feasible to adopt them on a general basis. For one thing, the plants could easily be damaged by the repeated beating. A more serious objection was that the average planter could not wait until the end of the maturation period to begin picking. The harvest in São Paulo coincided with the dry season from May to September. (This is one reason the requirement for damp ground was hard to meet consistently.) By mobilizing all the available manpower in late May, there was just enough time to go over all the groves before the rains began. Coinciding with the beginning of the rains was the start of budding and flowering, the first stage in the life cycle for the following year. If a crop were harvested late or not at all, the intensity of the flowering, and hence the size of the following crop, would be adversely affected.

The fact that cultivation and harvest methods remained fairly constant cannot be attributed to ignorance or blind adherence to routine on the part of coffee growers. The attempts to develop and introduce more advanced techniques were widely debated for many years in agricultural societies and regional conventions of planters. Reports of experiments appeared in specialized magazines and technical journals such as the *Revista Agrícola*, *Revista dos Fazendeiros*, *O Fazendeiro* ("especially dedicated to the interests of the coffee industry," according to its masthead), and the *Boletim de Agricultura*, a monthly distributed free by the state government to more than three thousand subscribers. The *Boletim* published state and federal legislation affecting agriculture and immigration, detailed coffee market conditions in Santos, Rio, and Europe, weather information, predictions of the future coffee crop, news of arriving immigrants, and labor market conditions, in addition to analyses of experiments to reduce coffee labor needs through mechanization. The Department of Agriculture district inspectors also disseminated information on new techniques as they periodically toured their assigned territories. The Paulista planter was thus well informed of economic conditions and technological developments and was eager to reduce his labor needs wherever it was feasible. This rational attitude was exemplified by the rapid and nearly universal adoption of mechanized and motorized coffee processing equipment concurrently with the transition from slave to free labor in the 1880s and 1890s.

At the time coffee cultivation was being introduced on a commercial scale in western São Paulo in the 1850s and after, processing technology, like the use of slave labor and the methods of cultivation and harvest, was the same as that used in the Paraiba valley. After drying in the open air the coffee was hulled in a wooden mortar and pestle device called the *pilão*. On larger plantations a more complex version driven by water power, called the *engenho de pilões*, accomplished this task. By the 1870s more advanced machines were developed to scrape the outer pulp from the berries prior to drying, break the hulls from the dry beans, sort the coffee by grade and size, and do other specialized processes. Some of these operations, such as depulping, had not been done previously. Others had been by slow or labor-intensive methods.

A Dutch coffee expert noted in 1883 that while the *engenho de pilões* was still in use, the western planters were rapidly adopting machines. By 1885 local and foreign manufacturers had introduced a variety of depulping, gleaning, hulling, polishing, and sorting equipment in a range of sizes. In 1888 a firm in Syracuse, New York, began production of the Engelberg Coffee Huller, which a mechanic named Conrado Engelberg had invented in São Paulo. It quickly gained popularity, along with such brand names as Arens, MacHardy, Lidgerwood, Martins Barros, and Rocha Passos.[33] Water wheels sometimes provided power. Much more common were steam engines of various sizes. Coffee hulls were a universally available fuel, supplemented by charcoal and wood. By the 1920s many larger plantations were installing electric generators, from which they obtained light as well as power. These machines reduced plantation manpower needs, and by the time slavery was abolished the pattern was set: capital-intensive processing facilities requiring a small but skilled labor force, and the large mass of unskilled field hands working with rudimentary techniques that remain essentially unchanged to this day.

The terminology of the coffee economy reflected the low technical level and labor-intensive nature of field work. One way Paulista planters referred to labor requirements was in terms of man-equivalents, called "hoes." For example, a planter hiring workers might find a family with an able-bodied father and son in his late teens (one hoe each) and three younger children (one hoe combined), with the mother occupied at home. Another family might have a man and wife in their early forties (one hoe each) and two teenage daughters (one hoe combined). A young couple with small children who needed the mother's care might supply just one hoe. Planters calculated that each hoe could care for about two to three thousand coffee trees, a ratio that varied according to specific conditions but that has remained generally current in western São Paulo from the beginning of the free labor era.[34]

Throughout the period here under study, manpower requirements were high, due to labor-intensive methods; constant, due to the perennial nature of the coffee plant and the continuous labor input its adequate care required; and stable, due to the persistence of essentially similar techniques for the entire coffee area of western São Paulo. The stability of labor needs was relative to the number of coffee trees in production at any given time. From 1886 requirements doubled by the early 1890s, doubled again by 1900, and doubled again by the late 1920s. And labor needs by zone varied in the proportions illustrated in figure 3. They never declined even in the Central zone and they grew considerably along with the successive stages of coffee expansion into the western frontier.

As the slave era drew inexorably to a close in the 1880s, São Paulo planters were forced to search for a solution to the labor crisis they thought would follow abolition. Prices were high, the railway network in place. And the virgin land available on the western frontier was, for all intents and purposes, limitless. In advance of final abolition they found a solution to the problem of manpower, a solution that not only eased the transition from slavery but also made possible the tremendous expansion of the coffee industry in the ensuing decades. The growth shown in figure 3 would have been impossible without the mass migration of working people into São Paulo's western frontier. The fact that the laborers came primarily from southern Europe was no accident. It came about due to the conscious policies of an economic and political elite in São Paulo whose fortunes—in the literal and in the general sense—depended on coffee consumed at the center of the world economic system. To an analysis of those policies and their results we now turn.

3

THE IMMIGRANT STREAM

Braços para a lavoura was the slogan that directed the immigration policies of São Paulo from the decline of slavery to the Great Depression. It is a telling phrase. The literal meaning of *braços* is "arms," referring to the physical labor Paulistas saw as the purpose of the program, the intended role immigrants were to play in the economic system. Their labor was to be in *a lavoura*—a generic term for agriculture, but one that everyone knew referred to coffee. Planters and the government considered work in industry, in commerce and other services, and even in agricultural occupations other than coffee production, as detrimental to the primary goal, rather than as the successful result of a more general policy of populating the country. Any diversion of the immigrant stream away from the plantations of the western plateau was a leak in the channels for recruiting, transporting, and distributing manpower that were established in the 1880s and functioned through the 1920s.

The early beginnings of immigration to São Paulo were not primarily the result of "push" factors in Europe, although long-term demographic pressure and short-term economic depressions helped make people available when they were needed in Brazil. Rather, it was the impending end of slavery that forced the coffee planters to look elsewhere for workers. The story of slavery's decline and fall has been well studied and needs little recapitulation here. In brief, the imperial laws that chipped away at bondage in 1850, 1871, and 1885 were accompanied by a sporadically intense abolitionist campaign, demographic attrition, and increasing unrest among the slaves themselves. All served to put the Paulistas on notice that the end of slavery was a matter of time. For the planters of the Paraiba valley, as well as for many in other stagnant or declining areas of Brazil, abolition was a severe blow. In western São Paulo, in contrast, the Golden Law of 13 May 1888 was almost an anticlimax, settling an irritating political question. This is because the Paulista planters had immigrants to replace the slaves.[1]

The immigration activities of São Paulo began many years before the end of slavery, and long before the decentralized republican political system was finally established in 1891. As early as August 1871, before the enactment of the law freeing future children born to slave mothers, the provincial governor called together several financiers and planters to form the Association to

Aid Colonization and Immigration, for the purpose of "facilitating for our planters the acquisition of free workers." Provincial laws of 30 March 1871 and 26 April 1872 were intended "to aid planters who might wish to obtain immigrant workers," and authorized financial support of up to nine hundred thousand milreis for that purpose.[2] In November 1871 the association contracted to introduce fifteen thousand workers, but by the end of the period only 480 people had come in under the program. The contract for fifteen thousand immigrants was then extended for five years, and from 1875 through 1879 a total of 10,455 persons were recorded as entering São Paulo.[3] This increase over the previous period was still only a trickle compared to the growing labor demand in the coffee zone.

In December 1881 the provincial assembly established a commission to plan construction of an immigrant receiving station. Nicolau de Souza Queiroz, a member of one of the important landholding families of the western plateau, was put in charge of the immigration service, and in that same year the provincial government acquired a building in the Bom Retiro section of the capital. Although the building was remodeled in 1883, it had a capacity of only five hundred persons, and it was inconveniently located far from existing rail routes.[4] On 21 March 1885 the provincial assembly authorized 100,000 milreis for the construction of a new receiving station, and a special commission chose a site at the junction of the railroad lines entering the city of São Paulo from Rio de Janeiro and Santos, the routes by which virtually all immigrants entered the province. Construction of the new building began in June 1886. By July 1887, with parts still under construction, the Hospedaria de Imigrantes began receiving new arrivals. When it was completed in 1888 the new hostel had a capacity of four thousand persons, and 475,603 milreis had been spent in its construction.[5] The building became the focal point of São Paulo's immigration program. It continues to function to this day as a center for processing immigrant and migrant workers to the state.

In March 1884, four years before the final abolition, the French botanist Louis Couty reported that immigration was the principal topic of discussion in the city of São Paulo. As an example of the Paulistas' concern, he cited a newspaper editorial to the effect that the inevitable attrition of slavery would force the province to seek new sources of manpower just to maintain coffee production at current levels.[6] Much of the public interest was directed to the provincial assembly, where several bills related to the labor problem were being debated. On 12 March 1884 the assembly passed a law providing direct subsidies of up to four hundred thousand milreis for the transportation expenses of immigrants who entered agricultural occupations. A provincial law of 29 March 1884 created an annual tax of one milreis per slave employed in agriculture, and twice that amount for slaves not employed in agriculture, with the proceeds to be used for the immigration service.[7] Thus slaveowners were directly taxed and the funds used to import free workers. Martinho Prado Júnior, representing the proimmigration coffee planters of the western frontier, was instrumental in the success of these legislative measures.

By the mid-1880s the negative publicity that would plague Brazil for years had already become a serious obstacle to the further development of European immigration. Returning Italians had impressed government officials with criticism of life in São Paulo, and in 1885 the Italian government issued a circular describing São Paulo as inhospitable and unhealthy and recommending that its nationals avoid emigration to Brazil. Another problem resulted from the abuses of independent recruiting agents in Europe. Provincial Governor João Alfredo criticized the current practice of paying recruiters a fixed sum for each person, citing the need to "weed out the speculators who, thinking only of profits, . . . try to transport the largest number of immigrants without caring for the quality of the people they import, and who take recourse in the perfidious incentive of impossible promises." He went on to suggest that an independent company be formed, "worthy of the favors of the province," which would assume control of the immigration service.[8] This recommendation became a reality in mid-1886 with the creation of the Sociedade Promotora da Imigração. The Promotora was similar in concept to the earlier Association to Aid Colonization: a group of private citizens, funded through contracts with the provincial government, would administer a nonprofit agency for the purpose of recruiting, transporting, and distributing immigrant manpower. While the attempt in the early 1870s was largely a failure, by 1886 it was an idea whose time had come.

João Alfredo publicized the need for an organization of this type, and it began operation during the governorship of Antonio de Queiroz Teles, the viscount of Parnaiba. But credit for the formation and the success of the Promotora belongs in large measure to Martinho Prado Júnior. This slave-owning coffee planter of republican political sympathies, representing the booming and labor-hungry Mogiana zone, was a key figure in the successful transition to free wage labor in São Paulo. He and his brother Antonio were among the planters who experimented with free European labor beginning in the 1870s. In the 1880s both Prado brothers were often in the public eye, dealing with various aspects of the labor problem. Martinho Prado became president of the Sociedade Promotora da Imigração when it was formed in July 1886. Codirectors were Nicolau de Souza Queiroz, head of the provincial immigration service since 1881, and Rafael Aguiar Paes de Barros, member of another important family of coffee planters.[9]

The directors of the Promotora immediately began promotional activities. One of the first accomplishments was the publication of a brochure detailing the attractions of São Paulo. This sixty-page booklet was published with a grant from the imperial Ministry of Agriculture, headed at the time by Antonio da Silva Prado, brother of Martinho. It had a brightly colored front cover to catch the eye, and a large fold-out map of São Paulo in the end-papers. Eighty thousand copies were printed in Portuguese, German, and Italian. The text made favorable comparisons wherever possible with Argentina, the United States, and European countries. There was no mention of race or the continued existence of slavery, and it was carefully pointed out that in São Paulo "the manner of dress, furnishings, food, and in general all customs, are European." The booklet detailed the facilities available to immigrant families: transportation from Rio de Janeiro or Santos to the city of São Paulo, up to eight days food and lodging in the reception station, including free medical treatment, and free rail transport to the final destination in the interior of the province. The booklet concluded that thirty thousand immigrants were needed immediately, with a preference for families and for farmers.[10]

In addition to these calculated propaganda efforts, the society assumed administrative responsibility for the entire immigration program. A provincial law of 3 February 1887 turned over the administration of the newly constructed hostel in the capital to the Promotora. Martinho Prado Júnior made a tour of northern Italy in 1887 to study conditions there and set up a branch office in Genoa to advertise in favor of emigration to São Paulo, process requests for subsidy payments, and screen potential coffee workers. The provincial legislature periodically approved funds to subsidize a specified number of immigrants, at a given rate of payment per individual. The Promotora then contracted with the government to bring in the workers. In this way public funds were channeled either to shipping companies or to individual immigrants to pay transportation costs.

Although the Paulistas could not have foreseen it in 1886, one of the most important functions the Sociedade Promotora eventually carried out was to provide continuity for the immigration program through the period of reorganization attending the fall of the empire and the subsequent establishment of the republican political system. After the military coup d'état of 15 November 1889, the bureaucratic structure of the Brazilian empire was left virtually intact, with provisional appointees assuming the highest positions. Planning was begun for reorganizing the provincial (now state) and national governments, but during the uncertain transition normal bureaucratic procedures were sometimes slowed or interrupted.

The new federal constitution promulgated in 1891 gave the Paulistas the wide-ranging autonomy they had sought, and during that year the state government was restructured. The new state bureaucracy absorbed many of the old administrative departments, while others were disbanded. By 1892 the new system was in full operation. The São Paulo Department (*Secretaria*) of Agriculture, Commerce, and Public Works was charged with a variety of administrative duties, including the state immigration service. Throughout the period of final transition to free labor, the fall of the empire, and organization of the republican regime, the Promotora continued to function more or less normally. In 1894 the São Paulo Department of Agriculture entered into the first of many direct contracts with shipping companies. In 1895 the Sociedade Promotora brought in its last groups of Europeans, and the Department of Agriculture took on an increased share of the program. The administrative transition complete, its purpose accomplished, the Promotora disbanded in the course of 1895.[11]

In the government of Brazil during the late empire and early republic, coffee interests had influential spokesmen, and the national government occasionally helped the Paulistas import workers. But at the provincial level such a statement does not adequately describe the power of the planters. Similarly, to say the planter class controlled the province is not to imply that some other interest group existed and was excluded. In fact, the economic dominance of coffee was unquestionable. Among the property-owning sectors of society the right of the planters to control the political system was unquestioned, and the mass of working people—slaves, freedmen, native Brazilian peasants, and immigrants—had no political voice. The government of São Paulo was itself the *instrument* of the coffee planters. Immigration policy must be understood in this context. The Paulista elite did not see the Sociedade Promotora as a private interest group using state subsidies for the exclusive benefit of a restricted segment of the body politic. Rather, it was an extension of the executive branch, a special administrative apparatus established in critical circumstances to serve an extraordinary purpose. As the São Paulo secretary of agriculture expressed the relationship in 1892, the Promotora "came forward as a powerful assistant of the government, with which it proposed to contract for the importation of the number of immigrants authorized by law. . . . The combined action of these two elements [the provincial government and the Promotora] has resulted in the extraordinary increase in public and private wealth in the state."[12]

The buildup of São Paulo's immigration program was coordinated well with the concurrent decline of slavery. Before 1887 few plantations had switched to the exclusive use of free workers, and slave labor was still a viable option for many coffee producers. Annual immigrant arrivals averaged less than six thousand in the 1882–86 period, but with the establishment of the Sociedade Promotora, the allocation of transportation subsidies, and the construction of the reception station, immigration shot up to more than thirty-two thousand in 1887 and nearly ninety-two thousand in 1888. As increasing numbers of Europeans entered the province, they began to replace slaves prior to abolition. According to contemporary reports the transition to free labor on the plantations went more smoothly than might have been expected. The 1888 coffee crop harvested in the months immediately after the abolition law was larger than the preceding or following crop for western São Paulo.

That was only the beginning. From 1889 to the turn of the century nearly three-quarters of a million more foreigners arrived in São Paulo, of which 80 percent were subsidized by the government. From abolition to the Depression nearly two and one-quarter million immigrants came in, compared to a population base in São Paulo in 1886 of one and one-quarter million. Some 58 percent of all immigrants in that period were subsidized by the state. Immigration to São Paulo alone accounted for 56 percent of the 4.1 million immigrants who entered Brazil from 1886 through 1934.[13]

Figure 4 illustrates the rise and fall of annual immigration to São Paulo. One of the significant features is a close relationship between immigration totals and the coffee prices trends shown in figure 2. During the era of high prices from the mid-1880s to the mid-1890s, average inflows became increasingly larger. As coffee prices fell in the last years of the nineteenth and the first decade of the twentieth century, immigration also declined. A sharp but brief rise followed a similar improvement in coffee prices prior to World War I. During the war the cutoff of transatlantic shipping and social dislocations in Europe caused immigration to fall sharply. During the 1920s immigration trends followed coffee prices upward until the Depression hit. Also during the 1920s a sizable flow of working people from other parts of Brazil to São Paulo began a pattern of internal migration, which continues to the present, but which does not appear in figure 4.

Figure 4 also illustrates data on steerage-class departures from the port of Santos, the only information available on return migration from São Paulo. There was no large-scale annual migration of coffee harvest workers to and from Europe of the type that characterized the Argentine wheat industry. And although Santos departures are only a partial reflection of total out-migration, because some people left by land routes to Rio de Janeiro, they provide a rough indication of trends. Returns resulted from the aggregation of individual decisions to leave, for diverse reasons. Thus the departure data show much less oscillation than the immigration totals, which were affected by funding and recruiting decisions of the São Paulo government, as well as by occasional restrictions imposed in the countries of origin.

The slow and steady increase in departures from the beginning of the period up to World War I should be seen in the context of the total resident immigrant population—the pool of potential returnees—rather than in a spurious calculation of "net" immigration in any given year. In- and out-migrations were not necessarily related population flows. "Net" figures are useful in assessing the long-term demographic impact of immigration, but in examining the short-term development of the labor market it is important to keep inflows analytically separate from outflows. By the turn of the century there were perhaps half a million immigrants in São Paulo, and departures from Santos were less than thirty thousand annually. By the pre-World War I years annual out-migration via Santos had increased to just over forty thou-

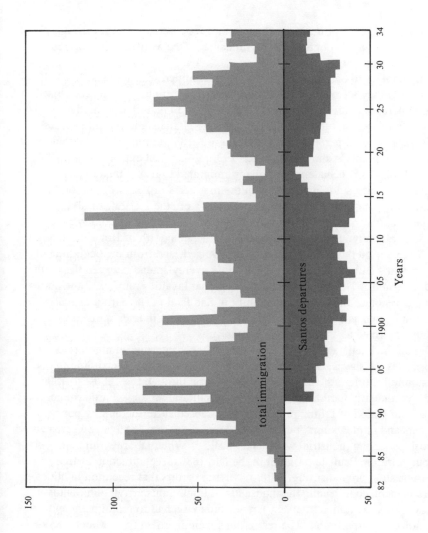

4. *Immigration to São Paulo, 1882–1934, and Steerage Departures from Santos, 1892–1934*

sand, and the resident immigrant population was probably more than one million. Seen in this context, the significance of the available data on return migration dwindles.

Immigration to São Paulo has long been identified with Italians. While it is true that they were the largest single nationality group, Italians comprised just 46 percent of all immigrants in the 1887–1930 period. During the transition to free labor and the ensuing coffee boom, Italians did indeed predominate, supplying 73 percent of all arrivals from 1887 through 1900. Of all Italian immigrants in the period 1882–1930, 74 percent entered before 1903. In the 1888–1897 decade more Italians emigrated to Brazil than to any other country, and one study notes that "in the first years of heavy migration to Brazil fully four-fifths of the emigrants came from the North [of Italy]." Italian records show that in the last quarter of the nineteenth century two-thirds of all emigrants to Brazil were from the area north of Rome. In the 1901–13 period those proportions were reversed, and from the beginning of World War I emigration to Brazil was more evenly spread between the north and the south.[14] Different dialects and regional loyalties reinforced the north-south division of the Italian community in São Paulo. The earlier arrivals became known as "Italians," while many who came in later were commonly identified as "Calabrians" (*calabreses*).

When the Paulista planters began seriously considering immigrants as substitutes for slaves, the Italian economy was stagnating. According to one economic historian, the depression was general through the 1880s, to 1896, and "particularly hard hit . . . was the agricultural sector." Furthermore, "the long period of falling prices not only caused suffering among poor farmers and farm laborers, but the deep depression from 1889 to 1893 created hardships among industrial workers as well."[15] When labor recruiters began to publicize the Paulista program in the late 1880s, the attraction of free transportation proved strong. After receiving reports that reception facilities were inadequate to handle the thousands of immigrants arriving in Santos every week, the Italian minister, Crispi, ordered a halt to recruitment and subsidized transportation. The restrictions were in effect from March 1889 until the Nicotera ministry rescinded the order in July 1891; the drop in Italian immigration in that period is reflected in figure 4.[16] After the ban was lifted, Italian immigration reached the highest levels ever recorded.

During the mid-1890s an upturn in economic conditions in Italy coincided with a severe downturn in São Paulo, as coffee prices fell sharply. The bleak reports of some returning immigrants reinforced negative consular reports, and emigration to São Paulo had been declining for several years before the commissioner general of emigration, Senator Luigi Bodio, issued an executive order in March 1902 prohibiting subsidized emigration to Brazil. The sharp drop in immigration in 1903 shown in figure 4 indicates the previous importance of Italians in the subsidy program, and the partial recovery after that year reflects the shift to other nationalities. The "Prinetti decree," as the order was called, after the current foreign minister, was never repealed, and it was a sore point in Brazilian-Italian relations for many years.[17] It referred only to the provision of free transportation; those paying their own way could still emigrate at will. Large numbers of Italians continued to go to São Paulo, but no longer could a family hope to emigrate at little cost after arrival in Genoa. Working people had an unenviable existence anywhere in the early twentieth century. The Prinetti restriction eliminated the opportunity for some poor Italians to test their fate on the Paulista coffee plantations, as hundreds of thousands of their fellows had done in the preceding fifteen years.

During the 1887–1900 period Spain supplied 11 percent of São Paulo's immigrants, Portugal 10 percent, and other countries just 6 percent. From 1901 through 1930 the nationality distribution was more diverse. The proportion of Italians fell to 26 percent, Spaniards made up 22 percent, Portuguese 23 percent; other nationalities rose to 28 percent. Of this last category the most important single group was Japanese, who began arriving in small numbers in 1908 and became a steady stream after 1917. In the 1911–30 period more than ninety-six thousand Japanese went to São Paulo. Japan thus followed Italy, Spain, and Portugal as the most important source of labor power for the coffee plantations. German immigration had been relatively important in the 1870s and early 1880s, and although some continued to enter the state they did not become important again until the 1920s, when twenty-eight thousand Germans arrived.

Also during the 1920s some twenty thousand Rumanians, nineteen thousand Lithuanians, and nearly ten thousand Poles entered São Paulo. A group retaining its ethnic identification in a way similar to the Japanese was the Syrio-Lebanese. While the Ottoman empire controlled the Middle East these people traveled with Turkish passports, and although they continued to be called *turcos* in popular speech, most were self-exiles from Turkish rule. Eighteen thousand of this group entered from 1911 to 1920. After World War I their geographical origin is clearer. Of 20,308 immigrants from the Middle East from 1921 to 1930, 16,253 were from Syria, 1,740 from Lebanon, 1,558 from Turkey, and 757 from Armenia. Some of these people undoubtedly worked on coffee plantations, but the Syrians were more commonly identified with itinerant petty commerce. The *mascates*, as these peddlers were known, supplied many of the household utensils and dry goods that coffee workers consumed.[18]

Throughout this period, the system established in the labor crisis of the 1880s continued to function virtually intact, with some adjustments in response to changing conditions. From its beginnings the provision of transportation costs was the key to the program. The immediate problem in the 1880s was to replace the slaves and then provide manpower for coffee expansion. Planters were understandably reluctant to subsidize immigrants whose arrival would do little to meet those goals. Thus the system was clearly aimed at recruiting workers who were indigent or nearly so at the time of their departure from Europe. In 1887 Martinho Prado Júnior pointed out that "only those individuals without resources, attacked by necessity in all its forms, emigrate to Brazil, and they do it by seeking free or reduced passage."[19] A decade later the secretary of agriculture repeated the common assumption that those who paid their own passage usually entered commerce or other nonagricultural occupations, "thus bringing in consumers, instead of elements of production." Without subsidized passage, he continued, "no one will come. Emigration is, in general, the result of poverty in the countries that presently provide us with immigrants." Referring to a diplomatic incident that led to anti-Italian riots in São Paulo in 1896, the secretary claimed: "the misery of the [Italian] peasant population is such that during the recent lamentable events that caused the Italian government to suspend emigration to Brazil, emigrants in the port of embarkation, bound for São Paulo, lacked the resources to return to their abandoned homes."[20] In 1908 an Italian consul noted that the immigrant coffee worker "generally emigrates to Brazil in the condition of have-not [*nullatenente*]."[21]

By offering subsidies the Paulistas made emigration possible for those at the lowest levels of the socioeconomic hierarchy in the countries of origin, but the program constituted a subsidy for the coffee planters as well. If individual employers advanced passage money, the workers arrived with a heavy debt burden. Such a debt was a disincentive to emigration, and private subsidies increased the capital requirements of the planters involved. Those in the frontier areas would have been especially hard-pressed to pay for their own workers directly, since they had recently made capital outlays to establish their plantations. By making the subsidy a grant rather than a loan and by channeling it through the government, the planters were able to spread the costs. Everyone who paid state taxes helped pay for the program. The unquestioned and even enthusiastic acceptance of the scheme among property-owning groups was again related to the overwhelming importance of coffee, not only in the regional economy, but also in the provincial tax structure.

From the perspective of the Paulista elite, one way of evaluating immigration policies was in terms of funds expended. During the last years of the empire, coffee consistently accounted for more than 99 percent of São Paulo's taxable exports by value. From 1881–82 to 1886–87 (coffee) export taxes supplied 51 percent of all provincial revenues, and income from coffee indirectly contributed an important share of other revenue sources as well. During the same period provincial expenditures on immigration were the equivalent of less than 8 percent of all revenues.

Table 1 shows similar data for the period from 1892, when the administrative structure of the state government was established, until 1930, when the national political unheaval of that year, coinciding with the onset of the

Depression, changed São Paulo's fiscal and administrative organization. As can be seen in column F, state immigration expenditures averaged nearly 9 percent of total tax revenues in the first decade of the republican regime. In later years the proportion oscillated considerably, averaging just over 5 percent for the entire 1892–1930 period. During the last years of the empire, from fiscal year 1883–84 through 1891, São Paulo spent a total of 10,102,000 milreis on immigration, equivalent to U.S. $4,507,400 at current exchange rates.[22] When that figure is added to the total in column G of table 1, it can be seen that from the beginning of its policy of actively promoting immigration to 1930 the government of São Paulo spent the equivalent of nearly U.S. $37,000,000.

Advocates always justified the immigration service as a means of supplying workers to the coffee plantations. In answer to occasional critics who argued that the coffee industry should subsidize immigration directly, planters and their political representatives repeatedly pointed out that revenues from the export tax on coffee paid for the immigration program many times over. Furthermore, the planters reasoned, the labor supply the immigration service helped provide was small return for the contribution of the coffee industry toward financing the state government.[23]

The data in columns C and D of table 1 show the basis for those claims and give an indication of the economic underpinnings of the continuing political power of the coffee planters in these years. For the entire 1892–1930 period, the state received nearly ten times as much revenue from coffee export taxes as it spent on all phases of the immigration program. For the first dozen years of the republic, coffee export taxes made up nearly three-fourths of the state's tax revenue, and although the proportion declined later, export taxes remained the single most important source of São Paulo's tax revenue.

In the first years after it was organized, the State Department of Agriculture, following the practice of the Sociedade Promotora, signed exclusive contracts with individual shipping companies. The first such contract originated from a law of August 1893 authorizing the importation of fifty thousand people, to be contracted to the lowest bidder. Angelo Fiorita and Company, which had long done business with the Sociedade Promotora, submitted the winning bid of five pounds sixteen shillings sterling per adult passage. The agreement the state signed with Fiorita in August 1894 set the pattern for later ones, and it illustrates the attention to detail characterizing São Paulo's program of subsidized immigration.[24] To qualify for subsidized passage, immigrants had to meet well-defined criteria of sex, age, and family structure.

According to the terms of the agreement, the company was to bring in the fifty thousand immigrants within eighteen months. They were to be Europeans and agriculturists (*agricultores*) by profession. The requirement that subsidized immigrants be of agricultural background was another continuation

TABLE I

São Paulo State Tax Revenues Compared to Coffee Export Tax Revenues and Immigration Expenditures, 1892–1930

Year	Total Tax Revenue[a]	Coffee Export Tax Revenue[a]	C as % of B	State Expenditures on Immigration Programs[a]	E as % of B	E in Current U.S. Dollars[b]
A	B	C	D	E	F	G
1892	36,452	26,553	73	1,507	4.1	362
1893	31,982	23,313	73	3,738	11.7	897
1894	34,592	25,561	74	1,220	3.5	244
1895	46,384	32,397	70	7,279	15.7	1,456
1896	41,840	29,599	71	4,645	11.1	836
1897	44,094	33,492	76	5,927	13.4	948
1898	37,549	26,026	69	2,739	7.3	411
1899	38,550	29,051	75	2,278	5.9	342
1900	38,270	29,282	77	1,129	3.0	215
1901	40,924	31,989	78	4,501	11.0	1,035
1902	33,003	24,918	76	2,094	6.3	503
1903	29,926	22,146	74	238	0.8	57
1904	33,215	24,817	75	668	2.0	167
1905	27,586	19,297	70	3,172	11.5	1,015
1906	34,830	26,195	75	2,610	7.5	861
1907	38,520	27,981	73	1,659	4.3	512
1908	32,414	22,190	68	2,001	6.2	620
1909	44,048	33,210	75	2,609	5.9	809
1910	30,665	17,470	57	3,096	10.1	1,022
1911	50,287	27,567	55	3,583	7.1	1,147
1912	60,405	36,665	61	5,949	9.8	1,904
1913	58,942	40,944	69	6,572	11.1	2,103
1914	48,985	34,760	71	3,277	6.7	950
1915	61,186	41,086	67	1,439	2.4	360
1916	59,036	33,538	57	1,769	3.0	407
1917	58,965	24,729	42	3,706	6.3	927
1918	52,123	18,266	35	2,526	4.8	632
1919	72,336	31,339	43	1,962	2.7	510
1920	77,423	28,181	36	3,492	4.5	733
1921	82,285	28,966	35	7,908	9.6	1,028
1922	89,629	29,248	33	5,787	6.5	752
1923	124,342	43,276	35	8,978	7.2	898
1924	141,965	52,544	37	16,966	12.0	1,866

TABLE I. *continued*

Year	Total Tax Revenue[a]	Coffee Export Tax Revenue[a]	C as % of B	State Expenditures on Immigration Programs[a]	E as % of B	E in Current U.S. Dollars[b]
A	B	C	D	E	F	G
1925	233,174	—	—	16,344	7.0	1,961
1926	235,611	128,232	54	15,407	6.5	2,157
1927	275,642	147,964	54	7,028	2.5	843
1928	273,105	119,352	44	2,639	1.0	317
1929	298,478	145,457	49	4,000	0.7	480
1930	255,625	132,550	52			
Total	3,304,388	1,650,151[c]	50	172,442	5.2	32,287

Notes:
  a. In thousands of milreis.
  b. In thousands of dollars, at current annual average exchange rates.
  c. Not including data for 1925, which are not available.
Sources:
  Column B: São Paulo, Departamento Estadual de Estatistica, *Publicação*, pp. 11–22.
  Column C: São Paulo, Secretaria da Fazenda, *Relatório*, various years.
  Column E: *Boletim do Departamento do Trabalho Agrícola*, no. 73–74, (1932), pp. 67–68.

of Sociedade Promotora policies. Throughout the following decades, nearly all subsidized immigrants listed their profession as "agriculturist." It was difficult to verify the occupation of immigrants in their home countries, however, and state officials commonly assumed that many people of urban origin misrepresented themselves as farmers in order to qualify for free passage.[25] All those who entered under the contract were to be in family units, carefully defined as follows: (a) married couples under age forty-five with no children; (b) married couples with children or wards, with at least one working-age male per family; or (c) widows or widowers with children or wards, with at least one working-age male per family. Dependent family members eligible for subsidized passage were the parents, grandparents, single brothers and brothers-in-law, and orphan nephews and nieces of the family head. Married women joining husbands already in Brazil were eligible, but cousins and more distant relatives were not. The state would not pay for families or single immigrants who did not fulfill those conditions, for those who declared their intention to settle in states other than São Paulo, or for those who had previously received paid passage to Brazil and later returned to their homeland. The company agreed to repatriate at its own ex-

pense anyone who did not fulfill the requirements, within thirty days after
the arrival of the individual in Brazil. The state was to pay full passage for
eligible persons age twelve and older, one-half passage for children age seven
through eleven, and one-quarter passage for those age three through six.
Infants under age three were transported free.

Among the hundreds of thousands of immigrants brought in after 1886,
some openly protested the crowded and unsanitary conditions on the ships,
on the Santos waterfront, and in the São Paulo hostel. Others charged fraud
and maltreatment on the plantations. Whatever the actual ideologies or af-
filiations of such critics might have been, government authorities categorized
them as "anarchists" or "strikers" (*grevistas*). In early 1893, for example,
the chief of police in Santos received information that a few "anarchists"
were aboard a Fiorita and Company ship under contract to the Sociedade
Promotora. The state deported three immigrants after investigating and
"verifying" the reports.[26]

In reaction to this and similar incidents, immigration officials began
watching carefully for such undesirables, and the 1894 Fiorita contract included a clause in the following language: "In the event that any immigrant is
denied entry for being an anarchist or on suspicion of being a member of that
association, the transporting company will be held responsible for the cost
of repatriation and whatever expenses the government or police of São Paulo
might incur with such immigrants." A similar clause became standard in
later contracts and laws regulating the immigration program. In this way the
state applied pressure on the shipping companies to screen out potential
troublemakers before leaving Europe.

The massive influx from Italy was by the mid-1890s causing some concern
in São Paulo.[27] In an attempt to balance the early preponderance of Italians,
the Fiorita contract of 1894 stipulated that not more than ten thousand of the
total fifty thousand immigrants could be Italian. In August 1895 Fiorita, an
Italian company itself, requested a revision to the effect that up to twenty-
five thousand immigrants—half the contracted total—could be from Italy.
The state granted the contract change, on the condition that Fiorita pay
twenty-five hundred francs monthly toward the expense of maintaining an
official inspection station in Europe. The company was required to put two
first-class berths or four steerage passages at the disposition of the São Paulo
government on all immigrant ships, to permit in-transit inspection and supervision. Pursuant to the agreement, in August 1895 the state opened an office
in Genoa, the principal port of embarkation from Italy to São Paulo.

The Genoa office set the precedent for a network of inspection stations
in foreign ports, for the purposes of promoting emigration to São Paulo,
ensuring that shipping companies complied with state regulations, and inspecting ships for sanitary conditions. The head of each office was called the
commissioner (*comissário*), and his functions and authority were similar to

the consular representatives of national governments. When an 1896 contract provided for recruiting ten thousand Canadians, a commissioner was appointed to set up an office in Montreal. The Canadian venture was unsuccessful to the point of embarrassment, however, and in December 1896 the commissioner there was transferred to set up an office in Málaga, Spain. In 1897 a subcommissioner was appointed for Naples, under the Genoa office, and a commissioner for northern Europe was later installed in Belgium. The latter office became more involved in promoting the sale of São Paulo coffee than in immigration activities.[28]

In later contracts and immigration laws the specific eligibility requirements for paid passage differed somewhat from the 1894 agreement, but the requirements that subsidized immigrants be farmers and be in family units remained in force. In addition to the standard provision that shippers would have to repatriate any ineligible immigrant at their own expense, the companies posted sizable bonds to ensure fulfillment of their contracts. In a contract with Fiorita signed in March 1896, for example, the state stipulated that immigrant families were to have at least one physically fit male between the ages of thirteen and forty-five for every two family members. The company protested that such a requirement made the contract impossible to fulfill, because young couples with several small children would be ineligible, and in June 1896 the family composition rules were relaxed to previous levels for all but Italians. At the same time the state demanded that in the first four months of the contract period the company should bring in at least ten thousand non-Italians or lose half of the twenty thousand milreis bond it had posted. By October Fiorita had not complied, and the fine was levied.[29] To prevent shippers from charging both individual immigrants and the São Paulo government, thus making double income and nullifying the intent of the subsidy program, the company was to submit a certified affidavit from the head of each immigrant family stating that he had paid nothing to the company for passage or for the transport of baggage.

During the period of large contracts with individual companies, São Paulo officials tried to enforce quotas not only for given nationalities, but for regions within European countries as well. The Fiorita contract of March 1896, for example, included a quota of not more than ten thousand Spaniards, and they were to come only from the Basque provinces, Navarre, Galicia, and the Canary Islands. In August 1897 the state awarded a contract to Fiorita for the introduction of thirty thousand Italians and ten thousand Austrians. Of the Italians, fifteen thousand were to be from Veneto, eight thousand from other northern regions, and seven thousand from the provinces of southern Italy. Also in August 1897 a contract for twenty thousand immigrants went to José Antunes dos Santos and Company with the total to comprise ten thousand Spaniards, five thousand Portuguese, and five thousand "northern Europeans" of unspecified nationality.[30]

When immigrant ships arrived in Santos, state officials examined passenger lists to ensure compliance with the subsidy agreements. Only qualified people counted toward fulfillment of the contracted quotas. By the end of 1899, for example, Fiorita had brought in a total of 43,418 individuals under the August 1897 contract, but 4,505 were not counted for subsidies because they were under three years of age, and the state refused to pay passage for an additional 8,268 persons because they did not comply with the contract stipulations regarding family composition, profession, or region of origin. Although most of those who did not qualify for subsidy because of their region or origin were allowed to remain in São Paulo, losses from such "rejections" spurred the companies to be more selective in their recruiting.[31]

By a law that took effect in September 1900, São Paulo made the first major changes in its subsidy program since the establishment of the republic. The previous pattern of large exclusive contracts was largely abandoned. Under the new policy the state legislature set maximum limits on the number of immigrants subsidized each year, and any company that fulfilled certain requirements for ship speed and sanitary conditions was allowed to transport as many immigrants as it wished until the annual limit was reached. Instead of the current price of passage, the state paid a set fee of fifty francs for each qualified immigrant. In subsequent publicity brochures the São Paulo immigration service noted that while the flat rate of fifty francs was sometimes less than the full price of steerage passage, it meant a considerable reduction in the amount the immigrant would have to pay out of his own pocket. In addition to making the administration of the program more efficient, the flat fee system reduced the overall cost to the state per immigrant.[32] To qualify for the new partial subsidies, immigrants could not have been in Brazil previously, and they had to be farmers, in family units, in good health, and of "good moral character." Each family was to have at least one able-bodied male member between the age of twelve and forty-five.

Since the shipping companies no longer financed the inspection offices in foreign ports, the 1900 regulation provided state support for the agencies. It also charged the commissioners with inspecting prospective immigrants and their supporting documents before embarkation and ensuring that the immigrants paid no more than the difference between the state's contribution of fifty francs and the full cost of steerage passage. Shippers leaving from ports where there was no inspection station could submit passenger lists, passports, and supporting documents upon arrival in Santos, taking responsibility for repatriating any immigrants rejected at that time. The state later awarded some smaller contracts to individual companies, but in the main the program operated under the system of open competition and partial subsidies after the turn of the century.[33]

Transportation subsidies gave the state considerable control over what occupations immigrants would enter after their arrival in São Paulo. There was less control over those who entered on their own. In the early years the eventual destination of the few nonsubsidized foreigners was not of much concern. After the turn of the century increasing proportions of the new arrivals paid their own way, while the reception station remained the focal point of the governmental program. In the fourteen years from 1908 through 1921, for example, 206,483 subsidized immigrants entered the port of Santos, and 98 percent of them went directly to the hostel in São Paulo. Of the 359,167 nonsubsidized immigrants who entered Santos in the same period, less than 23 percent went directly to the hostel. The remaining 278,242 nonsubsidized entries went their way without state tutelage. While it is probable that many of them eventually worked for a time on coffee plantations, many others entered the growing urban labor market, especially in the city of São Paulo.[34] In order to evaluate the state's program for importing and distributing workers into the western coffee zone, the central role of the immigrant hostel in the system must be examined.

Santos was considered only a transfer point, where new arrivals boarded trains for the eighty-kilometer trip to the city of São Paulo. Conditions in the port long contributed to Brazil's reputation as a humid, tropical country teeming with malaria and yellow fever. Working people from various parts of the world, having crossed the tropic belt on an ocean voyage of three to five weeks, often brought disease, which could spread quickly on the dirty and crowded waterfront. In 1899, for example, an outbreak of bubonic plague in Portugal spread to Santos, nearly closing the port. A sanitation program after the turn of the century improved Santos's public health record, but immigration officials wanted no facilities that might give new arrivals an incentive to tarry in the port. In the late 1880s the government leased an old theater building near the waterfront where new arrivals could spend the night if necessary, but it was a dilapidated shed that provided little more than shelter from the rain. The state eventually acquired offices for immigration inspectors near the docks, but did not construct or acquire new lodging for immigrants in Santos. Nor were regional branches of the immigrant labor service established in the western plateau itself, as was occasionally suggested. Although other buildings in the capital were sometimes used on a temporary basis to cope with the massive influx of Europeans during the 1890s, the Hospedaria de Imigrantes remained the only permanent facility of its kind.[35]

The hostel was an imposing structure occupying most of a city block, with a special railroad siding and platform for unloading immigrants and their baggage. The ground floor was taken up by offices, a currency exchange, a medical dispensary, kitchens, dining halls, and storage areas. The dormitory rooms were in the upper floor. A separate building near the street entrance housed the offices where new arrivals met future employers. The government provided interpreters to help Italian, Spanish, and later Japanese immigrants make some sense of the wages and various nonwage provisions of work

Immigrant hostel, São Paulo

contracts. Specific regulations varied over the years, but those who entered were generally allowed to remain four to eight days, during which they were provided with a place to sleep, two meals per day, and medical treatment. After an immigrant contracted for work he drew a travel ration of bread and salami for each member of his family the night before departing for the interior.[36]

A cursory description of the hostel can give no sense of the confusion and frustration many people must have felt there. The facility was originally intended to lodge a maximum of four thousand persons, but during the early years as many as ten thousand at a time were crowded in.[37] The immigrants were often treated more like cattle than people, as they were processed in, hired, and processed out. Mealtimes were not fixed because when the place was full the serving lines had to operate continuously most of the day. In

Newly arrived immigrants, courtyard of hostel

its first twenty years, during which nine hundred thousand people passed through, each dormitory was simply a bare hall providing space for six or seven hundred men, women, and children to sleep together on the floor, on mats issued on arrival and turned in on departure. Sanitary facilities consisted of one latrine divided into ten compartments for every two dormitory rooms, and a spigot and trough in the interior courtyard for drinking water and washing. Children especially suffered. Those from age seven through eleven received half the adult food ration, those from age three through six received a quarter ration, and those under age three received nothing but what their families could share. The children were more susceptible to diseases, which grew in filth and spread rapidly in crowded conditions. Annual reports on the immigration service often included the routine but poignant observation, "of those who died, nearly all were children under ten years of age."[38]

Watchmen patrolled the buildings day and night to reduce the incidence of theft, and guards at the entrances checked to ensure that no one left without authorization and no one entered without official business. Immigrants and consuls protested that the security system made the hostel into a prison from which the only escape was through signing on as a coffee worker and taking a train for the interior.[39] State officials justified the strict control on the grounds that free access would permit unscrupulous labor recruiters to take advantage of the new arrivals, making false promises and enticing people to work in the city rather than in the rural zone. This was a constant preoccupation of the immigration service, since its reason for existence was to supply manpower for the coffee plantations of the interior. In 1896 the secretary of agriculture went so far as to specifically prohibit the recruitment of domestic servants and wet nurses in the reception station.[40]

In 1906 the hostel was remodeled. Sanitation was improved, the kitchens modernized, cots provided, and some of the dormitory halls partitioned into compartments for family sleeping quarters. An Italian consul generally critical of the immigrants' condition reported that the renovation greatly improved the facility.[41] At the same time the hiring office was reorganized to reduce the cases of misrepresentation that had previously been common. The agency began recording the provisions of each work contract, and planters and their hiring agents were required to register with the employment office. If officials received reports of fraudulent hiring, maltreatment of workers, or failure to pay wages as contracted, the planter in question was not allowed to use the employment office to obtain more laborers.[42]

From the beginning of the immigration program in 1886–87 to 1892 no separate data are available on movement through the hostel, but since most immigrants were subsidized in those years, most probably used it. From 1893 through 1930 over 60 percent of all immigrants to São Paulo passed through the reception station. Those who entered were divided into three general categories. New arrivals from outside São Paulo made up the subsidized and nonsubsidized groups. Such people included those just off the boat in Santos as well as foreigners or Brazilian migrants who arrived at the establishment via railroad from other parts of Brazil. After a reorganization in 1900 the hostel began to admit people who were grouped in a third catch-all category known as "reentries" (*reentrados*), to distinguish them from the two types of new arrivals. Most of the "reentries" were people who voluntarily appeared at the gates of the hostel in search of jobs in the coffee plantations. These "reentries to obtain work in agriculture" (*reentrados para colocarem-se na lavoura*) were eligible for the same period of free food and lodging as were immigrants. Thus after 1900 the hostel functioned more generally as an employment service supplying workers to the coffee zone, in addition to processing new arrivals from abroad.

It is impossible to say how many of the "reentries" had actually been through the building previously. A nonsubsidized immigrant who chose to stay with relatives in the capital might after a time go to the reception station to get a job. Natives of São Paulo might enter for the same purpose. A migrant from northern Brazil might arrive by train or on foot and then go to the hostel. Receiving clerks classified all such people as "reentries" along with those who at one time had already been at the hostel. Because the building was located in Braz, the working-class section of the capital where many immigrants and migrants congregated, potential coffee workers had easy access to its facilities.

Data on the people who entered the hostel by category are presented in table 2. As with total immigration figures, the subsidized proportion declined over the years. After the hostel began admitting "reentries" that category quickly became a major contributor to total entries into the establishment. Beginning in 1908 "reentries" were especially important, culminating in 1914 with 45 percent of the total. A more detailed examination of records kept at the hostel clearly shows that most of the people who passed through were in large family units. Data on family composition are available in a complete series from 1902 through 1923. During those years 728,000 people went in and out of the hostel, 20 percent of whom were adults traveling alone and 80 percent in family units. The average size of families was 4.7 people, ranging from lows of 4.3 in 1903 (when few immigrants were subsidized) and 4.2 in 1918 (when immigration fell off due to the war) to a high of 5.4 in 1923. Family composition data by category of entry are available for only shorter series of years, 1902–10 and 1918–21, but they show the importance of subsidy eligibility requirements in determining the composition of the immigrant stream. During those years subsidized families averaged 5 persons each, nonsubsidized families averaged 4.8 persons, and "reentries" averaged just 4 persons per family unit. In the same time periods, only 3 percent of all subsidized persons entering the hostel were adults traveling alone, compared to 25 percent of the nonsubsidized category and 44 percent of the "reentries."[43]

The sex and age breakdown of those who entered the hostel from 1893 to 1928 are presented in table 3 grouped by periods for which comparable data are also available for the three categories of entries. Part A of table 3 shows that from 1893 to 1900 the sexes were more evenly balanced than later, as might be expected since nearly all entries in those years were subsidized immigrants. In later periods the pattern again appears. Subsidized entries were most evenly balanced by sex, followed by nonsubsidized new arrivals. Nearly three-fourths of the "reentries" were males. The age data on part B of table 3 show related tendencies. There were more children among the total entries in the early period than later. Greater proportions of the subsi-

TABLE 2

Entries into the São Paulo Immigrant Hostel, by Category, 1893–1928

Year	Total Entries	New Arrivals Subsidized		Nonsubsidized		"Reentries" (after 1900)	
		No.	%	No.	%	No.	%
1893	69,139	65,462	95	3,677	5		
1894	29,148	26,548	91	2,600	9		
1895	104,122	101,233	97	2,889	3		
1896	74,910	71,586	96	3,324	4		
1897	65,886	63,649	97	2,237	3		
1898	28,358	27,072	95	1,286	5		
1899	16,764	14,920	89	1,844	11		
1900	13,389	12,126	91	1,263	9		
1901	57,634	49,607	86	4,257	7	3,770	7
1902	25,436	19,311	76	3,498	14	2,627	10
1903	7,634	229	3	3,576	47	3,829	50
1904	17,253	7,005	41	5,755	33	4,493	26
1905	37,925	26,015	69	5,502	15	6,408	17
1906	36,966	23,885	65	5,426	15	7,655	21
1907	22,635	4,862	21	8,367	37	9,406	42
1908	30,315	9,433	31	7,422	24	13,460	44
1909	30,768	12,662	41	7,230	23	10,876	35
1910	32,024	15,517	48	6,137	19	10,370	32
1911	44,452	21,458	48	12,482	28	10,512	24
1912	66,779	42,628	64	14,645	22	9,506	14
1913	83,080	53,174	64	17,673	21	12,233	15
1914	46,924	15,385	33	10,609	23	20,930	45
1915	22,559	2,680	12	7,610	34	12,269	54
1916	22,134	6,844	31	5,314	24	9,976	45
1917	31,459	15,770	50	5,766	18	9,923	32
1918	16,980	6,062	36	4,161	25	6,757	40
1919	18,179	4,439	24	6,720	37	7,020	39
1920	31,887	7,493	23	15,500	49	8,894	28
1921	33,458	13,647	41	10,933	33	8,878	27
1922	26,405	8,626	33	11,196	42	6,583	25
1923	43,027	14,250	33	20,347	47	8,430	20
1924	52,395	23,145	44	20,336	39	8,914	17
1925	54,678	32,003	59	14,661	27	8,014	15

TABLE 2. *continued*

Year	Total Entries	New Arrivals				"Reentries" (after 1900)	
		Subsidized		Nonsubsidized			
		No.	%	No.	%	No.	%
1926	61,414	38,313	62	13,769	24	9,332	15
1927	66,092	28,393	43	24,325	37	13,374	20
1928	88,447	16,970[a]	19	45,720	52	25,757	29
Total	1,510,655	902,402	60	338,057	22	270,196	18

a. Including 3,065 subsidized by private parties.
Source: *Anuário estatístico do estado de São Paulo*, various years.

dized immigrants were children under age twelve, there were fewer children among the nonsubsidized group, and the "reentries" were overwhelmingly adults.

Since these data on family composition, sex, and age are consistent and mutually reinforcing, it is probable that similar patterns existed during the periods for which more complete records are not available. Furthermore, since nearly all recorded immigrants were subsidized in the early years for which hostel details were not published, it seems likely that the 350,000 immigrants who entered the state from 1886 through 1892 tended to be in large family units, with few unaccompanied adults.

Records kept by immigration inspectors in the port of Santos, the route of entry for some 85 percent of all immigrants to São Paulo, provide a more general picture of the sex and marital status of those who came in, without regard to subsidy category. Of the immigrants entering Santos age twelve and older in the 1887–92 period, 62 percent were males, and 30 percent of all entries were children under age twelve. Of Santos entries in all age categories in the 1893–98 period, 59 percent were male, and 61 percent of those twelve and older were married. Children under twelve made up 34 percent. There is a gap in the Santos records from 1899 to 1907, but for the years from 1908 through 1930 some 64 percent of all Santos entries were male, and 51 percent of those twelve and older were married. During this later period 23 percent were under twelve years old.[44]

This statistical profile of the immigrants arriving in Santos and those who passed through the hostel was very important for the viability of the labor system adopted in the coffee plantations of the western plateau after the end of slavery. Thus in addition to the long-term financial advantage to the coffee industry, the state subsidies helped bring in the specific types of workers the

TABLE 3
Persons Entering the Immigrant Hostel, by Category, for Selected Periods, 1893–1928

A. Sex Ratios

Period	Total Entries		Subsidized		Nonsubsidized		"Reentries" (after 1900)	
	Male	Female	Male	Female	Male	Female	Male	Female
1893–1900	225,654	176,062						
percent	56	44						
1901–10	179,179	119,411	90,270	78,256	36,759	20,411	52,150	20,744
percent	60	40	54	46	64	36	72	28
1911–21	257,214	160,677	102,088	87,492	72,279	39,134	82,847	34,051
percent	62	38	54	46	65	35	71	29
1922–26	145,730	92,189						
percent	61	39						
1927–28	104,263	50,276	27,247	18,116	48,938	21,107	28,078	11,053
percent	67	33	60	40	70	30	72	28
Total	912,040	598,615						
percent	60	40						

B. Age Divisions

Period	Total Entries		Subsidized		Nonsubsidized		"Reentries" (after 1900)	
	Under 12 Years	12 and Older	Under 12 Years	12 and Older	Under 12 Years	12 and Older	Under 12 Years	12 and Older
1893–1900	137,689	264,027						
percent	34	66						
1902–10[a]	79,206	161,750	48,185	70,734	15,281	37,632	15,740	53,384
percent	33	67	41	59	29	71	23	77
1911–1921	119,852	298,039	66,708	122,872	30,185	81,228	22,959	93,939
percent	29	71	35	65	27	73	20	80
1922–26	62,943	174,976						
percent	26	74						
1927–28	32,873	121,666	11,026	34,337	14,452	55,593	7,395	31,736
percent	21	79	24	76	21	79	19	81
Total	432,563	1,020,458						
percent	30	70						

a. These data are not available for 1901.
Source: *Anuário estatístico do estado de São Paulo*, various years.

planters wanted. A standard argument for continuation of subsidized transportation was that the labor system on the coffee plantations worked best when entire families were contracted as a unit, and that a greater proportion of nonsubsidized immigrants were single individuals. In 1920 the secretary of agriculture stated the official position in the following terms:

> As long as it is not possible to dispense with family units as the permanent plantation labor force, nonsubsidized immigration will never make the necessary numbers of workers available. The immigration of families . . . will only be satisfactory through the selection that subsidized immigration makes possible, and through the payment of passages by the state, which is the essence of the system. With nonsubsidized immigration, on the other hand, there is no selection, because there is no screening of immigrants before departure. Furthermore, it is difficult for families to travel together, because when immigrants must pay their own passage this becomes very expensive.

He went on to cite the high rate of labor turnover on the plantations, as workers took their savings and became independent farmers. The secretary concluded that "the state must permanently maintain subsidized immigration in order to replace those workers who leave the plantations to set themselves up on their own."[45]

Especially from the mid-1880s up to the turn of the century, the incentive of free passage helped determine the overall composition of the immigrant stream. This continued to be true for those who went to work on the coffee plantations, since most subsidized immigrants continued to enter the hostel immediately upon arrival, from where they spread into the western plateau. In addition to the free food and lodging and the availability of the employment service, geographical barriers and distances between the coffee areas and the coast helped channel workers through the hostel. Campinas, the nearest important coffee center, was one hundred kilometers from the capital over hilly terrain. Ribeirão Preto, in the Mogiana zone, the central point of the most intensively cultivated coffee area in these years, was five hundred kilometers northwest of the capital. The most practical means of getting to the plantations was by train, yet rail travel was costly for a coffee worker. In the late 1880s, when a day laborer might expect to earn 1$000 to 2$000 (1 to 2 milreis) for a ten-hour day, second-class train fare from São Paulo to Ribeirão Preto cost 12$980 (12 milreis and 980 reis). By 1920 daily wages rose to some 2$000 to 3$000, and the fare from the state capital to Ribeirão Preto was 16$300.[46] Throughout this period, transportation from the capital to the coffee zone might have cost a single laborer something over a week's normal earnings, and such a trip could have been a major expense for a large family. In this context, the free services of the hostel take on added significance, as does the statistical information from the hostel records.

When an immigrant, migrant, or "reentry" contracted for work, he and his family received a free train ticket to the station nearest his future place of employment. At the time the ticket was issued, immigration officials recorded the municipio of destination within São Paulo. Similarly, after 1896 the clerks kept track of those who entered the labor force of the capital city. Changing magnitudes and regional distributions of workers reveal which parts of the state benefited from the immigration program and make it possible to examine the relationship between the rural labor market and the spread of coffee into the western frontier. These data also provide an indicator of the geographical mobility of the rural labor force.

Summary data on the destinations of those who passed through the hostel are presented in table 4. Throughout these years the overwhelming majority continued on to the western plateau coffee zone. The economically stagnant Paraiba valley received relatively few. The data for the Capital zone show the importance of the urban labor market over the years. Of the 34,660 who went to "other parts of São Paulo," the Sorocaba zone received 12,241 for the entire period 1893–1929, the Baixa Sorocabana zone received just 8,310, and the Santos and southern coast zone received 14,109.

The immigration system brought in an abundant labor supply, composed of the types of people the planters wanted. The hiring office at the hostel then functioned to place those workers according to regional labor needs. Figures 5 and 6 show the geographical distribution of coffee trees in western São Paulo and the regional distribution of workers sent out from the hostel. The similarity of figures 5 and 6 is a striking reflection of the effectiveness of São Paulo's immigration program. Each zone of the western plateau received workers from the hostel in proportions roughly equivalent to its share of the coffee industry, even though those shares changed markedly over time. The one exception is the Araraquarense zone, intermediate in the process of frontier expansion, which apparently drew workers from the older areas contiguous to it during its period of growth in the 1920s. Absolute levels of labor demand grew only slightly in the three older zones during the 1920s (see figure 3, chapter 2). Thus their continued absorption of workers from the hostel reflects the need to replace earlier arrivals who moved on. This indirect evidence of geographical mobility is made more explicit by comparing destination data to labor needs in the coffee plantations of the west.

Since most of the people who came in the early years went to work on coffee plantations, the data on total immigration into São Paulo may serve as proxy indicators of labor supply conditions during the important early period, for which destination data are not available. From 1887 through 1892, 341,000 immigrants entered São Paulo. Based on the age distribution recorded for Santos entries during that period and for hostel entries in later years, it may be assumed that 70 percent of the 1886–92 immigrants, or some 240,000, were in the economically active group of twelve years of age

TABLE 4
Destinations of Persons Leaving Immigrant Hostel, by Region of São Paulo, 1893–1929

Period	Total Departures No.	Western Plateau No.	%	Capital Zone No.	%	Paraiba Valley No.	%	Other Parts of São Paulo No.	%
1893–1900	323,153 [a]	290,535	90	26,259	8	2,380	1	3,979	1
1901–10	285,291	257,302	90	18,945	7	1,250	0	7,794	3
1911–20	379,745	325,344	86	42,885	11	3,351	1	8,165	2
1921–29	491,842 [b]	428,192	87	42,975	9	5,953	1	14,722	3
Total	1,480,031	1,301,373	88	131,064	9	12,934	1	34,660	2

a. Since destination data are not available for 1896, the 74,910 total hostel entries for that year are included in this total, and spread among regions in a proportion equal to the average regional distribution for the 1897–99 period.

b. Not including 40,890 hostel departees in the years 1922–27 whose specific destinations were not published.

Source: São Paulo Repartição de Estatística, *Relatório*, and *Anuário estatístico do estado de São Paulo*, various years.

or older. Then using later destination data as a basis for extrapolation, at least 80 percent of the working-age immigrants, or 192,000, probably went directly into the western coffee zone upon arrival during the 1886–92 period. Based on estimates of the number of coffee trees in western São Paulo (figure 3, chapter 2), and a ratio of twenty-five hundred trees per adult worker, about 134,000 people were needed to care for the trees in the plateau area by 1892. Without attempting to adjust these estimates to allow for the ex-slaves and prior immigrants or for demographic increase of the working-age population, it seems probable that the labor supply in the coffee zone began to exceed demand early in the period of mass immigration. In view of the rapid increase in the number of coffee trees coming into production in the 1890s, it is apparent that many of the new arrivals became occupied in the care of newly planted groves.

By the same token, the growth of São Paulo's coffee industry in the last decade of the nineteenth century would have been impossible without the influx of immigrant manpower. Even if all the 68,400 slaves recorded in the rural areas of the western plateau in March 1887 had stayed on the plantations after abolition—an unlikely prospect—such growth could not have taken place without more laborers.[47] Mobilization of the subsistence-oriented peasant population scattered in the backlands of northeastern Brazil was unthinkable on the scale and speed of the immigration program. The decision to promote immigration from southern Europe was a quick, effective solution to the planters' labor problem. Considering the return, it was also inexpensive for the Paulista elite. When the Paulistas decided to go to Europe for their workers, the Brazilian peasantry, including many ex-slaves and the native mixed-blood backwoodsmen, was relegated to a marginal position in the regional economy. Native Brazilians worked as day laborers, cartmen, and household servants, but not generally as field hands after abolition.

By the early twentieth century the die was cast, and work in the coffee fields of the west was universally identified with immigrants. In an agricultural census of 1905, 404,316 rural laborers were counted in all of São Paulo, 56 percent of them foreigners. The proportion of foreign workers rose to 65 percent for the western plateau; of all foreigners counted, 98 percent were in the western plateau, where there was one immigrant worker for every 2,772 coffee trees counted in the same census. In thirty-eight of the ninety-seven municipios in the western plateau in 1905, foreigners made up more than two-thirds of the rural workers. In the same thirty-eight municipios, an average of 81 percent of the land in cultivation was planted in coffee, and together they accounted for 59 percent of the producing coffee trees in the western plateau. In contrast with this concentration of immigrant workers in the coffee-producing areas of the west, in the Paraiba valley zone only 1,711 of the 39,331 rural workers counted in 1905 were foreigners, just 4 percent of the total.[48]

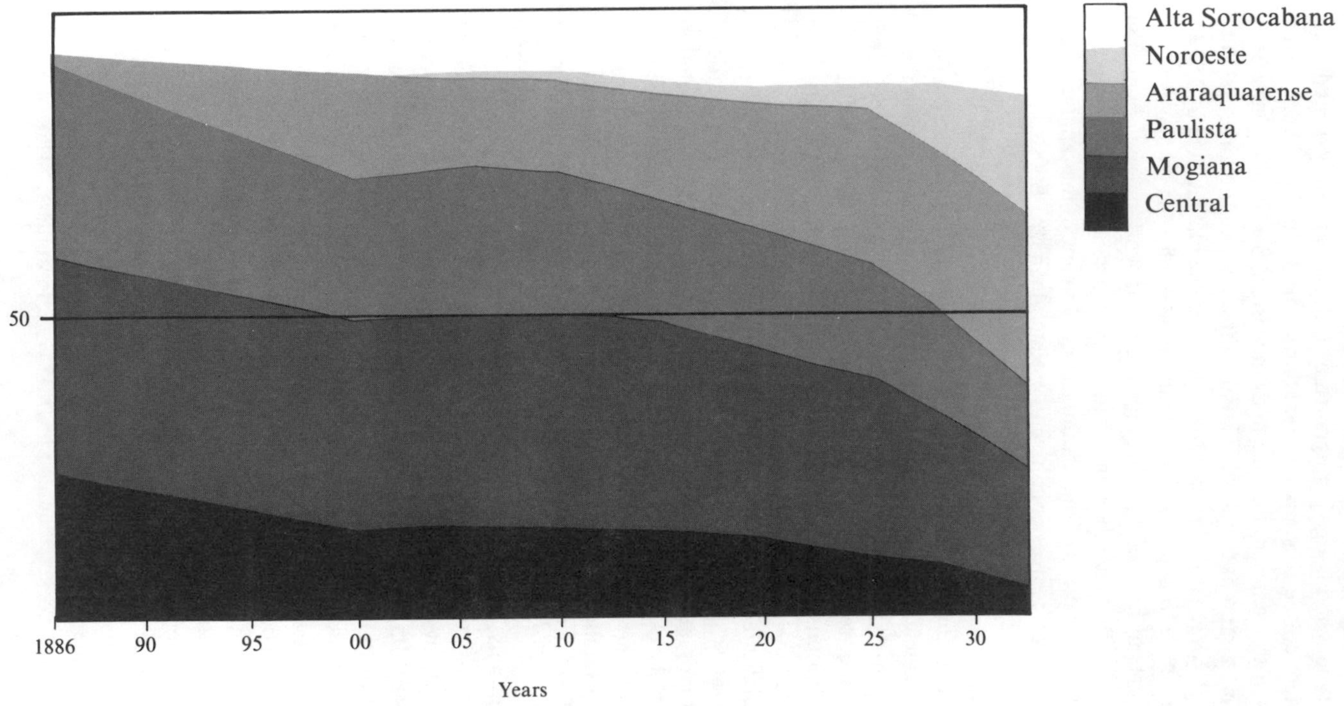
Alta Sorocabana
Noroeste
Araraquarense
Paulista
Mogiana
Central
50
1886
90
95
00
05
10
15
20
25
30
Years

5. Regional Percentage Distribution of Coffee Trees in Western Plateau, 1886–1932

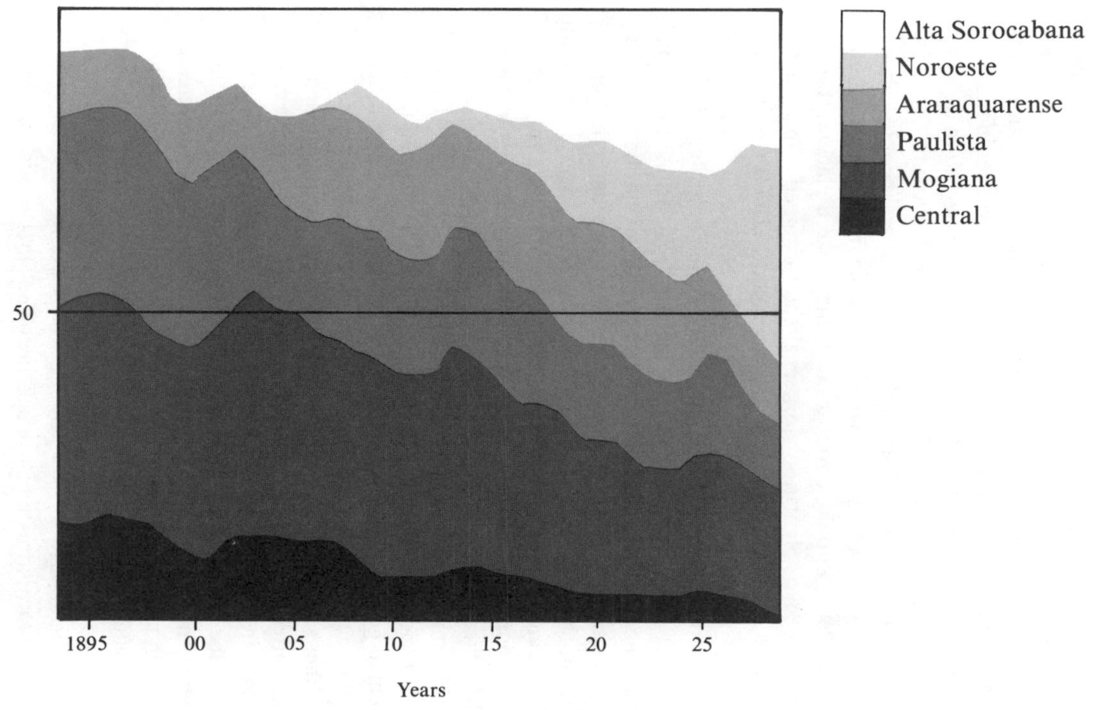
Alta Sorocabana
Noroeste
Araraquarense
Paulista
Mogiana
Central
50
1895
00
05
10
15
20
25
Years

6. Regional Percentage of Workers from Hostel to Western Plateau, 1894–1928

Using the data on coffee trees in existence, a stable ratio of twenty-five hundred trees per worker, and the internal destination data from table 4, it is possible to make comparisons between labor supply and labor requirements after 1892 and to make minimal estimates of the level of turnover in the work force of the coffee plantations. Hostel destinations are conservative indicators of labor supply for several reasons. These are not hypothetical projections or extrapolations but rather the recorded destinations of real people. The figures include only those who are known to have gone from foreign countries or the city of São Paulo into the coffee zone of the western plateau, most of them with employment as plantation workers already arranged. Since the data begin only in 1893, they do not include the estimated 192,000 working-age immigrants who probably went into the coffee zone between 1887 and 1892. Smaller numbers arrived before 1887, and many ex-slaves probably stayed on after abolition.[49] Also, these data do not include the nonsubsidized immigrants, internal migrants, and natives of São Paulo who continued to go to work on the plantations without passing through the Hospedaria de Imigrantes. Most importantly, there is no allowance for the demographic increase of the population already in the coffee zone and the continuous entry of children into economically active age brackets over the years. Adjustment for any or all of these factors would increase these estimates of the labor supply available to the coffee industry.

On the other hand, a very small proportion of those who passed through the hostel went to government-sponsored farm colonies, and a few others probably went directly into urban occupations in the expanding towns of the interior. Other small numbers obtained employment on sugar plantations or in other noncoffee rural activities. After World War I cotton achieved some importance in São Paulo, centered mainly around Sorocaba, in municipios outside the coffee zone. Workers going to the cotton plantations in the Sorocaba zone in the 1920s are not included in the western plateau destination data in table 4. Given the reason for the existence of the immigration program and the hostel labor office, it may be concluded that nearly all the workers who left that establishment for the western plateau went to work on coffee plantations.

Table 5 presents the estimated increases in coffee labor needs for periods from 1893 to 1929 (column B), compared to the numbers of people who went from the hostel into the western plateau in corresponding periods (column C). According to the age breakdown for entries into the port of Santos and into the hostel, a fairly stable proportion of 70 percent of the immigrants were age twelve or older, thus considered able to do the work of an adult in the coffee groves. Based on that proportion, column D of table 5 shows the probable number of working-age people involved. For all the periods shown, São Paulo's immigration and labor service supplied the western plateau with many more workers than were needed as a result of the growth of the coffee

TABLE 5

Estimated Increase in Labor Needs of the Coffee Industry of São Paulo's Western Plateau Compared to Persons Leaving the Immigrant Hostel for Work in the Coffee Zone, by Selected Periods, 1893–1929 (In Thousands of Persons)

Period	Estimated Increase in Labor Needs [a]	Persons from Hostel to Coffee Zone	Estimated "Adults" from Hostel to Coffee Zone [b]	D as % of B
A	B	C	D	E
1893–1900	37	291[c]	204	551
1901–10	19	257	180	947
1911–20	80	325	228	285
1921–29	141	428	300	213

a. Calculated from appendix table 3, at 2,500 trees per worker.

b. Calculated at 70 percent of column C, assuming that proportion of hostel departees was age 12 and older.

c. Including 63,675 for 1896, assuming 85 percent of all hostel departees went to coffee zone in that year, for which destination data are not available.

Sources: column B from appendix table 3; column C from *Anuário estatístico do estado de São Paulo*, various years.

industry. During the stagnant first decade of this century, nearly ten times as many workers were supplied as could have been accounted for by coffee expansion. Even in the booming 1920s the number of workers who went from the hostel into the plateau was more than double the concurrent increase in coffee labor needs. These estimates are calculated from the number of trees in production, and some coffee workers were employed in the care of unproductive young seedlings. But adjustment of the estimates to allow for such a factor would do little to alter the general conclusion.

Compared to the total numbers of workers needed in the coffee industry at any given time, the destination data provide even more convincing evidence of labor turnover. By 1910 an estimated 248,000 workers were needed in the coffee plantations. In the preceding sixteen years, from 1893 to 1909, 520,000 people went from the hostel to the western plateau, and about 364,000 of them were of working age when they made the trip. By 1929 about 442,000 workers were needed in the coffee industry. In the preceding eighteen years, from 1910 to 1928, some 684,000 people went into the western plateau from the hostel, including about 480,000 of working age. These data on the flow of workers into the coffee zone throw a different light on the technical need for intensive labor inputs discussed in chapter 2. With workers generally available, planters had less incentive to adopt labor-saving methods, even if practical techniques had been developed to reduce labor requirements for cultivation and harvest. Estimates of a decline in labor needs under improved methods would be little more than counterfactual speculation, however. Except for sporadic and scattered cases, workers were always plentiful. And coffee production methods continued to be labor intensive.

Since these destination data represent only a part of the potential supply of labor, the inevitable conclusion to be drawn from these comparisons is that there was considerable geographical mobility of the rural labor force. Otherwise the coffee plantations could not have continued to absorb the hundreds of thousands of workers who passed through the hostel over the years. Workers circulated in local areas, they went from stagnant older zones to the expanding frontier, and they left plantations to become independent farmers, to enter cities and towns, or to return to their homelands. (One indication of where they went is in the phenomenal growth of the city of São Paulo. The state capital went from a population of 65,000 in 1890 to 240,000 in 1900, an increase of 270 percent; then to 579,000 in 1920, an increase of 141 percent over 1900; and to 1,060,000 in 1934, an 83 percent increase over 1920.) Since the overall labor needs of the coffee industry never declined, such movement opened positions for other immigrants and migrants, and there was a continuing need for workers, even during the periods when the coffee industry was expanding only slightly.

Beginning during World War I the flow of working people from other parts of Brazil grew relative to overseas sources. From 1914 through 1929 a quarter of a million internal migrants passed through the São Paulo government's labor system, equivalent to 40 percent of the total of foreign immigrants in those years. Many other migrants entered the state without going through the labor office. Nonsubsidized immigration from abroad also became increasingly important. In 1914–27 only 40 percent of São Paulo's immigrants were subsidized, compared to about 85 percent in the 1890s. The new sources of manpower made the subsidy program less necessary than in earlier years, and support grew in government circles for discontinuing the subsidy policy. State officials also complained that expenditures on the immigration program chronically exceeded the amounts originally budgeted. Finally, in late 1927, Governor Júlio Prestes abruptly declared that the government would no longer pay transportation subsidies from other countries to São Paulo. The immigration service continued to operate the Santos inspection station and the hostel in the state capital, and workers could still use the labor exchange attached to the hostel. Some Japanese and internal migrants continued to arrive under subsidy programs already arranged, but the general policy of prepaid ocean passage ended by 1928.[50]

Since the 1880s the Paulista coffee planters had been accustomed to easily available sources of manpower, and they continued to expect the state to import thousands of workers each year at public expense, regardless of budgetary conditions or fluctuations in the rural labor market. Antonio de Queiroz Teles, namesake of the pioneer of the immigration program who oversaw the construction of the immigrant hostel in 1886–87, became a vocal critic of the subsidy cut; his arguments illustrate the planters' reaction. In a 1928 article in the journal of the Brazilian Rural Society, Teles claimed that "the sudden governmental decision caught our agricultural sector completely off guard, unprepared to make up quickly for the absence of new groups of immigrants, which had always been assured for more than forty years." He then repeated the familiar refrain regarding the role of the coffee industry in the regional economy: "It is a well-known fact that the income of the state of São Paulo comes largely from the coffee export tax. . . . We must recognize that our principal agricultural product is the mainstay of the state budgets. Since coffee contributes such a high proportion toward satisfying the public needs, it is only natural that a portion of that income, say 10 or 15 percent, should be spent on the immigration service, to benefit the coffee industry.''[51]

By the late 1920s, with the coffee export tax as a proportion of state revenues falling and nonsubsidized sources of workers increasing, such arguments were becoming increasingly hollow. The forty-year tradition was a success story from the perspective of the planter elite, but by the end of the era state officials concluded that the rationale of the coffee planters was no longer valid. The sources of workers changed from initial dependence on Italy to more diversified origins, including Japan, northern Brazil, and the growing labor pool of the state capital itself. Even after transportation subsidies declined in importance and disappeared, the state program continued to supply workers to the western plateau. The collapse of the international economy hit São Paulo severely soon after the subsidy system was ended. When the bottom dropped out of the world coffee market, previous assumptions changed. Older groves were abandoned, labor needs fell, immigrant inflow fell (well before the national origin quota system was instituted by the national government in 1934), and the regional economy entered a period of retrenchment. History had superseded São Paulo's complex program for recruiting, transporting, and distributing immigrant manpower. The onset of the Depression put the revitalization of the program out of the question.

4

SOCIAL RELATIONS OF PRODUCTION

The labor system that replaced the chattel slavery in the coffee plantations of western São Paulo constituted the specific matrix into which hundreds of thousands of immigrant workers entered upon arrival. That unique pattern, which can only be subsumed under the label "colono contract," defined the interaction between planter and worker—the social relations of the productive process. For planters, it was an incentive "package" making it possible to attract and maintain a free labor force during the decline of slavery, the ensuing coffee boom, and later periods of less favorable conditions in the world market. For the immigrant workers, the colono system and its variants determined the level of living and life chances. It has repercussions in the historical evolution of agrarian society in western São Paulo far beyond the specifics of producing coffee.[1]

The colono contract, developed in stages through experimentation with more conventional forms of free labor, was not the inevitable residue of earlier traditions. On the contrary, it was radically different from the preceding slave system. Nor was the colono system dictated by technical aspects of coffee. Over the past century the yearly production cycle, natural conditions, and technology have remained virtually the same in southeastern Brazil, yet the groves have been worked by slaves, sharecroppers, renters, small farmers, and migrant gangs of day laborers, in addition to the colonos. Because it was sui generis, restricted to western São Paulo, and practically universal there from the end of slavery to the Depression, the colono system is central to understanding the agrarian society for which it was the basis. One has only to go back to the mid-nineteenth century to find the origins of the social relations of production in São Paulo's postabolition coffee industry.

Efforts to replace slaves with free immigrants began as early as 1840. Several planters recruited and employed Europeans, but Senator Nicolau Vergueiro most actively promoted the scheme. The strikes of Swiss sharecroppers on his plantation in 1856–57 brought to light the defects of the system.[2] Vergueiro and his fellows were motivated by economic realities rather than by a humanitarian interest in ending slavery. These experiments took place near Campinas and Rio Claro, where commercial coffee cultivation had been introduced about mid-century. When the English and Brazilian governments effectively stopped the transatlantic slave trade in 1851, the planters on the frontier were increasingly hard-pressed to fill their expanding labor needs.

One of the basic problems to be solved was how to compensate free workers and how much to pay. Accounting procedures were rudimentary, and the wage bill an unknown expense. The slaves who did most coffee plantation work were bought, maintained, and replaced like capital goods. Nonslave laborers were the numerically unimportant group of *agregados*, who were more like informal serfs than salaried employees. Planters had little basis for knowing what incentives might have been necessary to attract Europeans and how much of the risk of coffee production they could get free workers to assume. The experiments began with *parceria*, a form of the sharecropping pattern found in many areas of premodern agriculture. The literal meaning of *parceria* is partnership, but the "partners" were hardly on an equal footing.

The planters paid the transportation costs of the immigrant families from Europe to São Paulo and advanced sufficient funds to sustain the new arrivals until they could harvest food on their own plots of plantation land. The worker was expected to reimburse the planter in full for these expenses, with an interest charge on the unpaid balance. Each immigrant was assigned a certain block of trees to cultivate, and he had no choice but to turn over the crop to the landowner after the harvest. The worker was to receive half the net profit from the eventual sale of the coffee from the trees under his care. The planter also allotted each family a house, for which they sometimes had to pay a small rent, and an area for raising food crops and a few domestic animals. The landowner was to receive half the production of these plots in excess of the subsistence needs of the worker.

The money income of the worker depended on the productivity of the trees under his care and on the prevailing coffee prices. Although the two "partners" were to share losses equally, only under very severe conditions might the landowner lose some of his investment. The sharecropper, on the other hand, rarely rose much above the subsistence level, and he was deeply in debt from the start. To him a killing frost or a bad turn of the coffee market meant not simply lower profits or the loss of an investment but threatened the loss of his livelihood. Most contemporary observers agreed that the living conditions of the mid-century sharecroppers were very bad. Given his precarious margin of existence, the sharecropper could not absorb the risks such a system entailed.[3] Under ideal conditions it would take several years to repay the cost of transport and the advance payments, making the sharecropper the effective equivalent of an indentured servant or a slave intent on buying his own freedom. This major obstacle was not removed until the mid-1880s when the government began to subsidize European immigration on a large scale.

In addition to being at the mercy of nature and the world market, the sharecropper was open to fraud on the part of the planter. After delivering the crop the worker had no control over its processing and sale. Senator Vergueiro's son José later claimed sharecropping had failed largely because of the worker's mistrust. The sharecroppers were "always suspicious, convinced that the landowner wanted to cheat in operations such as weighing, shipping, selling, etc. any of his production." Furthermore, the laborers looked upon the landowner's share as "a tax on the worker, which takes away any hope for the future."[4]

Physical violence and psychological subjugation maintained the slave system. There were reports of corporal punishment of immigrant sharecroppers, and oppressive paternalism was common, even to the extent of interfering in worker's private domestic affairs. Couty observed that "the colono will never substitute for the slave as long as the planter . . . wishes to intervene in the simplest acts of his life."[5] Such strict control could not become the basis of a viable free labor system if immigrants were to be attracted in sufficient numbers to replace slaves and allow for the growth of the coffee industry. Considering the debt burden and the uncertain income of the sharecroppers, positive incentives did not counterbalance the system's negative aspects. For the Paulista slavocrats one of the most important lessons of the early free labor experiments was that positive incentives had to replace coercion as the dynamic that made the labor system function.

The problem had to be remedied at two levels, the individual and the institutional. At the level of individual planters' attitudes, the appeal of the coercive approach to labor relations lingered through a generational turnover even after the abolition of slavery. The attempts at coercion ranged from monetary fines, to restrictions on freedom of movement, to cases of threatened and real beatings. Some planters probably found coercion efficacious in the short run, especially in isolated areas and with newly arrived immigrants not yet oriented to general conditions in São Paulo. But a consciously developed system of repression was not institutionalized, and the state did not exercise its legal recourse to force in support of such a system. The goal of the coffee capitalist was not to maintain a system of subjugated labor, but rather to produce his crop and make a profit. Through the abolition of slavery and world market slumps, the São Paulo planters were able to achieve their objective by developing a system of positive incentives that replaced the coercive foundations of the slave regime.

After 1860 the sharecropping pattern was changed in several ways. Rather than dividing the proceeds from the sale of the crop on a percentage basis, some plantations began to pay each worker a fixed piece rate for each volume unit of coffee harvested from the trees under his care. Second, the landowner gave up the right to one-half of the food crops workers grew in excess of their subsistence needs. Third, miscellaneous day labor was paid at a separately contracted daily wage. This variation was called the *contrato preço marcado*, or "fixed price contract." The price referred to was not the cost of labor, but the planter's proceeds from the future crop. Payment was set at a portion of the estimated future value of the coffee each worker harvested, assuming an average volume of picked berries for each kilogram of processed beans ready for market. Another name for this intermediate system was *por ajuste*, "by adjustment." What the planters still considered a variant of share-cropping had in fact become a piecework system. This was an important step toward the colono contract that eventually became standard.[6]

One apparent advantage in the change was to diminish the uncertainty under which the immigrants labored. Under sharecropping, the many risks involved in the coffee industry had been shared between landowner and worker. Under piecework the risks were divided. The size of each crop might fluctuate considerably, but the planter's annual costs *per unit* were relatively fixed, regardless of how abundant or sparse the yield per tree or unit of land. On the other hand, he assumed the risks involving coffee market conditions and the exchange rate. The landowner thus reaped the benefit of favorable turns of the market and absorbed the losses in the short run if the market went bad. The worker was freed from such short-term market fluctuations, and the possibility of fraud in the processing and shipping stages was diminished.[7] The piece rate, however, did not give the worker a contractually fixed annual income, nor assure him a certain wage per day. The worker was left with those risks involving frosts, drought, and the delicate nature of the coffee shrub. A frost in 1887, for example, caused the production of the entire western plateau for that year to fall 36 percent below the 1881–90 average. If a piece rate worker was in a severely affected zone there might be no harvest, and his wages for the year could drop to near zero.

At the same time as the piecework system was generally replacing share-cropping in the 1860s and 1870s, some plantations went one step further in reducing the uncertainty of the free worker's income. They separated the pay for the annual cultivation of the coffee groves from the harvest piece rate.[8] This was the final step in the evolution from sharecropping to the colono contract. With this change the colono was no longer subject entirely to natural fluctuations, since payment for cultivation was independent of the size of the crop. Each colono could contract to care for as many trees as his available family manpower dictated. Thus the colono's risk was reduced and his income made more stable, while still allowing flexibility based on varying ability, initiative, and family composition.

The employer assumed the degree of risk the worker lost with the separation of cultivation from harvest payments. The planter's cost for the newly established category of cultivation wage, the *trato*, was determined by the number of coffee trees on the plantation, rather than by the size of the crop. Continuation of the separate harvest piece rate still cushioned the planter from the effects of a small yield. In years with a sparse crop, the colono would have to spend nearly the same amount of time picking as in years of high yield, with less return per hour of work. But the planter's harvest costs remained fixed per unit of coffee produced. Another advantage for the planter was that the colono's income varied with the amount of labor he and his family could apply to both harvest and cultivation. The incentives built into the system were designed to extract the full potential from the labor pool on each plantation, still leaving the workers with a marginal element of risk.

Throughout the early period of institutional evolution the number of free workers remained small relative to the slave labor force. After 1857 Vergueiro's plantation and some others returned to the use of slaves, and active promotion of free labor in western São Paulo went into decline. The employment of immigrant workers never completely died out, but the number of plantations with free labor "colonies" fell from twenty-nine in 1860 to thirteen in 1870. In 1884 an estimated one thousand free families were working on São Paulo plantations under a variety of forms of payment.[9]

Around Campinas in 1884, free labor plantations with older groves still paid by harvest piece rate, with cultivation included. Plantations with new groves, where production was higher per tree, paid separately for cultivation. When the Sociedade Promotora began advertising in Europe in 1886, its brochures mentioned only the mixed colono contract, with cultivation separated from harvest. Just prior to the abolition of slavery an official from the neighboring province of Minas Gerais described the colono contract as virtually the only system Paulista planters were using to employ newly arrived immigrants.[10] Sharecropping and the piece rate *contrato preço marcado* died out in western São Paulo by the time the abolition of slavery was imminent, and throughout the period from the late 1880s to the 1930s, the colono contract was the standard form of coffee plantation labor organization. Specific details varied somewhat, but in general the colono's total income included the following combination of money wages and nonmonetary perquisites.

Money wages came from three separate sources. First, there was the contractually established payment for the care of the coffee trees through the annual production cycle. The coffee groves were divided into sections based on the standard unit of division of one thousand trees, and when he arrived at the fazenda the head of the colono family was assigned a block of so many thousand trees, called a *talhão*. The *talhão* was marked off by numbered stakes or painted stones, and for the duration of the one-year contract each family cultivated its own block exclusively. Each colono family contracted for a minimum of two thousand trees to as many as twelve or fifteen thousand, depending on the number of "hoes" available. Contemporary economic studies of coffee calculated an average of about five thousand trees per family.

Included in the annual *trato* were four to six hoeings per year to keep the groves free of weeds; the task of replanting and caring for seedlings to replace occasional dead trees; the *coroação*—raking the debris into rows in preparation for the harvest; and the *espalhamento do cisco*—spreading the surface debris evenly after the harvest. This last operation took place in October and November, and its completion signaled the end of the yearly agricultural cycle. The annual *trato* salary, which accounted for roughly one-half to two-thirds of the income of the colono family, depended on the number of trees in each family's *talhão* and the contractually established wage rate per thousand trees. It had no direct relationship to the amount of coffee those trees produced nor the price the planter eventually got for his coffee.

During the year colonos received periodic cash installments on their annual cultivation wage to cover current living expenses. Such partial payments were often made quarterly, but pay periods ranging from monthly to semiannually were also reported. Administrators recorded each payment in the *caderneta*, or account book, which the colono kept, as well as in the plantation ledgers. Every year after the *espalhamento do cisco*, accounts were settled for the preceding year. In arranging contracts for the following year colonos could take on more or fewer trees, negotiate for higher wages, or leave the plantation if they chose. The colono used some care in deciding how many trees to take on. If he fell behind due to illness or sheer exhaustion, the planter had the contractual right to bring in day laborers to complete the job—often other colonos with free time—and charge the expense against the account of the delinquent worker.

The second important source of monetary income came from the coffee harvest. Again the family contracted its labor as a unit, receiving a fixed sum for each fifty-liter alqueirc picked. (The alqueire of volume was not directly related to the area measure of the same name.) Under sharecropping the harvest of each family was limited to the block of trees under its care. One of the advantages of separating harvest and cultivation wages was that it permitted more efficient use of the work force during peak labor demand. From May through August overseers mobilized the entire *colônia*—all available workers including women and children—to harvest the groves at the most appropriate stage of maturity and in the shortest possible time. The colono family's haryest wages were earned anywhere on the plantation, rather than being restricted to the *talhão* it cultivated for the rest of the year. The colono got a receipt (*vale*) for each alqueire of berries delivered to the cart road at the edge of the grove. At the end of the harvest the family head presented his collected receipts to a bookkeeper for recording in his account book and the plantation ledger.[11]

The harvest portion of the colono family's income, unlike the *trato* por-

Medium-sized coffee plantation, with drying yards, assembled labor force, headquarters buildings, groves in distance (note bell for calling colonos to work)

tion, fluctuated considerably from year to year. These changes were due primarily to the wide annual variations in yield per tree. It was not unusual for harvests to fluctuate as much as 100 percent from one year to the next, due to weather changes and the delicate nature of the plant. In the regional context, the harvest was more lucrative for the colono in new land with a higher average yield per tree, even though the unit cost to the planter may have been the same. This was one of several factors attracting workers to the frontier.

The third source of money income, much less important than the other two, came from occasional day labor, including work in the coffee processing facilities, carting coffee from the fields and to the nearest train station, repairing outbuildings and fences, and other miscellaneous tasks. These jobs were normally left to a few *camaradas*—semipermanent workers paid by the day or month, who were more usually native Brazilians than immigrant

Plantation of Lupercio Camargo, São Manuel, Alta Sorocabana zone, showing pasture and stream, colono houses with fenced yards, coffee drying yards, headquarters buildings and fruit orchard, pasture, coffee groves

Europeans. When coffee workers were called to supplement the camaradas during times of peak labor needs, the colonos were paid at a contractually stipulated daily wage rate.

These three types of income made up the colono's money wages. Any analysis of the standard of living of the coffee workers or their ability to accumulate savings is incomplete without considering the sources of nonmonetary income that were integral parts of the system.

One important type of nonmonetary income was housing. In 1870 payment of house rent to the landowner was still part of the free worker's living expenses.[12] By the time mass immigration began in the late 1880s, and for the entire period the colono system was widespread, free housing was a standard provision of work contracts. In the early years colono houses were sometimes of crude mud and wattle construction with dirt floors. But the standard type of colono housing, which can be seen today in many parts of western São Paulo, was of masonry and stucco with brick floor and tile roof. Such houses commonly had two bedrooms, a living area, and a kitchen, and were often built in duplex form. Whatever the type of housing provided, the colono did not have to use part of his wages to pay for it.

One of the legacies of the early sharecropping experiments was the practice of providing plantation land for the colonos to grow their own food, primarily corn and beans, but sometimes including rice, potatoes, and other crops as well. Along with permission to plant food crops went the provision of pasture land for a limited number of livestock, in the valley bottoms more susceptible to occasional frosts. In the immediate vicinity of their houses, colonos grew vegetables and kept chickens and hogs. One of the changes that took place in the evolution from sharecropping was that the plantation owner gave up his original right to half the food production in excess of the workers' own consumption. Colonos could retain the food products and sell any surplus to rural supply stores called *vendas* or in regional markets. If outside markets were not accessible, colonos were sometimes forced by circumstances to sell surplus food to their employer, often at prices below the going market rate; but the planter had no contractual right to any of the products colonos grew on his land.

In many cases the surplus cereals and livestock the colono sold provided an important additional source of cash. Such extra income could be added to savings or used to buy the items not produced on the plantation, such as wheat flour, salt, sugar, kerosene, clothing, and tools. As an example of the importance the workers themselves attached to the nonmonetary portions of the labor contract, an Italian vice-consul in Ribeirão Preto reported in 1903 that colonos preferred a plantation where money wages were precarious but where food crop privileges were generous, over one where wages were paid in full and on time but where food crops and livestock were restricted.[13] A French analyst noted in 1909 that "what really enables the colonists to make both ends meet is the crops they have the right to raise on their own account. . . . They often think more of the clauses in their contract which relate to these crops than to those which determine their wages in currency."[14]

The coffee worker paid no rent—either in money, products, or labor—in return for the nonmonetary provisions of the colono contract. Nor did he compensate the landowner through loyalty or occasional unpaid services, as in a patron-client relationship. The house, food plot, and pasture were considered separate from and in addition to the wages for cultivation, harvest, and day labor. Land was an abundant resource in the regional coffee complex of western São Paulo, and by allocating land in this way the Paulista planters could offer these incentives to the workers and keep monetary wage bills lower than they might have been otherwise.

The most important variation of the colono contract was the system used to open new coffee groves in virgin land. Migrant gangs of native Brazilian workers were brought in to chop down the largest trees and burn off the surface vegetation. After clearing and burning, the land was put in the care of an immigrant worker known as a *formador* under a system known as the *contrato de formação*, loosely translatable as "development contract." The formador agreed to plant the contracted area and care for the young plants, keeping the ground free of weeds and replanting any dead seedlings. The young trees began to bear in small quantities in the fourth year of growth. From the fourth to the sixth year, depending on the length of the contract, the formador kept the proceeds from the sale of these small coffee crops. At the end of the period the formador turned the producing groves over to the landowner, who then contracted their care to colonos under the standard annual contract.

During the boom of the late 1880s the landowner paid the formador a small sum per plant at the end of the development period, but after the mid-1890s the declining rate of coffee expansion, lower prices, and the competition among workers to assume development contracts combined eventually to eliminate such payments. The development contract thus enabled the landowner to open new coffee groves and provide for their care through the initial unproductive years at low cost. For the worker the most important part of the contract was the permission to use the space between the rows of young coffee seedlings for growing corn and beans. In keeping the young coffee free of weeds he simultaneously cultivated his own food crops, most of which he sold in local markets. It was also common for formadores to keep herds of hogs, which they allowed to feed on corn planted among the charred tree stumps and coffee seedlings.[15]

A development contract could be a lucrative venture for an immigrant worker, but it entailed risks not involved in the annual colono contract in mature groves. The colono was limited in the amount of food he could produce, but received a money wage for the annual cultivation. Relatively more of the income of the formador came from the sale of cash crops or livestock, but he received little or no payment for weeding coffee.[16] Another difference was that the formador lived in an isolated shack but was free from the direct control of an administrator. The colono lived in a permanent house near other colono families and was under closer supervision from plantation headquarters.

The nonmonetary portions of the coffee worker's income are difficult to quantify, and thus generalizations about the colono's "real wages" (total income compared to living costs) are difficult to make. There is no way of knowing how much a colono "saved" by receiving free housing, for example, since there was no debit and credit entry in his account book to allow for rent. To the extent that the colono produced his own food, the cost of corn and beans was immaterial to him. And to the extent that he sold surplus cereal and animal products in local markets, the colono *benefited* from in-

*Colono houses, plantation of Cornelio Procopio, São João da Boa Vista,
Mogiana zone*

creased prices for those products. In economic terms, the colono was a wage
earner, a subsistence farmer, a producer of agricultural commodities, and a
consumer all at the same time.

A cost-of-living study done in the city of São Paulo in 1934 provides a
basis for evaluating the importance of the colono's nonmonetary income. Data
from the sample of 185 urban working-class families show that housing and
food accounted for 75 percent of expenditures. Similar surveys of low-income
families in the United States in 1874–75, 1888–89, 1901, and 1917–18 indicate that food and rent were about two-thirds of expenses.[17] Extrapolating
from these surveys in São Paulo and the United States, it may be estimated
that perhaps 70 percent of a colono family's total income came in the form
of housing, food crop land, and pasture privileges.

In these circumstances, variations in money wages for the care and harvest of coffee are not by themselves valid indicators of fluctuations in real

Colono houses and coffee groves, plantation of Durval Fortes, São Manuel, Alta Sorocabana zone

wages, the more so since money wages were often adjusted in proportion to other forms of income. On one plantation colonos might have been given the use of more land for food crops, for example, but have received lower money wages than on a neighboring plantation where less free land was provided. Even on individual plantations several combinations of wages and non-monetary perquisites were sometimes available. In 1903, for example, an Italian vice-consul told of a plantation near Casa Branca, in the Mogiana zone, where cultivation wages were offered in six levels, ranging from 50$000 per thousand trees per year in choice land with permission to plant food crops between the rows of coffee, to 85$000 per thousand trees in third-quality land without interrow cropping privileges.[18] It seems likely that despite the 70 percent variation in money wages, the various combinations were roughly on the same total income level, since colonos could choose from the various possibilities on the same plantation.

In an area as large as a single municipio the range of cultivation wages could be even wider. An 1899 report on conditions in São Carlos, in the Paulista zone, revealed the following variations in wage rates on the 226 coffee plantations in the municipio:

no. of fazendas	cultivation wage per thousand trees (milreis)
12	70
8	75
124	80
25	90
47	100
2	110
4	120
4	150

The mode was 80$000 per thousand trees per year, and the mean was slightly higher. The "great majority" of the reporting fazendas paid for the harvest at 500 reis (written $500) per alqueire, with a few offering $600 or $700.[19]

Because of these wide variations, isolated wage reports are not generally comparable to those for other times and places. For the early years of free labor no comparable series is available, and sporadic reports provide little basis for identifying trends. In 1886 and 1888 cultivation wage rates were reported to be about 50$000 per thousand trees per year, with harvest payments ranging from $260 to $300 per alqueire. By 1895, according to a Department of Agriculture survey, cultivation wages rose to about 90$000 per thousand trees, and harvest payments doubled to some $600 per alqueire.[20]

The rates on a single representative plantation shown in table 6 provide a basis for following fluctuations in money wages in the first three decades of the twentieth century. From the beginning of the series to 1911, wages were stable, rising along with coffee prices in the 1912–14 period and declining slightly during World War I. The steady rise during the 1920s generally accompanied rising coffee prices and internal inflation up to 1929. This plantation in the Mogiana zone was probably running out of good food crop land by the 1920s, so the increased wage rates may in part reflect an effort to attract workers by offering proportionally higher money wages. With the onset of the Depression wages fell sharply, reaching about half the 1929 levels by 1933.

In 1911 the state created a Labor Department, still under the secretary of agriculture, and consolidated under it the various aspects of the immigration and labor program. The wages planters offered colonos at the hostel and published in the bulletin of the Labor Department in the ensuing years show a continuation of earlier patterns: there was a wide gap between maximum

TABLE 6

Colono and Camarada Wages on the Star of the West Coffee Plantation, Municipio of São Simão, São Paulo, 1901–1933

	Colono Wages			
Year	Cultivation, per 1,000 Trees per Year	Harvest, per Alqueire	Occasional Labor, per Day	Camarada Wages, per Day
1901	80$000	$500	2$500	3$000
1902	80$000	$500	2$500	3$000
1903	80$000	$500	2$500	3$000
1904	80$000	$400	2$000	2$500
1905	80$000	$400	2$000	2$500
1906	80$000	$500	2$000	2$500
1907	80$000	$500	2$000	2$500
1908	80$000	$500	2$000	2$500
1909	80$000	$500	2$000	2$500
1910	80$000	$500	2$000	2$500
1911	80$000	$500	2$500	3$000
1912	100$000	$600	2$500	3$000
1913	100$000	$600	2$500	3$000
1914	100$000	$600	2$500	3$000
1915	100$000	$500	2$500	3$000
1916	95$000	$500	2$500	3$500
1917	95$000	$500	2$500	3$500
1918	95$000	$600	2$500	3$500
1919	100$000	$600	2$500	3$500
1920	120$000	$600	2$500	4$000
1921	140$000	$700	3$000	4$500
1922	160$000	$700	3$000	4$500
1923	170$000	$900	3$000	5$000
1924	210$000	1$000	3$500	5$000
1925	310$000	1$000	4$000	7$000
1926	310$000	1$200	4$000	7$000
1927	320$000	1$000	4$000	7$000
1928	490$000	1$000	4$000	7$000
1929	510$000	1$500	5$000	7$500
1930	400$000	1$000	4$000	6$000
1931	200$000	$800	3$000	5$000

TABLE 6. *continued*

Colono Wages

Year	Cultivation, per 1,000 Trees per Year	Harvest, per Alqueire	Occasional Labor, per Day	Camarada Wages, per Day
1932	200$000	$800	3$000	5$000
1933	180$000	$800	3$000	4$500

Sources: 1901–29: *Boletim do departamento estadual de trabalho*, no. 71 (2nd quarter, 1930), p. 158. 1930–33: *Revista do DNC*, 1, no. 6 (December 1933): 702–3.

and minimum wages, and rates tended to rise and fall uniformly on a region-wide basis, including older zones, intermediate areas, and the frontier.[21]

In view of the difficulty of comparing wage rates to cost of living, one way of obtaining an idea of representative family incomes under ideal conditions is to examine the reports of foreign consular officials, planters, and other contemporary analysts. These examples illustrate the variety of income combinations that the colono system made possible, given different wage rates, income from the sale of food crops, and family size.

In 1897 the São Paulo secretary of agriculture reported the annual income of a representative colono family with two "hoes" as follows:[22]

Cultivation of 5,000 trees @ 100$000 per 1,000 trees	500$000
Harvest of 500 alqueires @ $600 per alqueire	300$000
Thirty days of miscellaneous labor @ 3$500 per day	105$000
Sale of 4 carros (4,800 liters) of corn @ 25$000 per carro	100$000
Sale of 10 bags (1,000 liters) of beans @ 16$000 per bag	160$000
Total income	1:165$000

This report did not include an estimate of how much such a family might have to spend on food it could not produce, clothing, tools, and other necessities. An 1895 survey indicated that normal expenses would amount to about half of such a family's income, which would leave this hypothetical family with a net annual income of 582$000.[23]

In 1901 Giuseppe Mortari, an Italian immigrant who owned a plantation near Taquaritinga in the Araraquarense zone, gave the following account of the annual income and expenses of a colono family made up of a husband and wife and one son capable of working full time:[24]

Income:

Cultivation of 4,000 trees @ 80$000 per 1,000 trees	320$000
Harvest of 480 alqueires @ $500 per alqueire	240$000
Sale of 5 carros (6,000 liters) of corn @ 20$000 per carro	100$000
Sale of 5 bags (500 liters) of beans @ 8$000 per bag	40$000
Sale of 10 bags (1,000 liters) of rice @ 4$000 per bag	40$000
Sale of assorted poultry, animals, and animal products	150$000
Total	890$000

Expenses:

Purchased food products, clothing, tools, and other supplies, calculated @ $500 per person per day	547$500
Net annual income	342$500

Such a family would be able to save 38 percent of its income. At the average exchange rate for 1901 (see appendix table 6), the money income of 890$000 was equivalent to U.S. $204.70, and the savings of 342$500 was equivalent to U.S. $78.78.

In 1903 an Italian vice-consul in Ribeirão Preto gave a less favorble accounting of the possible income of a similar family (two "hoes" plus housewife) contracting to care for more trees but at a lower wage rate:[25]

Income:

Cultivation of 5,000 trees @ 60$000 per 1,000 trees	300$000

Harvest of 450 alqueires @ $400 per alqueire	180$000
Sale of 3 carros (3,600 liters) of corn @ 30$000 per carro	90$000
Sale of 5 bags (500 liters) of beans @ 8$000 per bag	40$000
Sale of assorted poultry, animals, and animal products	140$000
Total	750$000

Expenses:

Food, clothing, household supplies, etc.	550$000
Net annual income	200$000

Also in 1903, the Department of Agriculture inspector for the Mogiana zone made an income estimate for a colono family with four "hoes." The family could contract for the care of more trees and could harvest more coffee, and its food crops would be much more extensive than the plots of smaller families:[26]

Cultivation of 10,000 trees @ 80$000 per 1,000 trees	800$000
Harvest of 1,200 alqueires @ $500 per alqueire	600$000
Sale of 15 carros of corn @ 40$000 per carro	600$000
Sale of 40 bags of beans @ 8$000 per bag	320$000
Total income	2:320$000

The inspector noted that an estimate for animal products and for free housing would increase the total substantially. His calculations made no allowance for expenses, but if the $500 per person per day used in the contemporary Italian sources can be extrapolated to this family (four field workers plus house-wife), annual expenses would have been about 912$500, leaving a net surplus of 1:407$500. This latter figure is 61 percent of the total income, and equivalent to U.S. $337.80 at the average exchange rate for 1903.

The advantages that the colono contract ideally offered the immigrant worker included the reasonable assurance of a minimum annual income, the reduction of living expenses through free housing and near self-sufficiency in food production, the possibility of accumulating savings through money income and low cash expenses, and the possibility of maximizing income per family by fully utilizing the labor of all members. The same combination of potential advantages was not to be found in either sharecropping or fixed wage labor systems. The terms "ideal" and "potential" are used advisedly here. The inability or refusal of the planter to pay wages as contracted, a harvest wiped out by frost, or a large debt to the employer could reduce or eliminate the colono's money income. An immigrant family with many mouths to feed and few able-bodied workers was at a considerable disadvantage. Prolonged illness might reduce the breadwinner's earning capacity, and professional medical care was either nonexistent or prohibitively expensive.

The granting of "concessions" did not necessarily involve a reduction in the planter's potential profit nor an increase in his wage bill. In the transition from slave to free labor, the planters created incentives through an acceptable distribution of risks and a rational allocation of the resources at their disposal, particularly abundant land, rather than through a simple distribution of income in the workers' favor. No benevolent paternalism was involved, much less blind adherence to time-honored routine. The colono contract should not be confused with tenant farming, renting, or sharecropping. It was also not a wage system, in the sense of a unit of pay per unit of time worked. It was a unique combination of annual wages, piecework payments, daily wages, and nonmonetary provisions—the specific social relations of production in the coffee industry during the era of mass immigration to São Paulo.

Once they were created, the colono contract and the system for importing and distributing labor had effects in both the short and the long term that the Paulistas had hardly considered in the heady 1880s. One of the short-term effects was to help stimulate the expansion of coffee into São Paulo's western frontier, independent of world market conditions or exchange rate fluctuations. This was because the food cropping provision operated as an incentive for planters to open new groves in order to attract workers from an abundant but mobile labor pool. Even when prices fell and credit contracted after 1896, the geographical mobility of the immigrant workers continued to affect planters' decisions to expand.

The colono much preferred to plant his corn and beans between rows of coffee rather than to maintain a food plot apart from the groves. If the food plot was separate he had to divide his time between the two areas. Only when the coffee was weeded to the overseer's satisfaction was the colono free to tend his own crops on his own time. A standard alternative was for the family to divide its labor force, with the men and older offspring primarily weeding coffee and the wife and younger children caring for subsistence plots. In either case, the family could care for fewer coffee trees and food products than if the two activities were combined in one area. As an agronomist summed up the situation in 1898, "the colono demands, as a sine qua non of his permanency, that he be assigned new groves where he can plant corn. In this way he has a source of free grain, since all the necessary cultivation of the corn is counted as coffee weeding, which is paid for by the employer."[27]

Coffee seedlings were planted two to three meters apart to allow for full development. Until the plants reached maturity the open space between them could be used for subsistence crops. Even where open space remained after the fifth year, planters knew that food crops would compete with the coffee root systems and drain the soil of nutrients and moisture. Thus the inter-row cropping the colono preferred was normally permissible only in young groves. After the first groves of a plantation reached maturity, interrow crop-ping could be maintained by periodically planting additional blocks of land in coffee and including some of the new area in each colono's assigned area for weeding. In this way coffee expansion became a device for retaining the labor force, rather than a response to favorable coffee prices.

In 1899 Santos Werneck asked readers of the *Revista Agrícola* to consider a hypothetical entrepreneur who buys land, contracts for its clearing, brings in colonos to care for the seedlings, and in the fifth year looks forward to the first harvest and some return on his investment. At that juncture the workers come to him in a group and demand land on which to plant corn and beans, now that the coffee groves are becoming too shady for interrow planting. The planter considers the drawbacks to giving the colonos some of his vacant land: the grassy areas are of poor quality, and would support only three or four years of cropping before becoming exhausted, at which time the colonos would demand new land. Besides, the pasture land is needed for animal forage. Allotting the colonos good quality forest land would deprive the planter of territory he might eventually want to plant in coffee. Separate food plots in either pasture or forest would divert a certain portion of each family's labor away from coffee, lowering the number of trees a family could care for and making it necessary to hire more colonos and build more houses to maintain the same number of coffee plants.

The landowner in Werneck's scenario concludes that since he will have to incur some expense in order to keep his workers, he should make the expense as small as possible and get some eventual return for it. The obvious expe-dient that comes to mind is to open new land to coffee, and let the colonos plant food crops between the rows.[28] Interrow cropping was preferable not only for the colono—it was also the most rational choice for the planter, if he had virgin land onto which to expand. Furthermore, the planter made his deci-sion in response to current labor market conditions, rather than in anticipation of world coffee market conditions four to six years in the future when the new groves would come into production.

In 1902 Augusto Ramos pointed out that in the conflict over interrow cropping, what was an end for the planter was only a means for the colono. The planter's goal was to maintain his labor supply and produce coffee, while the colono's interest lay mainly in food crops. Ramos admitted that coffee work, from the colono's point of view, symbolized "meager, disputed, and at times uncertain wages." Corn, on the other hand, symbolized abundance and well-being. It meant polenta (the cornmeal mush staple of the Italian colono's diet), feed for chickens, plenty of eggs, fattened pigs, salt pork, and smoked meat. From the sale of his excess food products he bought clothes, wine, and other needs. Coffee was dependence, subservience, the source of justified but disagreeable conflicts, mistrust, and disciplinary measures; corn was freedom of action and economic autonomy.

From this conflict of objectives and interests, Ramos wrote, arose the consequence that "nearly all the planters have been forced to expand their coffee groves, even against their will and at times against their true interests, in order to prevent the disorganization of labor on their properties." Furthermore, the reserves of new land usually sufficed only for a short while, and "once they are exhausted the plantation enters a personnel crisis: crisis of quantity, crisis of quality, crisis of stability, crisis of order." Ramos recognized that in response to low coffee prices after 1896 some planters had fallen behind in their wage payments to colonos. When this happened workers began to sell off their small supplies of livestock and more of their food supplies than they should have, to obtain needed cash. The result was further disruption of the rural labor market as colonos left to seek a more solvent employer or to return to Europe, there to spread the story of their travail and to discourage emigration to São Paulo.[29]

In addition to expansion to permit interrow cropping by colonos, a more general clash of individual interests with the collective good contributed to the increasingly severe overproduction problem. For well-managed plantations with good land and productive trees, whose owners were free of debt or paying reasonable interest rates, profit margins during the 1896–1910 "crisis" remained favorable, though below the boom days of the preceding decade. The Department of Agriculture inspector for the Mogiana zone, for example, calculated average profits in 1903 to be about 9 percent per year. The inspector concluded that while the planter had little reason to be satisfied with current low coffee prices, "he does not curse his luck, because he confesses to making profit in spite of his trouble." But those who had borrowed capital at annual interest rates of 12, 18, and 24 percent stood to lose money under current market conditions.[30] Coffee could still be an attractive investment, but it was not as lucrative as it had once been.

In these conditions, one way for an individual planter to make the best of the situation was to increase overall profits by increasing total production. Coffee expansion increased labor needs, but planters who continued to open new groves could make advantageous interrow cropping concessions to attract

Mature coffee with interrow corn

the necessary colonos. By this process workers were drawn away from the smaller plantations and from the older areas where much of the good coffee land had been occupied. Plantations that could not extend their coffee groves were thus at a double disadvantage: they did not have the option of increasing overall profits through expansion, and they could not offer food crop incentives on a competitive basis with the expanding plantations.

This divergence of interests among planters and increased competition for workers came at a time when general economic conditions were less favorable than they had previously been. Due to the extreme dependence on coffee exports, low coffee prices adversely affected all sectors of the economy—urban and rural, commercial and industrial, public and private. The general slowing of economic activity after 1896 made life increasingly difficult for the working groups, with contradictory results in the rural labor market. On the one hand, employment in the coffee zone was available to people forced

Colono (left center) receiving vale *from cartman for one* alqueire *of berries picked*

out of nonagricultural work as marginal small industries failed, urban construction decreased, and railroad building slowed. On the other hand, becoming a coffee colono was only one of several options open to victims of the economic slowdown. The most important alternative course of action for the immigrants was to return to their homeland.

Departures of steerage passengers from the port of Santos never fell below twenty-three thousand persons annually from 1896 to 1915, and the annual average for that twenty-year period was just over thirty-two thousand (figure 4). The departing immigrants included not only those who had been unemployed or employed in nonagricultural activities, but an important contingent of ex–coffee colonos as well. In the words of a contemporary newspaper columnist: "The exodus of Italians is critical. They return to their homeland poor and disillusioned. . . ."[31] Carlos Botelho objected that the increase in the numbers of returnees to Europe could not be blamed on the coffee planters. "If some reduction of wages has been attempted," he wrote in 1899, "it has been compensated by liberal planting concessions, even among mature coffee plants." Botelho claimed that increased permission to plant food crops was profitable for the colono, despite the fact that the market value of cereals had also declined somewhat in response to worsening economic conditions. As for the interrow planting privileges in new groves, "it is almost as if the colonos were paid to produce food for themselves, since they receive the cost of weeding their cereal crops in the form of coffee cultivation wages." As an additional incentive, "even cartage from the field to the storehouses is provided free on most plantations."[32]

Those landowners who tried to reduce wages and nonmonetary incentives risked a reduction in their labor force. An example of the planters' fears comes from a letter that Eduardo da Silva Prado wrote to Rui Barbosa, one of the important political figures of the early republic, in 1901. Eduardo Prado, the younger brother of Antonio and Martinho Prado, was himself a coffee planter in the older area around Campinas, where relatives of Rui Barbosa also owned coffee properties. Prado explained the situation: "It is not possible to think about reducing production costs. At the least attempt in that direction the colonos would respond by abandoning the plantations, returning to Italy or going to the Rio de la Plata. Your Excellency is aware that in the past two years [1898–1900] the movement of colonos leaving São Paulo through the port of Santos has been very large, and all indications are that this return movement would take place en masse if the planters reduce in any way the remuneration the colonos are accustomed to receiving."[33]

São Paulo officials were well aware of the close relationship among immigration, repatriation, the size of the labor pool, and colono wage levels. From the beginning of the mass immigration program there was a conscious effort to import workers in such numbers that competition among them would keep wages low and provide ample manpower for the expansion of the coffee industry. But along with competition among the workers, there was competition among thousands of coffee planters for the services of the arriving immigrants. Finally in 1896, at the end of the boom but before the extent of the impending "crisis" could be foreseen, the secretary of agriculture predicted that colono stability would soon cease to be a problem, not because the workers' geographical mobility was diminishing, but because the continued importation of workers "will cause the rural labor market to become well saturated, to the point of establishing equilibrium between labor supply and demand."[34]

In the following years a more realistic view replaced such sanguine assessments. The planters began to recognize that not only was instability a permanent feature of the colono system, but that one consequence of instability was a chronic attrition of the labor force. The main thrust of the state immigration program then became replacement to fill the inevitable gaps in the

army of coffee workers, rather than the creation of a reserve army of unemployed. Optimistic predictions of the "saturation" of the labor market
were not heard after 1896. In 1898, for example, the secretary of agriculture
urged that the inflow of immigrants be maintained, "if not on a scale sufficient to lower wages, at least so that wages would not be permitted to rise,
filling the gaps that result from the repatriation of agricultural workers."[35]
Finally in 1900 third-class departures from Santos exceeded the total immigration into São Paulo for the first time since the mid-1880s, and the secretary
of agriculture called attention to the "deficit" as an important factor in the
labor scarcity experienced in some areas of the western plateau.[36]

Just after the turn of the century, Department of Agriculture district inspectors confirmed that coffee workers were increasingly hard to obtain and
keep. In October 1900 the inspector in the Paulista zone reported that "the
labor shortage in this district is notable, due to the departures of colonos at the
end of this year's harvest." In December, from the Mogiana zone: "Crops
are being sacrificed in many municipios, due to the lack of workers."[37] Some
representative comments during 1901: "In Jaú the labor shortage is being
felt, to the detriment of agriculture." "There is a great shortage of workers in
Mogi Mirim, Leme, etc. . . . ." In August, in the Paulista zone, the harvest
was taking place normally, "due to the assistance provided by the new immigrants being brought in." But in the older Central zone, "the coffee harvest
is progressing . . . more slowly in some municipios than in others, mainly
because of the labor shortage."[38] In April 1902, from the Paulista zone:
"Although the crop is small, in some municipios there is a shortage of
colonos to do the work."

In July 1902 the inspector in the Alta Sorocabana zone reported that with
prices low, planters "were thinking more carefully about attaching the colono
to the land by giving permanent or temporary concessions of plots for the
cultivation of cereals, etc.," rather than depending on transitory permission
to plant between the rows of coffee. In April 1903, in the Central zone, "a
great number of coffee groves are abandoned and invaded by overgrowth.
This can be explained mainly by the labor shortage." And the Mogiana district inspector noted that many planters were reluctantly granting colonos
permission to plant food crops between the rows of mature coffee trees. In
such cases, he claimed, "the colonos are becoming like true parasites on the
landowners. [The planters] tolerate these practices detrimental to coffee and
to the fertility of the land, and consequently to its value, in exchange for labor
for the care and harvest of coffee, for which there is often a shortage of
workers."[39]

These were neither inflammatory attacks in the press nor impassioned
speeches in the legislature. They were routine and unsensational reports published in a technical journal. Some labor shortages occurred, despite the
smooth functioning of the immigration and labor distribution program. Such

shortages were regionally limited but felt sporadically throughout the coffee zone. They were also transitory. At other times the district inspectors reported that workers were "abundant and cheap" as new immigrants were directed to areas where they were most needed and contract conditions shifted in the planters' favor.[40]

In the late 1890s the number of trees in the western plateau continued to expand, due to increased planting during the earlier boom. As low prices continued into the twentieth century it became apparent that laissez faire price mechanisms were not operating to decrease or even to stabilize production. In 1902 when the Paulista Society of Agriculture discussed the idea of state intervention to restrict expansion, members considered unfounded the objection that "the colono, without new groves, will demand an increase in wages. It is precisely the new groves that incite the colono to move constantly from one plantation to another, without staying on any. This constitutes the greatest source of disorder for the rural labor force." Members noted that since the newly opening areas offered high money wages in addition to interrow cropping privileges to attract workers, expansion had the additional effect of making wage reductions impossible in the hard-pressed older districts. In fact, the argument went, if coffee expansion were legally restricted the effect would be a stabilization of the work force through the elimination of the main incentive to move. Finally the society passed a resolution in favor of legal restrictions "with near unanimity."[41]

State officials chose a prohibitive tax to limit expansion because the governor could impose it by fiat, whereas an outright fine would have had to be approved by the legislature after debate and possible obstruction by representatives of the expanding frontier areas. São Paulo executive decree 1,090 of 9 January 1903 imposed a tax of two thousand milreis for each alqueire or fraction thereof of land planted in coffee for the first time. Old groves or dead trees in existing groves could be replaced without penalty. The decree was to remain in effect for five years.[42] At a special session of the state legislature in early 1903, Governor Bernardino de Campos explained that he had decreed the tax primarily for the purpose of "liberating the planters from the vicious circle in which they find themselves—of opening new groves, under enormous burdens, as a means of retaining workers to care for the [older] groves, which they already have difficulty maintaining."[43] Just three weeks after the governor decreed the end of coffee expansion, a convention attended by one thousand planters in the city of São Paulo objected strongly to the possibility of financial penalties for extending the groves, and passed a resolution against the law.[44] Despite such objections, the measure remained on the books and was renewed for another five-year period ending in 1912.

The state attempted to enforce at least the spirit of the decree, and it probably helped limit the expansion of coffee during those years. During the 1903–12 period the number of producing trees in the western plateau increased by only 4 percent, well below previous growth rates. With the opening of the Noroeste zone, the beginning of the Alta Sorocabana railroad into virgin land in the west, and higher prices from 1910 to 1913, coffee again expanded during the last years the tax was on the books. Due to the delay between planting and maturation the effect of the limitations should have been felt at least through 1916; yet from 1909 to 1916 the number of producing trees in the western plateau as a whole increased by 112 million, from 627 to 732 million. That 18 percent increase compares to growth in the Noroeste zone of 280 percent (2.7 million to 10.3 million trees), and an increase in the Alta Sorocabana zone in the same period of 39 percent (56.7 million to 78.2 million trees).[45]

The bumper crop of 1906 was one of the many specific phenomena that disrupted the rural labor market over the years. That crop reflected cumulative expansion prior to the 1903 tax, and ideal weather during the periods of flowering and development contributed to a harvest more than double the size of previous and subsequent crops. For the planters it carried the threat of disaster, because overproduction was already a problem and prices remained low.[46] For the workers, however, a bumper crop meant a substantial increase in the harvest piecework portion of their income. Many coffee workers apparently decided to take their windfall and leave Brazil. The 41,349 steerage passengers leaving Santos in 1906 was 20 percent higher than the average for 1901–5 and 30 percent higher than the average for 1907–11 (see appendix table 4). Some colonos probably set themselves up as small farmers after the 1906 harvest or entered artisan or commercial trades. During the following year, although the crop was much smaller than the 1906 total, the district inspectors again reported labor shortages. In parts of the Mogiana zone the problem was so acute that some planters were temporarily changing their harvest techniques in an effort to gather as much of the 1907 crop as possible before the rains began. Rather than using the standard stripping method, colonos were sent into the groves armed with poles with which to "beat the trees barbarously to make the berries fall to the ground," thus damaging the plants.[47]

The coffee price rise from 1910 through 1912 relieved some of the pressure for planters to improve their profit margin by reducing the wage bill. Practices stimulating worker mobility, such as delays in payment or refusal to settle accounts to the satisfaction of the colono, probably diminished. After a serious but transitory setback caused by the 1918 frost, expansion continued on a broad front through the 1920s. Only the Central zone failed to expand after 1910 (as shown in figure 3, chapter 1). In absolute terms, the post-1910 boom surpassed the expansion of the 1890s. The capacity for coffee production in western São Paulo increased by about 600 million trees in the twenty years after 1910, compared to an increase of some 400 million trees from 1886 to 1900.

Throughout these years the colono system remained unchanged. The food cropping privilege continued to stimulate planting and attract workers away from the older areas. In 1916 an anonymous writer in the magazine *O Fazendeiro* (''The Planter'') described a persistent pattern established more than twenty years before:

> The expansion of the coffee industry, in its tendency to seek fresh land in previously unexploited areas, is drawing the workers now located in the older areas toward the interior. The workers do not stay in the older zones because they can no longer obtain there the income, equal or perhaps greater than their money wages, from the cereals by which the virgin lands amply repay the labor of those who cultivate them.
>
> The result is that the plantations of the older municipios are slowly becoming depopulated. And the planter, in order not to lose his work force, must raise wages and close his eyes to the quality of the workers luck gives him. On the plantations where there are new groves alongside the old, the problem is easier to solve. A small increase in the rates for the care of the older groves and for the harvest is usually sufficient to retain the colono, who is compensated by the allotment of new trees where he can plant corn and beans. Where there are only old groves, however, and especially where the soil is exhausted, it is very difficult to get workers, and the prospects for the future are not promising.[48]

The writer noted that fortunately new immigrants preferred the settled areas to life in the remote and unfamiliar frontier. As experienced colonos departed to seek better opportunities in the far west, the continued operation of the state immigration service helped fill the resulting gaps in the work force of the older areas.

After World War I, reports of labor shortages again became more common. In 1919 the *Revista dos Fazendeiros* claimed the labor force was one-third below adequate levels, and that 60,000 colono families were needed to work in coffee. Assuming an average composition of 4.8 persons per family, 60,000 families would represent a population of 288,000. At a meeting of the São Paulo–based Brazilian Agricultural League in May 1922, members complained that ''we lack the manpower to complete the present harvest, and the small number of workers present are only available at high prices.'' In 1922 the Paulista Society of Agriculture reported that conditions in the coffee industry were generally very good, ''except for the labor shortage, which continues to be a serious problem.'' At another meeting of the Agricultural League in April 1923, it was reported that some 35 percent of the trees in western São Paulo were inadequately cared for due to labor shortages.[49]

High coffee prices in the later 1920s brought improved economic conditions. High immigration totals from 1923 through the end of the decade were augmented by increasingly large inflows of native Brazilians from states north of São Paulo. As was the case during the 1910–13 price rise, planters had less reason to complain about labor problems, but declining productivity in the older areas was aggravated by the appearance in 1924 of the coffee borer insect, which quickly spread through most of the Central zone and adjacent areas of the Mogiana. Beginning in 1925, the Department of Agriculture required planters to go over the groves in the infested area after the normal harvest in order to eliminate the borer in the larval stage, when it lay dormant in unpicked berries. The "reharvest" did limit the spread of the pest, but it also increased the labor requirements of planters whose groves were already less productive than those on the frontier.

In 1905 production in the Central zone averaged forty-seven fifteen-kilogram arrobas of processed beans per thousand trees, compared to average production in the Mogiana and Paulista zones of fifty-four arrobas and for the three frontier zones of sixty-seven arrobas per thousand trees. By the 1910–14 period, average production in the Central zone fell to forty-three arrobas; in the Mogiana and Paulista it was sixty-one arrobas; and for the Araraquarense, Noroeste, and Alta Sorocabana combined, it was sixty-two arrobas. Damage from the 1918 frost was widespread in the plateau, and despite a huge bumper crop in 1927, average production fell in the 1924–28 period to just thirty-seven arrobas for the older Central zone infested by the borer, forty-one arrobas for the Mogiana and Paulista, and fifty-three arrobas per thousand trees in the three frontier zones combined. (In the Paraiba valley, where native sharecroppers eked out a minimal existence on exhausted land, coffee productivity for 1924–28 was just twenty-five arrobas per thousand trees.)[50] These average figures for large areas can tell little about each individual plantation. The rural labor market was regionwide, however, and each planter and colono lived with the knowledge of the regional context. By the later 1920s the coffee cycle in western São Paulo was on the decline.

While planters' claims regarding the adequacy of the labor supply fluctuated over the years in response to changing immigration totals and coffee prices, the problem of the geographical mobility of the colono was more constant. In 1929, for example, a writer in the journal of the Brazilian Rural Society traced the recent evolution of the São Paulo coffee industry. "By time periods and by geographical zones," he wrote, "the dislocation of the economic activity of the Paulistas, and with it the dislocation of the labor force, can be seen." Criticizing colono "nomadism," the writer described some of the negative effects of repeated movement. Often the colono had insufficient time to develop his food crop and livestock resources, which he needed to supplement money wages. When he moved he liquidated as much of his property as possible, but the resulting cash was often insufficient to sustain him until he harvested the first food crops at his new place of employment. Until his crops came in, he tried to live off the money wage portion of the work contract but had to borrow from the planter or local storekeeper in order to get by. Faced with the prospect of indebtedness he again decided to move on, in an attempt to escape from the cycle. In order to attract replacement workers, the planter had to continue to provide food crop privileges, pasture, and other incentives, in addition to money wages for all his colonos.[51]

This analysis on the eve of the Great Depression echoed themes recurrent since the beginning of the free labor era more than four decades before. During those years the coffee planters of São Paulo did not sit idly by while their labor force dissipated. Over the years they proposed and attempted to implement various types of solutions to the problem of geographical mobility, with varying degrees of success. The remedies generally fell into three categories: importing new workers to replace those lost, restricting the mobility of the existing labor force, and providing positive incentives to attract and retain workers already in Brazil.

The resounding success of the immigration program in the decade after 1887 engendered complacency on the part of planters. There was little concern over losing colonos, because new immigrants were sent to the coffee zone by the thousands every month. The fact that the great numbers of new arrivals easily found employment is indirect evidence that "nomadism" was already an important characteristic of the labor system. And the planters' actions in the face of the labor market glut of the 1890s encouraged the development of the mobility syndrome. According to an 1899 report, there was always an abundance of immigrants in the hostel, and "the planters easily, without the least trouble, rid themselves of the more demanding, those with little strength for the work, etc." Manpower was so plentiful that as wages began to fall in some areas, "anyone who had contracted colonos for high wages dismissed them and went off to obtain replacements for those who would not accept a cut in pay."[52]

With the successful policy of importing manpower for coffee expansion and the replacement of workers who moved, there was little incentive for planters to change the arbitrary and authoritarian attitudes many retained from the slave era. Colonos had virtually no legal protection, let alone the support of "public opinion" in the coffee zone, and there were sporadic reports of beatings, incarceration, arbitrary dismissal, and other forms of mistreatment during these years.[53] In 1896, as he proclaimed the success of the immigration program in compensating for worker instability, the secretary of agriculture observed that the system of constant large inflows was a more practical means of solving the problem than trying to coerce the colonos into staying in one place. Coercion, he warned, would have a negative effect, causing immigrants to avoid São Paulo and the governments of supplying countries to restrict or prohibit emigration to Brazil.[54]

The success of the immigration system could not be sustained at earlier levels after 1897. The newly arrived workers were no longer always sufficient to replace those who moved on, and some planters reacted by attempting to restrict the colonos' freedom of movement. It soon became apparent, however, that with many alternatives open to an unsatisfied coffee worker, with rapid rail transport available to fleeing colonos, and without an organized police force to hunt down and return escapees to their former employers, there was little a planter could do, short of outright imprisonment, to stop a colono from leaving. A landlord who dared to take that or some other drastic measure soon earned a bad reputation and was forced to depend on inexperienced new immigrants as the rate of labor turnover on his plantation increased.

A common method of disciplining colonos was to levy monetary fines on those who broke paternalistic plantation rules such as those against noise after curfew or unauthorized visitors, or who failed to fulfill the provisions of the work contract to the satisfaction of the overseer. The fine would take the form of a minus entry in the account book, thus reducing wages. One Italian visitor reported cases in which planters arbitrarily used fines to reduce their own indebtedness to the workers.[55] In their subservient position colonos had little choice but to submit, especially since the right of the planter to impose fines for certain infractions was clearly established in the labor contract. The incidence of fines had apparently declined by the early twentieth century. An Italian consul reported in 1908 that "if fines are rarer than in the past, it is mainly because of the labor shortage and the facility with which workers find employment. A fine considered unjust, a case of mistreatment, is more often than in the past the cause for the desertion of a family."[56]

It was standard practice for the planter to advance new arrivals food or cash during the initial period of adjustment, and a family with several small children to feed and few members of working age might find it difficult to repay the initial loans. Expenses such as those for medical care might also put a colono family in debt when, indeed, a doctor could be found to treat them. But planters learned early that large debts were an incentive for colonos to flee, rather than an efficient means of holding them. The regionally organized and legally enforced system of debt peonage characteristic of some plantation labor systems was not developed in western São Paulo.[57]

To the extent that debts were used at all to retain colonos, those the planter owed to the worker were probably as common as those the worker owed to the planter. Sometimes employers would make only partial payments or fail to pay at the specified intervals, and the colonos would have to stay on the plantation in hopes of collecting wages. As Silvio Coletti summarized the debt situation, "just as the strongest bond which keeps the colono on the plantation is to find himself the creditor of the landowner, so also desertions are caused especially by the colono himself falling into debt." The Italian consul added, however, that nocturnal escape involved certain risks: the planter might back up his authority with physical violence if necessary, recruiting men from loyal retainers on the plantations, usually native Brazilians not directly involved in coffee production. If the planter or his *capangas*, as such private police were called, learned of a planned escape, the least the colono could expect was "the summary justice of a beating."[58]

At times the planters failed to pay, not primarily to hold their colonos, but because they did not have the necessary cash on hand. The Italian consular inspectors by no means considered insolvency a valid excuse for defrauding workers of wages due. But they recognized that most planters, in order to ensure an adequate labor supply, preferred to pay punctually and in full.[59] A "reverse" debt system would function satisfactorily for the planter only when no attractive alternatives were open to the workers, or when they had reason to believe they would be paid reasonably soon. While it may have worked to retain colonos as a stopgap measure in some situations, failure to pay wages as contracted probably did more in the long run to encourage workers to move on than to restrict movement.

Most colonos who moved did so freely, sometimes on the spur of the moment but more usually at the end of the yearly contract period. An Italian journalist in 1891 explained the colono's attitude in the following way: "Your employer does not satisfy you, or you don't like the plantation? Change employers. The employer is satisfactory and you recognize the plantation is a good one? Go in search of a better one."[60]

As long as they could count on obtaining new workers from the hostel, some planters withheld payment to reduce their total wage bill, unconcerned by the consequent need to replace colonos who left in disgust or desperation. To limit such practices, or at least to placate the consular officials who received and publicized colono complaints, federal laws of 1904 and 1907 stipulated that agricultural wages took precedence over all other debts paid from net profits. This guarantee was ineffective because the planter's debts to his coffee broker, who supplied operating capital, often reduced "net profits" to a negative figure. The planter could then claim he had no funds to settle the colonos' accounts. If labor market conditions indicated that an insolvent planter should placate the colonos' demands, he might ask his broker for an advance on the next crop to pay his current wage bill, and the cycle would begin again.[61]

There were occasional instances of groups of coffee growers attempting to agree on maximum wages, in order to limit the competition for workers. In April 1903 the district inspector in the Alta Sorocabana zone reported that local planters had met and "decided to pay no more than 60$000 for the annual care of 1,000 coffee plants and not more than $300 to $400 per alqueire for the harvest piece rate."[62] In June 1903 some planters in the Paulista zone agreed to similar wage ceilings, but the district inspector there was pessimistic about the possibility of maintaining controls because of the lack of solidarity among the planters. Each considered his own labor problem unique, and if wage ceilings made workers increasingly scarce the plan would break down, especially since current wage rates ranged from 70$000 to 80$000 for annual cultivation and $500 to $600 for the harvest.[63]

The fact that planters felt the need to call such meetings and that district inspectors considered them newsworthy suggests that such organized attempts at wage restrictions were not common. Nor is there reason to believe that wage ceilings, whether arranged in public or in secret, had more than a transitory effect. In 1923, twenty years after the 1903 attempts to hold wages down, the Brazilian Rural Society heard one of its most influential members claim that the mobility of the labor force was the unintended result of offering higher wages.

Carlos Leôncio de Magalhães, owner of a vast estate near Araraquara, decried the disorganization of the labor market, brought about by chronic manpower shortages and the fear of not having sufficient harvest workers. With characteristic hyperbole, Magalhães said that toward the end of the 1923 harvest, "all the colonos of São Paulo advised their employers they intend to leave, as they do every year. The employers, or rather, the plantation administrators, become alarmed and suggest to the landowner that it is better to pay more than to be left without colonos. And the landowners, with rare exceptions, agree." Only the railroads and labor recruiters, he said, benefited from the constant transfers of manpower. The planter had his wage bill increased and was in constant uncertainty. The colono who moved repeatedly had no time to develop food crops and livestock, from which he could make considerable profit. "I beg your pardon, dear colleagues," Magalhães told the assembled coffee planters, "this is the truth. I am sorry to say that we ourselves cause the anarchy of the colonos, out of fear."[64]

Attempted wage ceilings, like nonpayment of wages, probably acted against the long-range interests of the planters as well as those of the colonos. More characteristic were propaganda efforts to attract workers looking for better opportunities. A typical example is a 1905 report from the Alta Sorocabana zone:

> The good understanding our planters have [of the situation], raising wages to 100$000 per 1,000 trees, giving the colono the advantage of excellent land for food crops, raising the wage of day laborers, treating the colonos well, and paying punctually on a monthly basis, has brought to São Manuel a great number of workers. Due to the abundance of manpower, many planters have planted a variety of crops, so that here everyone finds employment and advantageous wages. This has caused considerable development of agriculture and commerce. And many planters, taking advantage of the improvement in the exchange rate, are paying their colonos in pounds sterling.[65]

One restrictive measure that remained only a proposal was the institution of antivagabond laws to limit mobility and force people with no visible means of support to go to work. The model for this plan was the system by which the Argentine elite had eliminated the nomadic bands of gauchos from the pampas region. Although the Paulistas were aware of the Argentine precedent, no such legal measures were taken to restrict the movement of the rural lower classes in São Paulo.[66]

Nor did the state establish a police force charged with hunting down colonos who had unilaterally broken their contracts. In 1898 Count Pietro Antonelli, the senior Italian diplomatic official in Brazil, toured western São Paulo and visited many plantations. Contrasting what he saw with his European experience, Antonelli was struck by the fact that he did not meet a single policeman in his travels in rural São Paulo, except for a few guard posts in towns.[67] In subsequent years the action of the official police force remained restricted to the urban areas. In 1928 a member of one of São Paulo's wealthy and powerful landowning families claimed that there was no way of enforcing the provisions of work contracts and that colonos commonly moved with no regard for legal sanctions. He proposed the creation of "a small police force with the express duty of accompanying immigrants from their arrival to the final conclusion of their obligations in agriculture."[68] Still the state took no action to extend its theoretical monopoly on the use of force into the area of rural labor relations.

The establishment of a police system to enforce labor contracts would have required the approval of the landholding elite, but employers competing for workers were reluctant to permit legal limitations on their ability to attract colonos from other areas. At a meeting in 1913 a planter proposed a new clause in work contracts "which would punish with a heavy fine those planters who hire colonos who have left other plantations without satisfying the provisions of the contract. Furthermore, the new employer who violates said provisions would be required to pay damages to the previous employer of the colono in question." Action on the measure was postponed.[69]

At the next planter's convention, held in 1914 in Ribeirão Preto, a planter presented a stronger proposal, providing that anyone hiring a colono who had a debt outstanding with a previous employer would be responsible for that debt. Furthermore, the debt would have to be liquidated before the new employer could pay wages to the colono in question. The motion posed a clear threat to the current practice of hiring with no questions asked those colonos who fled from prior debts, and it stirred heated debate. Antonio Piccarolo, an Italian journalist and right-wing socialist, claimed that if Brazil "wants to stay within the bounds of universal law, she can never promulgate laws in accordance with this proposal." Some planters wanted to postpone a vote on the matter, but Francisco Ferreira Ramos, for many years a leader of the Paulista Society of Agriculture, objected that the resolution presented "such danger, is so monstrous, that it must be liquidated immediately.'' In the face of such vociferous opposition, the instigator of the furor withdrew the motion without a vote.[70] A prior-debt clause similar to the 1914 proposal was eventually included in the Brazilian civil code promulgated in 1916, but the vague language provided loopholes that limited its effectiveness.[71]

The absence of legal authority in the rural areas, of course, was a two-sided matter. The attitude of the government was that on the plantation the landowner's authority was supreme. Just as there were no official police to force the colono to work, so were there no police to protect him from the arbitrary action of the employer and the ''summary justice'' of capangas. But the influence of armed ruffians in the service of the landowner was restricted to the plantation itself and the immediate surrounding area. After the first years of the twentieth century, reports of capanga brutality diminished, as positive incentives increasingly replaced the vestiges of the coercive slave regime.

The coffee workers were aware of the reputations of individual planters. ''Good'' employers were those who treated their colonos with respect, provided adequate housing, food crop and pasture land, and paid wages in full and on time. ''Bad'' employers were those who provided few amenities, used capangas to enforce their arbitrary will, and often failed to pay wages in full when they were due.[72] With a variety of wage and working conditions, occasional labor shortages, and the continued mobility of the labor force, economic rather than legal pressures worked to attenuate the control the planters effectively exercised over their laborers.

The most fundamental and continuous source of positive incentives was the colono system itself, especially the food crop and pasture privileges. Occasional uncertainty of wage payments and variations in the adequacy and quality of the nonmonetary provisions of the colono contract were the frequent subject of controversy. But planters could not eliminate any of the basic elements of the system, and workers continued to expect them. In fact, planters proposed and implemented additional perquisites from time to time.

Often such ''extra'' services were related to the need to attract workers. The Italian consular agent Silvio Coletti had few illusions about the harsh realities of work on the coffee plantations and no qualms about reporting the negative aspects of colono life. In 1908 Coletti reported that ''the move from one plantation to another is normally facilitated by the new employer furnishing the colonos the necessary carts and draft animals to transport their household goods, grain supplies, and domestic animals.'' Another example of supplementary incentives was discussed at the planters' convention in 1913. Souza Campos, from São Carlos in the Paulista zone, claimed that ''agriculture in São Paulo is suffering increasing difficulties due to the absolute shortage of workers on the plantations.'' He told the assembly that in his visits to the hostel to hire colonos he had begun to guarantee prospective employees that if they were not satisfied with conditions on his fazenda he would supply them with free train fare back to the city of São Paulo.[73]

Some additional considerations were intended to retain workers already on the plantation. At a 1912 meeting Augusto Barreto, from Mococa in the Mogiana zone, presented a plan he had used successfully for many years on his own plantation. Barreto's scheme was a "longevity bonus" of 2.5 percent of the colono's contractual annual wage credited in his account book every year, with the accumulated total paid at the end of five years. For each succeeding five-year period the bonus was increased an additional 2.5 percent. If the original head of the colono family died and his widow and children stayed on, they would continue to accumulate bonus wages as before. And provided he returned to the plantation within one year, a colono could take a leave of absence to visit his homeland without a break in the accumulation of his bonus payment. Responding to an objection that under such a plan the colono would become a virtual partner of the landowner, Barreto explained that the bonus was not a share of profits, but rather a percentage of the colono's own wage. In the final resolutions the members of the meeting "suggested" the plan as one possible solution for the instability problem.[74]

Extra benefits were exceptional, but these cases show that while some employers attempted repression and fraud others resorted to increased incentives. Together with the persistent controversy over the food crop provisions of the colono contract, these examples provide evidence that not all planters considered repression a viable solution to their labor problems. A landowner could not retain workers for long by force or by ties of economic dependence. At the regional level, if an excessive number of workers removed themselves from the labor force, the coffee industry itself would be seriously threatened. Coffee planters would have preferred less uncertainty and less labor turnover, and they preferred to avoid the necessity of recruiting replacement workers for those who departed. This was especially the case after the initial labor market glut of the 1890s had passed. Even where repression was attempted, the goal was to retain workers rather than to drive them away. Thus the workers themselves usually made the individual decisions to move, which resulted collectively in the geographical mobility of the coffee labor force.

A general exception to this voluntaristic view of the system was in cases of protest by coffee workers, expressed in wage demands or strikes. Rumors that spread among the rows of colono houses or on Sunday trips to the general store left little permanent record, and so information on rural labor unrest is sparse. There are nevertheless hints that strikes and strike threats occurred frequently, and they shared several common features. They usually took place in late April or early May, not to commemorate international working-class solidarity, but because planters were more vulnerable to such pressure at the beginning of the coffee harvest. They were concerned with purely economic issues. And the results, whether success or failure, remained localized and short-lived.

Ideologically motivated working-class militants, most of immigrant origins, became active in the city of São Paulo. Their small successes became, in the standard formula, a "case for the police."[75] Despite the presence of hundreds of workers on many individual plantations, several factors inhibited the development of ideological or political activism among coffee colonos. Most important was the paternalism that was always a potential and often a real instrument of control and cooptation. A standard policy to limit collective action, for example, was to separate resident laborers into several scattered groups of houses. Permission to use the coffee-drying platforms for an occasional Saturday night dance, in contrast, made colonos grateful for small favors and cost the employer nothing. Workers who complained or appealed to their fellows for support could be summarily expelled with the help of a few native Brazilian capangas. The resulting loss of manpower was a small matter compared to the risk of retaining an "agitator" who might disrupt plantation routine. In any case, there were usually new arrivals available in the hostel in São Paulo, eager for work and uninformed, who could replace "troublemakers." Colonos understood this as well as the planters, and so the threat of expulsion did not have to be acted upon often to enforce tranquillity in the landlord's domain.

Another source of cleavage was between immigrants and Brazilian workers. The actions of a few natives as brutal enforcers of the planter's will was only one source of animosity between ethnic groups. Over the years, dark-skinned Brazilians suffered prejudice and discrimination at the hands of planters and immigrants alike, and native peasants and ex-slaves were relegated to marginal roles in the rural society of the coffee zone. But within the lower economic strata the disdain between races was in some measure reciprocal, and both white immigrants and black freedmen were degraded by the Brazilian elite. The low status of the coffee colono resulted from the identification of work in the groves with the condition of the field slave in the earlier era. An immigrant told an Italian inspector in 1902, for example, that when colonos objected to such conditions as being required to stay in the fields even during rainstorms the Brazilian employer responded: "Shut your mouth and be quiet. You Italians are slaves, and we natives are the masters." And the following example illustrates the disparagement lower-class Brazilians felt for field hands. On a plantation in the Campinas area in 1912, a French journalist overheard a black servant refuse an order she considered below her station, with the response, "What do you take me for, an Italian?" The Frenchman considered the incident humorous but understandable, since "the Italian immigrant today does the work that in former times was done by slaves."[76]

The immigrants, for their part, rejected being classified as the equivalent of slaves. They valued hard work and cast a disparaging eye on what they considered to be the lack of ambition of the Brazilian camarada. While race prejudice probably also tinged their attitudes, racial distinctions apparently concerned consular officials more than workers themselves. Silvio Coletti complained that even more damaging to the immigrant's moral level than geographical isolation was "the contact with Negro and caboclo (mixed Indian and Portuguese) elements, who are instinctively brutal, thieving, and violent." In another report, Coletti said that the cultural degradation of the immigrant "does not even respect racial differences. Marriages between Italian men and Negro women, and what is even more serious, marriages between Italian women and Negro men, are not infrequent."[77] These statements by a middle-class Italian bureaucrat cannot be imputed to the working-class countrymen he observed marrying Brazilian blacks.

One possible incentive for some immigrant women to marry blacks was the two groups' different attitudes toward women. An Italian journalist reported in 1891 that when he visited plantation living quarters he saw "the women of the blacks sitting in their doorways with their hands on their laps." The houses of the Italian workers, in contrast, were "hermetically sealed," with only a few old people in view caring for small children. The immigrant colonos of both sexes above ten years of age were in the fields hoeing coffee.[78] Native camaradas looked down on colonos for putting their wives to work in the coffee fields whenever possible. Immigrants, on the other hand, considered the native workers' practice of keeping wives at home to be a waste of labor power. Thus a European woman who married a black man may have been ostracized from her own ethnic group, but she stood to gain in status vis-à-vis her husband and in leisure time.

In addition to the division between black and white, there were national and regional distinctions within the immigrant group, which limited working-class solidarity. Italians were by far the largest single nationality, but they continued to identify themselves by their regional origins within Italy. Moreover, there were Spaniards, Portuguese, and later Japanese, Syrio-Lebanese, and people from several eastern European countries, all retaining their own ethnic, linguistic, religious, and cultural identification. The common status of coffee colono was an inadequate basis for breaking down these distinctions, given the turnover of the rural labor force, the geographical isolation of the plantations, the rudimentary development of noneconomic institutions on the frontier, and the pervasive control of the planters.

In 1913 strikes that could not be easily contained broke out simultaneously on several huge agricultural enterprises near Ribeirão Preto. The case required joint action by a group of planters; and the local police, foreign consular officials, and a recently established legal agency within the Department of Agriculture all became involved. The strike and its outcome illustrate several aspects of rural labor relations.

Coffee prices rose in 1910 and 1911, after more than a decade at low levels. The increased revenues fueled internal price inflation, but wages failed to keep pace with the rise in the cost of living. In 1912 coffee prices again began to fall. The drop was accentuated in 1913, but without a corresponding decline in the cost of supplies colonos could not produce for themselves. In their 1912 contracts colonos in the Ribeirão Preto area demanded and got higher wages, but no raise was forthcoming when new contracts were signed in early 1913. In late April, just before the harvest was to begin, workers on the plantations of Francisco Schmidt, the English-owned Dumont fazenda, and several others declared a strike for an upward revision in the wage provisions of their contracts. The word spread quickly, and within a few days several thousand colonos had laid down their hoes. Previous strikes had had some success, including one in Bragança Paulista several hundred kilometers to the southeast in early April 1913. But the stakes were much bigger in Ribeirão Preto, both in the potential for disruption of the harvest and for long-term maintenance of control by the planters. When the landowners met in Francisco Schmidt's palatial residence on the first of May and decided to resist the demands in a united front, the strikers were doomed to failure.[79]

The police chief of Ribeirão Preto threatened to expel the strikers, but in the face of several thousand united and militant colonos he took little action. Pietro Baroli, the Italian consul general in São Paulo, was soon on the scene attempting to negotiate a settlement, and his presence probably helped save his compatriots from capanga and police brutality. For his trouble, Baroli was roundly criticized in the press of Ribeirão Preto and São Paulo. The Patronato Agrícola, a state agency established in the previous year to head off complaints to consuls and resolve labor disputes, took the legalistic position that contracts already agreed to by both parties must be respected. Within a few days the Paulista Society of Agriculture met in São Paulo to consider the matter, and the members sent a telegram to Ribeirão Preto expressing "unanimous solidarity" with the hard line taken by their colleagues.

The situation remained tense for two weeks while the planters arranged to bring in other workers from the hostel and from elsewhere in the western plateau. Police were detailed to protect the strikebreakers, many of whom were recently arrived Japanese. The consul Baroli planned to ask the immigrant hostel to take the strikers and get them jobs on other plantations, but he reconsidered when the account books of the protesters, in which any later contract would have to be recorded, were marked "striker" (*grevista*) in red ink. His eventual solution was to repatriate several hundred workers and their families at the expense of the consular office. In the aftermath, an Italian-language magazine in São Paulo concluded that "the colonos had no preparation whatsoever: no class consciousness, no solidarity, no organization, no means of resistance," and knowing this, the strike was a futile action.[80]

The Patronato Agricola acted in the planters' favor in the 1913 strike. It went on to become an important government institution tempering the *droit de seigneur*, which left the worker virtually at the mercy of the planter's will. Economic considerations had attenuated planter control to a degree, and Italian and Spanish consuls had done what they could to respond to abuses of the colono system; but not until 1912 did the state intervene to protect workers' legal rights in an institutionalized way. The Patronato Agricola, which went into operation in June of that year, was to enforce state and federal laws concerning rural workers' contractual rights and obligations, as well as those of the employer; seek peaceful solutions to questions of rural labor relations; supervise the system of individual colono account books; and perform related functions including "bringing to the attention of the proper authorities the complaints of agricultural workers regarding crimes against their person, family, or property." Sampaio Vidal, who submitted the bill creating the Patronato to the legislature, made clear that it was a direct response to the activity of foreign consular officials as well as to the ongoing publicity campaign by consuls and journalists against São Paulo and against work on the coffee plantations of the west. Vidal recognized that the efforts of the consuls were necessary because the colono had no other recourse when the planter violated the work contract or the worker felt otherwise wronged. Thus the Patronato Agricola was established to keep consuls out of labor disputes and to reduce the material available for negative publicity.[81]

The agency handled 424 cases the first year, with only the director and one lawyer on the professional staff. The staff grew until by 1923 there were eight lawyers investigating complaints all over the western plateau. A typical case load for the Patronato was that for 1914. The 437 complaints that year comprised 254 for late payment of wages, 78 for violation of contract, 27 for theft of baggage, 18 for violent expulsion, 17 for coercion, 15 for unfair fines, 7 for "bad treatment," 6 for crimes against property, 1 for improper accounting procedures, and 14 cases brought by planters against striking workers. In that same year, 161,925 milreis in claims were collected from planters and paid out to colonos. At the going rate of 3 milreis per day the total was equivalent to nearly 54,000 person-days in wages. In the years from 1912 through 1929 the Patronato handled 11,962 cases, an average of 704 per year, and the total amount taken in claims and redistributed to the damaged parties was 4,055,043 milreis. Officials claimed that a large but undetermined additional amount changed hands in informal settlements after the initial intervention of the Patronato.[82]

The Patronato Agricola did work in the colonos' favor, and it seems unlikely that workers would have continued to avail themselves of its services over the years if the agency were no more than window dressing. By giving the workers some protection from arbitrary action by employers, the Patronato served the purpose its proponents had in mind. The secretary of agriculture proclaimed that broader success in 1914: "The complaints of the foreign colonos, which logically used to go to the consulates, now are almost all directed to the Patronato, thus depriving the consular files of complaints against out country, with evident advantages for our prestige as a state that seeks manpower for the plantations and good people for settling its land."[83] Directly or indirectly, consular and journalistic criticism of planter's attitudes and actions had some positive effect in easing the lot of the coffee colono.

The colonos were politically powerless, socially inferior, and economically weak relative to the planter class, but they were not wage slaves replacing the chattel slave of the earlier era. With several alternatives normally open other than continuing submission to the whim of a given landowner, the worker retained some control over his own labor power. The causes of geographical mobility can be seen as relative advantages among alternative courses of action as the colono perceived his options. Affecting his decision to move or stay was a combination of "push" factors—the negative aspects of colono life; and "pull" factors—positive incentives intended to attract workers from an abundant but mobile manpower pool. The planters feared labor shortages, and they competed among themselves for workers. Thus they continued to extend food cropping and other concessions to the colonos, and they responded in some measure to pressure from consuls and the press. The harsh realities of the coffee workers' existence must be set in the broader context of labor market conditions. Positive incentives, meager and uncertain though they may seem in historical retrospect, were an essential element of the social relations of production that developed in the São Paulo coffee industry after the abolition of slavery.

After the turn-of-the-century crisis of overproduction and low prices shook the Paulista planters out of their complacency, the colono system came under frequent attack. Experts in agricultural economics argued that it had served a valuable purpose in easing the transition to free labor but should be altered in response to the worsening economic conditions in the coffee industry. Some advocated a return to sharecropping as a way of again distributing risks for the benefit of the planters. Others claimed that by simply renting coffee land to workers for a fixed annual sum the landowners could free themselves from the cost and problems of administering plantations and from the vagaries of the coffee market. In a detailed proposal for a rental system presented to the Brazilian Rural Society in 1929, the director of the São Paulo Department of Labor openly expressed his envy that Paulista coffee planters had not been able to develop into a class of idle-rich absentee rentiers as had their counterparts in the Argentine pampas and in the British colonies.[84] Despite such proposals, continued competition among planters for an ample but mobile labor force limited the possibilities for change. The colono contract remained in general use in the São Paulo plateau until the collapse of the world economy in the 1930s. Even then the tradition of four and a half decades was slow to break down. The colono system—or parts of it— lingered on, but the conditions in which it developed and persisted were no longer present. Gradually since the 1930s, camaradas who are paid fixed monthly wages, sharecropping, renting, and migrant gangs have replaced the colono contract pattern.[85]

Today much of the coffee in northern Paraná state, the new coffee frontier, is produced by small and medium-sized farms in a dependent relationship to the owners of processing plants in regional towns.[86] In the 1950s minimum wage and social welfare legislation finally penetrated the São Paulo coffee zone, and workers suffered instead of gaining. To avoid such measures planters dismissed their resident workers, sometimes destroying rows of colono houses to make the expulsion final. Today the rehabilitated plantations of São Paulo use contour planting and chemical fertilizers to conserve the land once exploited with such profligacy. Most work is done by gangs of women who leave their children in the shacks of suburban slums before dawn, ride a jolting truck to the fields, and return after dark with a meager wage paid by their employer—the labor contractor who owns the truck. The modern planter deals with the owner of the truck, has few employees on his own payroll, and is little bothered by minimum wage laws.[87]

The people who hoe the coffee groves today just as slaves once did are called *bóias frias*—"cold lunches." The label is a graphic reflection of their socioeconomic status. For a Brazilian, to eat a cold midday meal from a metal bucket is a symbol of poverty, even desperation. Old men in wide fedoras sit in the plazas of the towns of the western plateau and reminisce in Italian accents about the *vida farta*, the "good life" of their days as coffee colonos. Their memories are selective, accentuating the positive. Those who failed under the colono system left no such idealized legacy. Still, the old days— with jobs on the frontier, with alternatives and even opportunities, with families eating a hot meal at midday in their little house near food plots and coffee groves—compare favorably with the lot of the "cold lunch" today.

5

LAND POLICY
AND RURAL LABOR

Land is the foundation of agricultural societies. The market value of land
and the commodities produced on it are sources of economic gain. Control
over land resources confers political power. And one measure of social status
is control over land and the wealth it produces. In the words of one student
of the subject, "'patterns of land tenure are, in fact, patterns of social relations, inasmuch as they define man's relation to man in the use of land and
the goods derived from it.'"[1] Where subsistence agriculture is practiced and
land supplies many of the family's needs directly, access to land can confer
a degree of independence from markets and the money economy that cannot
exist in the urban environment. In the case of São Paulo, if a family had land
on which to grow corn and beans to feed itself, the market price of those
products mattered little. One of the essential features of the colono contract
was that the planter temporarily ceded the productive value of land to the
colono, while retaining legal title and control. In order to understand the more
general development of agrarian structure in rural São Paulo, it is necessary
to look beyond the specifics of the colono system to an analysis of the patterns of land tenure that evolved concurrently with the coffee boom and
the influx of immigrants.

In legal systems recognizing private property, the state theoretically re-
tains ultimate control—directly in public land, and indirectly in private land
through the recognition of titles and the principle of eminent domain. When
a landed elite controls the politico-legal apparatus of the state, public and
private land policies might be expected generally to coincide. In the late
nineteenth century the power of the coffee planters and related groups was
so great as virtually to exclude other interest groups from a voice in political
processes in São Paulo. With the social changes of subsequent decades, the
urban, commercial, industrial, intellectual, and even proletarian sectors
became increasingly vocal and politically active. But the power of the landowners remained dominant and decisive, particularly in matters pertaining
to land policy.

Before discussing the evolution of legal institutions of tenure and elite
attitudes toward control of the land, it would be helpful to present some aggregate quantitative evidence as to how much land was occupied, cultivated,

or available for exploitation in São Paulo. The 1900 survey, which showed 21 percent of the area of the western plateau claimed in plantations and just 4 percent of the plateau area planted in coffee, has already been mentioned in chapter 2. Later censuses confirmed that the occupation of São Paulo was incomplete well into the twentieth century.

The total land area of São Paulo is about 10,216,500 alqueires. In 1905 the state carried out a census encompassing all types of rural economic activity, including coffee production. According to the 1905 census, 5,014,000 alqueires were claimed in private properties in the entire state, or 49 percent of the total land area. The 602,806 alqueires under cultivation were equivalent to just 12 percent of the land claimed in private property and 6 percent of the total land area. There were 361,572 alqueires reportedly planted in coffee groves in São Paulo in 1905, up from 313,159 in 1900 but still only 3.5 percent of the total land area of the state.

There were 5,736,888 alqueires claimed in private property in São Paulo in 1920, equal to 56 percent of the total land area. But just 820,176 alqueires—8 percent of the total land area—were under cultivation. By 1920 there were still vast reserves of arable land in the western plateau. By 1934 the area in cultivation in São Paulo had risen to 1,406,252 alqueires, or 14 percent of the land area. At the same time, the rural properties claimed nearly 3,263,000 alqueires in forest and scrub forest—land classified as arable, available for cultivation in the future.[2] These data reinforce the impressions of planters, politicians, consular officials, and foreign visitors: arable land was abundant.

The development of land tenure institutions in São Paulo must be seen within this context of the continued availability of unclaimed or unused land, both within the settled parts of the western plateau and beyond the western pioneer fringe. Furthermore, it is necessary to distinguish between official policy as reflected in the legal system on the one hand, and the real patterns of land control and use on the other. If policy is transferred into specific legal instruments and the law has actual effect, there may be close parallels between these two aspects of land tenure. But where the law is ambiguous or incomplete and the power or the will of the state to implement it is weak, de jure and de facto land systems may be related in only a tenuous way. A review of the historical development of land tenure legislation and its application can help elucidate the relationship between the legal and actual land systems.

During the colonial period the Portuguese crown alienated large areas to private individuals in land grants known as *sesmarias*. The system was haphazard, used as much for the political purposes of the crown as to promote actual occupation of the rural zones. Sesmarias were rarely surveyed or marked off, and many were never cultivated or otherwise occupied by the grantee. Sesmaria titles were often tenuous and disputed, but they remained the basis of many land claims through the nineteenth and well into the twentieth century. In addition to sesmaria grants, private individuals claimed land in the colonial period by a more informal method, which also remained an important element of later Brazilian land law. This was the principle of *posse* (literally, "possession"), or squatter's rights, the establishment of claim to land by virtue of de facto occupation or control. The term posse came to refer to both the basis for establishing ownership and the tract of land so claimed. The early European colonists occupied much land in Brazil by posse, despite the fact that such claims had no legal status in the colonial era.

After 1822 no further sesmarias were granted. Independent Brazil had no land law, and thus no legal means of alienating public lands, from that year until 1850. In the interim, the posse system continued to function beyond state control. Extralegal claims were extended over vast areas of unoccupied territory, and rival parties settled boundary disputes privately, often using threat and force. Finally in 1850 the Brazilian parliament passed a law intended to reassert the ultimate power of the state over land. The law provided for the revalidation of all claims based on the colonial sesmaria, and the registration and legitimization of all posse claims. Under the law the public domain was to be surveyed and mapped, and could only subsequently be alienated by sale. Squatting, the extralegal usurpation of public land, was forbidden.

The 1850 land law was a nearly unmitigated failure. Few sesmarias were ever revalidated or posses legitimized as the law required. The government abandoned the survey of public lands in 1878 after accomplishing very little. Wholesale encroachments onto public lands continued, and these new posses were entered into local notarial registries through an assortment of fraudulent practices.[3] Since the government did not attempt to contest the flagrant usurpations of the public domain or to penalize landholders for failing to comply with the 1850 law, the question arises as to why posseiros bothered to validate their claims at all. The answer has to do with the economic function of landownership. If a posseiro could establish legal title to land (even if by fraudulent means), he could use it as collateral for loans, bequeath it to his heirs, or sell it. But for the purpose of exploiting land for the production of subsistence or commercial products, legal title was less significant. Where land functioned primarily as a factor of production rather than as a commodity in its own right, de facto possession was the important consideration.

Throughout the nineteenth century and extending well into the twentieth, there existed in Brazil a group of posseiros who had no voice in the legislative process, no influence with local notaries, and little interest in land as a commodity. These were independent peasants who occupied land because it would provide them with subsistence. They could hope to produce enough of an economic surplus to barter or sell in local markets to supply the limited range of necessities they could not produce themselves. They were resigned to occasional encroachment on their holdings by more powerful men with other intentions, and many eventually fell into a semidependent relationship to a large landowner who might assume control over an area. But in such fertile areas as São Paulo there seemed to be plenty of land for the use of all who needed it, and in the hinterlands of the western plateau there were large areas where no government or individual held sway. Just as the 1850 land law did little to curb the movement of the capitalists onto public lands, it also did little to restrict the modest ambitions of the small farmer with no legal title to his subsistence plot.

Commercial coffee cultivation was introduced in the São Paulo plateau about the same time the imperial land law was passed. The wholesale usurpation of public domain in the western frontier in the following years is a flagrant example of the failure of the 1850 law to provide for the orderly alienation of public lands. People from more settled areas simply moved into an unoccupied area in the frontier zone, felled a few trees to mark their claim, brought in gangs of workers to clear a portion of the area and plant coffee on it—and a plantation came into being.[4] The possibility that someone else may have previously used the land to graze a few cattle, or that some of it may have technically been part of a sesmaria given out a century before, was of little concern. A more immediate problem was often to clear the land of the nomadic Indians who had lived in the area for centuries before the encroachment of the Brazilians.

Land in the Paulista plateau subsequently acquired value, and titles became increasingly important. If a posse with no legal status was sold, the resulting bill of sale and notarial record, with a description of the purported boundaries, could be used as evidence of ownership in later transfers, to settle disputes, or for commercial purposes. Other titles were established in registry books by fabricating fictitious posseiros who had occupied the land prior to 1850 and later transferred it to the current claimant. The state had little control over the extralegal tenure system that developed in western São Paulo in the second half of the nineteenth century. The most important criterion for establishing commercially valid land titles was de facto occupation.[5]

In 1891, at a time when the coffee boom was reaching a fever pitch, the federalistic constitution of the new republic placed all public land and tenure regulation in the jurisdiction of the states. São Paulo established the Office of Land, Colonization, and Immigration under the Department of Agriculture in October 1892 to take charge of title validations, surveying, and alienating public land. An example of official ignorance as to the true land situation during this period was revealed when the state granted provisional title to one hundred thousand hectares, presumed to be in the public domain, to a private colonization company. One clause ordered the concessionnaire to "restore at any time lands that might be duly claimed by anyone who could prove title to them."[6]

The law of 1850 remained technically in effect, but São Paulo authorities recognized the need for new legislation. As the secretary of agriculture described the situation in 1892, the rich soil of São Paulo had attracted "a great number of individuals desirous of possessing, by any means, great extensions of territory in this state." He blamed the current difficulty in discriminating public land on the 1850 law and its subsequent regulations. Under those regulations only titles registered by 1856 were recognized as valid. Subsequent to 1856 the purchase of public land was beyond the means of most small farmers, although those who could buy land or establish title by some subterfuge were in a more advantageous position. The consequence, he said, was on the one hand "the spread of each ancient posse like an oil stain on paper, making possible innumerable partial sales," and on the other hand the illegal but perhaps justified de facto occupation of public domain by small farmers who could not otherwise gain access to it. The secretary urged the passage of a new law that would "end the cruel uncertainty in which so many inhabitants of the remote parts of Paulista soil live."[7]

Finally in 1895 the state legislature approved a new land law. The measure had no legal force, however, until a regulating decree could be issued. Such a bill passed the state assembly in 1896, but it was held up in the state senate. In 1897 the secretary of agriculture again urged the quick approval of the necessary legislation so that the validity of posse claims could be established and public lands alienated in an orderly manner. Without a registry of land titles, he said, it would be impossible to institute a land tax, "which will lead us, although slowly, to the subdivision of the great estates."[8] It had become apparent in the course of the debates on the land regulations that planters and land speculators opposed limitations on the size of posse claims and high prices for subsequent purchases of public land. Not until January 1900 was a regulating decree finally promulgated that provided the basis for São Paulo's land tenure system in subsequent years.[9]

The regulation of 1900 was in large measure an updating of the 1850 law. It provided for the registration of all rural properties, the revalidation of the colonial sesmarias, the legalization of posses, and a survey of the public domain in anticipation of its sale by public auction. Any posse to which title was obtained prior to 1878 was declared legitimate with no further formality. It there was no clear record of the boundaries, the posseiro could claim an area of contiguous virgin land equivalent to double the area he already had under cultivation, up to a maximum of two thousand hectares of arable land and four thousand hectares of grassland. Most importantly, the criteria for the legitimization of posses established between 1878 and 1895, reiterating a provision of the 1850 law, were "habitual residence and actual cultivation" (*morada habitual e cultura efetiva*). In other words, technical violations of the 1850 law were swept away, and subsequent posses achieved legal status. By requesting the state land office to survey his posse and by paying the cost of measurement and demarcation, a squatter could receive legal title to the land he claimed. The law stipulated a small additional fee per hectare for legitimizing posse lands in excess of one thousand hectares. The principle of squatter's rights thus became a central element in São Paulo's land tenure legislation. Only posses established after June 1895 were considered in violation, but in the provision for the eventual sale of public land squatter's rights were again reinforced. Anyone "who cultivated, had made improvements on, or habitually resided upon public land, even though without legal title" was to receive preference when the area in question came up for sale.[10]

The São Paulo land regulation of 1900 was also similar to the law of 1850 in its lack of effectiveness. Before the state could proceed with the survey and sale of the public domain, an official record was to be established of land claimed by private parties. This was to be done through the registration of all types of titles and posse claims in specially established land offices within one year of 12 February 1900, when the law was published. The original deadline for filing claims was then 12 February 1901. But the regional offices were not opened until October 1900, so the deadline was extended to October 1901. In the first four months that the offices were open, just ninety-seven properties were registered in the entire state, and none of them had dubious titles subject to survey and the legal procedure of legitimization.[11]

The secretary of agriculture speculated that the reasons for the lack of compliance were the history of past land legislation, the assumption that the current law would never really be enforced, and the fact that there was no clear penalty for noncompliance. Technically, land claims not registered in the stipulated period were to revert to the state, but until the registration was completed there was no way of knowing what land was claimed in posse and what was clearly public domain. The secretary urged that the deadline not be extended and that surveying crews begin marking off public land based on the final results of the registration, however deficient. He also recommended the institution of a tax on land recorded elsewhere, such as in mortgage and notarial records, which did not appear in the state government's registration roles.[12] This proposal was tacit recognition that many planters held commercially valid titles that they used as loan collateral, without bothering to obtain validation from the state.

As the registration deadline approached, such a legalistic course of action became clearly impossible. The deadline was extended for an additional six months, to 1 April 1902, but still few squatters bothered to record their claims. The filing deadline was not extended after that date, and state officials gave up the attempt to obtain a record of property claims. The registration of land titles and sales remained the business of private notaries at the local level. The secretary of agriculture recognized in 1901 that the real purpose of the whole system—to make it possible to alienate public land in a rational and legal way—was not being fulfilled. In an attempt to get some idea of the public land available for distribution in each municipio, the secretary requested informal reports on the subject from municipal councils, justices of the peace, and other local authorities. Of the 150 municipios then existing, the Department of Agriculture received replies from only 32. Most of the reports simply noted the existence of public lands of undetermined area and value.[13]

After the public domain had theoretically been under the control of the São Paulo government for more than a decade, the only real effect of state land laws had been to give legal status to posses occupied between 1850 and 1895, just as the earlier imperial law had recognized posses taken prior to 1850. The general attitude in the rural areas was that the trouble and expense of legally validating a posse was unnecessary, since eventually the state would again approve posses ex post facto. In the meantime, the question of the extent and location of public lands was still unresolved, and new encroachments continued in the frontier zones.

State authorities decided to proceed with a public land survey, but on a piecemeal basis and in areas not involved in coffee cultivation. When the first teams surveyed the rural areas adjacent to the state capital, they encountered many technically illegal squatters. The secretary of agriculture suggested that since wholesale evictions were out of the question and since surveys should be continued, waiving legal technicalities and giving the squatters official title to their posses would serve the best interest of all parties. Such a policy would recognize the inevitable, limit further encroachments in the surveyed area by giving the posses definite boundaries, and end the legal uncertainty under which the posseiro lived.[14]

In 1904 the survey continued, but still there was no attempt to regularize the land tenure situation in the western coffee zone. While measuring an area in the coastal lowlands near Santos, the survey teams encountered no less than 169 extralegal posses within an area of some seventeen hundred hectares. This experience in an economically unimportant area was used to justify an ad hoc policy regarding posse claims. The secretary of agriculture again recommended that the state recognize squatter's rights in such cases. The principle was legally reconfirmed in a rider attached to the state budget bill for 1906. According to this law the state would give preference in the sale of public lands to posseiros who had established "habitual residence and actual cultivation" for a period of five years. The price of such posse land was set at ten milreis per hectare of forest land and two milreis per hectare of grassland. Maximum areas allowed under the law were five hundred hectares of forest and four thousand hectares of grassland in each posse.[15] Thus the government abandoned the previous pattern of fixed cutoff years such as 1856 and 1895, which had been central to previous legislation. The new piecemeal approach gave legal status to posses occupied for five years prior to the official survey or the filing of a validation claim.

In the following years surveys went ahead slowly in the coastal lowlands and in the Sorocaba zone where coffee was not important. These were not cadastral surveys whereby all properties were measured and recorded but simply attempts to reconnoiter land presumed to be in the public domain. In 1908 the survey effort was extended into the western frontier, bypassing that part of the plateau already within the coffee-producing area. As the secretary of agriculture explained the need: "With the advancement of the tracks of the Noroeste and Sorocabana railroads into unpopulated areas, the invasion of intruders into state lands in the area took place, making the guarding of the public domain urgent." The state organized two new survey teams, one for each of the new rail lines. In the following year the secretary noted that the surveys were needed, not only to permit the orderly occupation of the new areas, but also to confer "the tranquillity of secure ownership on the posses of those backwoodsmen [*sertanejos*] who have settled the Far-West [*sic*] of São Paulo through so many years of work and sacrifice."[16]

The survey teams in the frontier areas issued public notices giving posseiros ninety days in which to file land claims prior to the demarcation of the public domain. Faced with the possibility of having the government reclaim their posses, many private parties came forward to comply with the order. As the surveys progressed, the team in the Alta Sorocabana encountered ninety-six separate posses in the valley of a stream tributary to the Paranapanema River, in an area of 13,647 hectares. Of the posseiros in question, ninety-one justified their claims by virtue of residence and cultivation for a five-year period. All ninety-one paid the required surveying fee and the price of the land and received full title. The other five posses in the valley reverted to the state and were subdivided into twenty-five smaller plots of fifty to sixty hectares each, to be sold at public auction. The surveyors in the frontier area of the Araraquarense zone received about one hundred land claims during 1912–13, and in the process of verifying the areas of the posses found "many irregularities, to the complete detriment of the public domain."[17]

In 1916 the Department of Agriculture finally began a cadastral survey of São Paulo. This first effort to map the private property of the state in a systematic way came thirty years after the start of the coffee boom. Unlike the public land effort, the cadastral survey initially concentrated in settled areas. It was begun in five municipios, including Ribeirão Preto in the Mogiana zone, Araraquara and Jaboticabal in the Paulista zone, Taquaritinga in the Araraquarense zone, and Salesópolis, a relatively unimportant municipio in the coastal mountains east of the state capital. The most notable feature of the cadastral survey was its failure. One serious technical problem was the absence of systematic base points from which distances and angles could be measured to plot the relative location of rural properties and the borders separating them. More fundamental was the resistance of landholders and squatters. The survey parties immediately encountered all sorts of boundary irregularities, conflicting claims, and extralegal posses. The cadastral survey was not completed even in the five original municipios, and the entire project was apparently abandoned in the course of 1917.[18] The lack of official commitment to the surveys was revealed in 1920, when the state transferred many of the technical personnel from the survey teams to the newly established road commission. In the postwar period the planning and construction of automobile roads in São Paulo took precedence over the demarcation of the public and private domains.

A law approved in 1921 and regulated in August 1922 further liberalized the requirement for validating posse claims. By this new law, land could be given free to a private individual—whether Brazilian or foreign national—under any of the following conditions: if the posseiro (1) claimed the land more than one year prior to the effective date of the law, (2) held a nonvalid title that antedated the law, or (3) obtained the land through a judicial decision.[19] Again the state government bowed to the inevitable and reaffirmed the validity of squatter's rights by recognizing as legitimate the posses occupied between 1895 and 1921.

In 1924 landholders in the Alta Sorocabana frontier obtained a court order preventing further public land surveys. In obvious frustration, the head of the survey team in the area reported that the government could recognize all the posses in the large area as private lands, in which case the state would lose the payments due under the legitimization procedure. The alternative was to declare some or all of the posses illegitimate, in which case the affected posseiros would obtain a court order annulling the decision and rendering the entire survey and demarcation effort meaningless. "In either case," he concluded, "only private parties will benefit, to the detriment of the state treasury."[20]

From 1903 through 1924 the Department of Agriculture surveyed less than one million hectares of São Paulo's total land area of nearly twenty-five million hectares. In the following years the surveys made only minimal progress, and state authorities remained on the defensive. The problem became the preservation of the known public domain, rather than the establishment of control in new areas. In 1926 the secretary of agriculture recommended that guards he hired to patrol the public land already surveyed, to prevent people from cutting down forests and to protect against the encroachment of squatters. He also suggested that a lawyer be added to the staff of the land office who would defend state interests in legal disputes arising in the demarcation of public lands. By 1930 official maps of São Paulo's public domain were little improved over the previous decade. The land office was increasingly preoccupied with litigation over the legitimization of posses, the falsification of local land registry books, and other legal problems.[21]

This overview of São Paulo's land tenure legislation during the old republic illustrates the continued absence of effective state control over public land. Throughout these years land was occupied, bought, subdivided, sold, mortgaged, and inherited under a locally organized system of land tenure that recognized effective occupation or control as the ultimate criterion of ownership. An imperial decree of April 1865 called for the establishment of registry books for recording transfers of real property under the control of private notaries in each *comarca*, a judicial division comprising one or more municipios. The books were marked off in columns providing for an order number, date, parish of location, address or name of the property, boundaries and other distinguishing features, name and residence of buyer and seller, type of transfer (such as sale, inheritance, foreclosure for debt, purchase at public auction), basis for title, value of the contract, and conditions of sale. The first time a transfer was notarized, standard formulas for proof of ownership were parental gift, inheritance, purchase from (with name of previous owner), or simply that the land was held "in posse." Later sales often referred to the original notarial record or to "private papers" to validate ownership. These scanty records, controlled by notaries whose income came from fees charged to the registrants, were the basis for the legal system of tenure. At the time the registry books were opened, much of the São Paulo plateau was not even explored, much less occupied by Brazilians. Subsequently, land was first taken over by simple squatting. Only later, as institutional penetration followed the economic exploitation of the virgin land of the west, was the notarial record of ownership begun.

The Brazilian pattern of land division compounded the uncertainties of legal tenure. There has been little effort historically to apply a surveying system based on constant starting points. Instead, such surface features as ridges and streams have been used as reference points for borders vaguely described in relation to roads, fences, and the undefined limits of other properties. A plot of land sold near Campinas in 1867 had the following typical boundary description: "Begins on the highway that goes to the city of Limeira, at the crossroads that goes toward the posse, where there is a cross, in a straight line to the headwaters of the deep stream; from there downstream to the bridge of Gertrudes Barreto, or Joaquim Pires, taking the road from the bridge toward the highway, then following the highway to the crossroads where the boundaries begin." The following representative description from Ribeirão Preto in 1925, late in the coffee cycle, is a striking reflection of the persistence of informal and vague tenure: "Twenty alqueires, more or less, with twenty thousand coffee trees, more or less, including gaps and replanted trees, and other improvements, with the following borders: Begin at Exgotto

Creek, bordering on Luiz Delphino, until hitting the border of the 'Aguas Claras' plantation of the Paulino brothers, bearing to the right until you come to a *jenipapo* tree, continuing to the coffee groves of Augusta Morandini. From there turn right to Exgotto Creek, following it to the starting point.'' Also included in the sale were sixty additional alqueires of scrub woodland "bordering on Augusta Morandini, the Paulino brothers, and others."[22] As usual, no distances between turning points were given, much less compass directions.

By the twentieth century the older zones were filling up, and boundaries were more commonly stated in relation to neighboring land. A sale in Campinas in 1900 was described thus: "A piece of land with five alqueires, more or less, bordering on one side with land of Manuel Vargas, on the other side and the rear with the land of the sellers, and on the front with the land of an Italian." In 1914 a sale in Campinas of "nine alqueires, more or less" was recorded as bordering "on the land of Constantino Zingra, Antonio Jorge, Napeleão Porsa, Julio so-and-so [*de tal*], Portelo Montagnieri, João Camo, Thomaz Achili, Julião so-and-so, a black, and finally with an unnamed stream." The land was sold by Raymundo Carrara and his wife, Romana Carbinetta, to Antonio Zanchetta and his two minor children, Giuseppe and Antonio Zanchetta.[23] By 1914 Italians were no longer anonymous in land registries, but black Brazilians could be.

In land sales registered with notaries, the total area was usually not mentioned in the nineteenth century. Sometimes explicit reference was made to uncertain area, such as a plantation near Campinas in 1868 recorded with the notation "the area is not measured, and so is not known exactly." Later the area was more often guessed at, but occasionally with such notations as in the sale of "forty-five alqueires of arable land" near Ribeirão Preto in 1904: "The sellers do not take responsibility for the exact number of alqueires of land included in this sale."[24] Well into the twentieth century references to area commonly carried the caveat "more or less." Ephemeral and irregular boundaries, combined with the lack of surveys, often made land titles ambiguous even when they were recorded in notarial registries. This situation reinforced the importance of actual occupation as the final determinant of who was to use the land, particularly on the frontier.

There were many conflicts over land claims, to be sure. The importance of establishing commercially valid title was reflected in the development of professional land manipulators, known as *grileiros*. Like his namesake the cricket (*grilo*), the grileiro jumped erratically from place to place, setting up posse claims in the frontier, falsifying documents, trading in tenuous or fictitious titles, and befriending notaries, politicians, and judges. Posseiros intent on opening plantations on the frontier sometimes employed grileiros or their techniques to validate claims in local registry books. Family ties, political power, and other sources of influence were important in making such validation possible. Subsistence-oriented small farmers usually had less need for the services of the grileiro, but in cases of conflicting claims unscrupulous land agents often could, for a fee, establish legal title to reinforce squatter's rights. Grileiro agents became so important in the settlement of the Noroeste zone in the 1910s and 1920s that Penápolis, one of the important towns along the new railroad, acquired the nickname "Grilópolis."[25]

With the continued availability of land along the frontier there was little pressure to develop land more intensively or carefully. The extensive, apparently wasteful pattern persisted as the rational allocation of the resources available, at least in the short run and from the perspective of the individual planter. Off the plantations, land continued to be available to small farmers through posse or purchase; on the plantations, land continued to be temporarily ceded to colonos for food crops. There was little pressure for more systematic and uniform legal institutions of land tenure. On the contrary, both the large plantations and small farmers were able to take advantage of the informal patterns that evolved.

The question remains as to whether or not the Paulista elite tried to monopolize land and limit the development of small farming. On the face of it, planters who worried about the geographical mobility of the labor force might have been expected to see small farming opportunities as unwanted competition in the effort to attract and retain colonos. Also, state agencies charged with importing and distributing manpower might have objected to immigrants becoming independent farmers rather than plantation laborers. The Paulistas did recognize a relationship between labor supply and the development of small farms. During the last years of slavery the immigration program was set up to provide plantation workers, in explicit rejection of earlier programs promoting self-sufficient colonies. After the successful changeover to free labor, however, small farming was more often seen as a potential *solution* to the coffee labor problem than as undesirable competition.

This alternative to the colono system was known in São Paulo as the *viveiro* plan. Literally, viveiro means nursery, the place where young plants are nurtured. On the coffee plantation the viveiro provided seedlings to replace trees that disease or old age rendered unproductive, or those to be transplanted in new groves. With a similar connotation in the context of labor supply, viveiro came to refer to a local source of manpower upon which coffee planters could draw as needed. With a general awareness of the availability of land the idea was based on propositions that planters and government authorities considered self-evident: the ultimate goal of the European peasant transplanted into rural São Paulo was to establish himself as an independent farmer, and the coffee planters wanted a stable and abundant supply of manpower at the least possible overall cost. The viveiro concept had an attractive simplicity as an alternative or supplement to the colono system. There were repeated efforts to develop such a pattern of small farms on both public and private lands.

Soon after the Department of Agriculture was established in 1892, the inspector of lands, colonization, and immigration revealed the official attitude that small farms would complement the plantations rather than compete with them: "The government, through the promotion and development of small holdings, will do much to assist the large plantations, which will be the principal source of wealth of our country for many years to come."[26] In 1895 the secretary of agriculture criticized the labor importation system in the following terms: "The direction of the immigrant stream exclusively or nearly so toward plantation agriculture, as has been the practice up to the present, does not satisfy the need to settle our land except in outward appearance." He proposed that perhaps the state could provide a subsidy to landowners for each immigrant family permanently settled on subdivided plots of plantation lands. The advantage of such a program "would be to establish permanent population centers near the plantations where [the planters] could obtain needed manpower."[27]

The planters themselves echoed these statements of official policy. At an agricultural congress held in the city of São Paulo in 1896, "colono stability" was one of the principal problems discussed. The agenda noted that the promotion of small holdings was the "sure means of definitively stabilizing the worker in the state" and that the small farmers would form a "reserve of personnel to assist in the coffee harvest." Fernando Santos Werneck, a member of an important landowning family and a student of the economics of coffee production, told the assembled planters that the total annual wage bill in the São Paulo coffee industry could be conservatively estimated at one hundred million milreis. Of that total, he claimed, at least half, "in view of the proverbial frugality of the Italian, stays in the toe of the sock or the bottom of the chest of the colono, who waits for the right time to exchange it for gold and send it home." To keep the colono in São Paulo and put his savings into local circulation—thereby helping to stabilize the workers, increase local food production, and lower coffee wage bills—Santos Werneck recommended the active promotion of small farms.[28]

As the coffee market slump that began in 1896 worsened in the following years, authorities warned that some of the labor force might be thrown out of work if many planters went bankrupt and abandoned their coffee groves. "It is indispensable that work be found" for colonos who might become unemployed, said the secretary of agriculture, and "the unique measure that becomes necessary is to subdivide the land, placing it within reach of the small resources of the agricultural worker. . . . It is necessary to establish small holdings and bring in immigrants for manpower, dividing them as necessary between the coffee industry and food production."[29] Commenting on

a demand in the local Italian-language press that land be made available to
colonos at low prices and with long-term credit, the *Revista Agrícola* said
in 1898 that such a program would be in the interest of São Paulo and its
government, "because only in this way will we achieve the stability of the
Italian colono in Paulista soil as a farmer, instead of seeing him leave with his
savings for Italy or, many times, for the La Plata republics, where he estab-
lishes himself as a rural proprietor with money earned here in the coffee
industry."[30]

In 1898 the São Paulo Department of Agriculture established a training
school near the city of Piracicaba, in the Central zone, on land donated by a
local planter. Instruction began in 1901, and in subsequent years the institution developed into the most important center of agricultural education in
Brazil. The year the school opened, its director reported favorably on an
experiment of a planter in Uberaba, Minas Gerais, just over São Paulo's
northern border. The man had subdivided his plantation into plots of ten alqueires for sale to resident colonos, on the condition that they make certain
minimum improvements and not resell the land for a period of three years.
The director declared: "I believe that the uncultivated parts of rural estates
can be subdivided as a means of eliminating the *wage* [labor system], the
disadvantages of which are notorious. Under the wage system we will never
succeed in connecting the worker to a given property. There is only one thing
that will hold the colono to the land: a direct participation in profits."[31]

Department of Agriculture bureaucrats also recognized the desirability of
establishing viveiros of workers to supplement or replace the plantation
colonos. Toward the end of the 1901 coffee harvest, for example, a district
inspector reported that "the present labor system has delayed the completion
of the harvest. Only when the plantations no longer need to keep more than
the number of workers necessary for normal maintenance and can depend on
outside labor for the harvest, which agricultural villages could supply, will
the planter see his expenses reduced and be able to shorten the time needed to
bring in the crop." At the end of that same year the six district inspectors
met and resolved "to study the labor question, promoting the establishment
of colono-proprietors within reach of the coffee centers, and of sharecroppers
on the plantations, especially in the [western plateau] zones cultivated by
imported manpower."[32]

In August 1907, toward the end of the harvest, the district inspector in
the frontier along the Araraquarense railroad reported that due to the lack of
manpower some plantations had managed to bring in only one-third of their
crop. He said the harvest in his district would probably not be completed
until the end of October, and that "if this does not mean a labor shortage I
do not know what it could mean." He added indignantly, "I make this observation because I heard someone maintain the extravagant opinion that we
have no need for more workers." More fundamental than the widely recog-

nized labor shortage, the inspector continued, was the need for "a new system of labor organization, which would provide the plantations with supplemental labor during the harvest. In order to achieve this it will be necessary to facilitate for the colono the acquisition of land, so that he also will be a landowner, even if only on a small scale. In this way he will be occupied through most of the year with his own farm, and be available when it comes time for the coffee harvest."[33]

Secretary of Agriculture Carlos Botelho discussed in a 1906 memorandum to municipal agricultural commissions the potential role of small farming in reducing the geographical mobility of the rural workers: "It is public knowledge that there exist in our state enormous tracts of unused lands situated where they could be used advantageously by small farmers, due to their proximity to railroads. On the other hand, everyone knows of the exodus that takes place among the colonos after each yearly coffee harvest. They take the savings from their work and use them out of the country because often they do not know of the existence of available land here." Botelho reminded the commissions that they were expected to publicize the subdivision of plantations in their areas and the availability of small farms for sale to ex–coffee workers.[34] In addition to such indirect promotion of small farming and the many examples of public and private advocacy of the viveiro plan over the years, there is more direct evidence that some plantations were, in fact, subdivided for sale.

Among the pioneers in experimenting with the viveiro solution on private property was Prado Chaves and Company, the coffee-producing and trading firm of the da Silva Prado family. Luiz Bueno de Miranda, the general manager of the company's plantations, subdivided and sold four hundred alqueires of the Pau a Pique plantation near Campinas in five- to ten-alqueire parcels, trying to ensure that each plot had pasture, woodland, and a water supply. Dario Leite de Barros, in a 1907 report, considered the program important because it indicated a willingness to legally alienate portions of large landholdings in place of the standard practice of granting temporary use of food plots to colonos while jealously maintaining full ownership. Barros observed that Pau a Pique was "surrounded by happy farms established by more or less independent ex-colonos." Satisfied with the results at Pau a Pique, Miranda went on to a larger project at the Queluz plantation near Capivari in the Central zone. There he subdivided one thousand alqueires, putting six hundred up for immediate sale and keeping four hundred in reserve. Just six months after the lots were placed on the market, some three hundred alqueires had been sold to Italians, Austrians, Germans, and native Brazilians. Similar subdivision experiments were reported in the Araraquarense and Mogiana zones.[35]

In 1908 a district inspector reported on a subdivided plantation in Casa Branca, in the Mogiana zone, on which "numerous colono families have established themselves and bought land, which they now cultivate, supplying the city of Casa Branca with the varied production of their cereal plots.'' When the Santa Escolastica plantation near Campinas was subdivided in 1909, the owner sold off two hundred alqueires in family-sized parcels at prices up to 600 milreis per alqueire. A writer in *O Fazendeiro* said that at those prices the breakup of the plantations made good economic sense, and the original owner could still retain as much land as he considered necessary to preserve the family patrimony.[36] Land prices varied in São Paulo depending on total size, soil quality, distance from markets, and the nature of improvements. A normal range is thus difficult to establish, but 600 milreis per alqueire indeed seems high. An informal sample of fourteen farm sales recorded in Campinas from 1906 to 1912, ranging widely in improvements and in size from three to twenty alqueires, had an average purchase price of 270 milreis per alqueire. A 1908 source listed the price of good coffee land in the western plateau at 200 to 500 milreis, depending on soil type and distance from railroads. According to a survey by the federal Ministry of Agriculture in 1911, the going price of good coffee land in Campinas ranged from 200 to 300 milreis per alqueire.[37]

Many of the examples of private subdivision achieving public notice, especially in the Central zone, took place on plantations that by the early twentieth century had mostly older and less productive coffee groves, and consequently more trouble competing for colono manpower. Subdividing all or part of their land was a way for planters in the older areas to liquidate assets before the inevitable forces of nature took their toll. The capital realized could then be applied to opening a new plantation in the frontier zone or used in alternative economic activities. From the immigrant worker's point of view, this process facilitated the acquisition of land. When a planter subdivided, he sold off his noncoffee land first, and later even areas once planted in coffee could be used for food crops, sugar cane, cotton, and other products using nutrients the coffee plants had not drained from the soil.

As part of its ongoing propaganda campaign, São Paulo occasionally published booklets detailing the legal protections and material assistance available to immigrants and the opportunities open to them in São Paulo. One such booklet, published in Italian around 1910, included a table with information on small farm subdivisions on private property in the western coffee zone. Of the thirty-five "colonies" listed, nine were in the Central zone, three in the Mogiana, fourteen in the Paulista, six in the Araraquarense, and three in the Alta Sorocabana zone. Together they contained 1,792 farm plots populated by 9,317 individuals comprising 1,811 families, for an average of more than five persons per family. Italians were listed as the "predominant nationality" in nineteen of the subdivisions, Portuguese predominated in six, native Brazilians in four, German-Swiss in two, Spanish in two, and

Austrians and Russians in one each. For thirty-three of the "colonies" the distance from the railroad was given. The average distance was six kilometers, with the nearest situated right along the railroad and the furthest located some thirty kilometers from a station.[38]

In addition to publicizing the existence of such private subdivisions, the state promoted their establishment in a variety of ways. The Department of Agriculture provided technical personnel to survey and stake off such land free of charge—verifying, at the same time, that the landholder held valid title to the land surveyed—and paid a premium of ten thousand milreis for each group of fifty families permanently settled on privately established farm colonies. The government also provided credit for small farmers to buy plantation land by paying the original landowner up to twenty-five milreis per plot of twenty-five to fifty hectares, depending on soil type and distance from railroads, and collecting the purchase price from the buyer over a five- to ten-year period. On the western frontier, especially during the development of the Noroeste and Alta Sorocabana zones, private individuals and land companies took advantage of such facilities to open virgin territory to small farmers.[39]

Discussing the potential of the Alta Sorocabana frontier in 1917, an anonymous writer in the magazine *O Fazendeiro* urged the government to do more to promote settlement by small farmers. "Every colono who has accumulated savings," he wrote, "should become a landowner, or at least work in partnership with landowners. The large properties must be broken up, and each colono family must have the amount of land it can cultivate. Only in this way will the well-being of the worker be obtained and the national wealth be rapidly increased."[40] Such a statement is hardly the expression of a tradition-bound, *latifundista* mentality. On the contrary, it exemplifies the economically rational and self-interested attitude of the Paulista elite, faced with the abundance of land and the geographical mobility of the plantation labor force.

A discussion of the land and labor situation in 1923 echoed attitudes and assumptions little changed in three decades. Carlos Mendes, writing in the journal of the São Paulo–based Brazilian Rural Society, reiterated the problem of peak labor needs during the coffee harvest, and said:

> The footnote to the large property should always be the small farm. . . . We can only attenuate the great damage of prolonged harvests in two ways: either allot sufficient land to have a numerous population on the plantations, or create small farms alongside the large plantations. With the first of these solutions, although there is the advantage of establishing that population in such a way as to guarantee enough manpower for the harvest, . . . there are the great disadvantages of not having

the colono definitively tied to the land and, above all, of requiring land that many fazendas no longer have; or if they have such land it represents a capital investment that will yield no income [if parceled out to colonos].

For the viveiro solution, on the other hand, Mendes had only praise: "When each large plantation is surrounded by small farmers it will have, for its difficult periods, the excess workers who, exactly during the best time for the coffee harvest (July–August), have little to do at home. The food crop harvests are completed, and the preparation for the next sowing has not yet begun."[41]

The campaign platform of Washington Luiz Pereira de Sousa for the governorship of São Paulo in 1920 provides an indication of the political elite's attitude regarding small farms at a time when coffee growers in the older zones were having increasing difficulty attracting workers. Washington Luiz and his allies, representatives of the planter class that had governed São Paulo in unbroken succession since the establishment of the republic, recognized the supreme role of coffee and the familiar system of agricultural organization in making the greatness of São Paulo possible. "Therefore," the platform declared, "it is the unavoidable duty of the government to resolutely protect [the coffee industry], providing it with the manpower it needs." But in those areas and in those circumstances where the old patterns no longer worked and where coffee was no longer productive, the planter "must work toward the transformation of the agricultural system. The duty of the government is to collaborate in this transformation, so that the landowner does not lose his capital and so that agriculture does not decline. It is not a revolution that I suggest, but an evolution, which is already about to take place. Only he who does not want to look does not see it."

The platform approved the breakup of the large landholdings, the move toward smaller farms, and the consequent diversification of agriculture, especially in those areas where the coffee cycle was approaching the end of its course. The state would encourage this development, the statement went on, through its program of providing surveying teams free to planters wishing to subdivide, credit facilities for the purchasers of farm plots, free distribution of land in the public domain, and the construction of access roads in newly opened frontier areas.[42] During Washington Luiz's subsequent term as governor the conditions for validating squatter's rights were further liberalized, and members of the public land survey teams were transferred to the state road commission.

In addition to the various activities for promoting small farming on private land, the state took a more direct role in the effort to substitute or supplement the colono system with viveiros of workers. This was through the colonial nucleo program, the establishment of colonies of small farms under direct government tutelage. For most of the nineteenth century the imperial government had promoted such colonies in the provinces south of São Paulo, and in the later years of the empire the program had been successful in settling some European immigrant farmers, especially Germans and Italians, in semiautonomous, subsistence-oriented communities in areas that had previously been only sparsely inhabited by white men. In the late 1870s the imperial government attempted to establish similar colonies near the city of São Paulo, but they failed to achieve the desired results.[43] Official colonization in São Paulo stagnated for several years. When the program was revived, the goal was no longer to set up semiautonomous communities but to aid in the settlement of the state by free workers and attract immigrants to the coffee areas. In short, the rationale for the state-sponsored nucleo program in São Paulo after the mid-1880s was the viveiro concept.

A law of March 1884 providing funding for immigration subsidies authorized the provincial government to establish up to five colonial nucleos near railroad lines in the principal agricultural districts. In 1885 the province acquired land for a nucleo in the municipio of Lorena in the Paraiba valley and one near Rio Claro in the Paulista zone. In 1887 the imperial government began a new program in São Paulo by opening the Antonio Prado nucleo near Ribeirão Preto and the Rodrigo Silva nucleo near Porto Feliz on the western edge of the Central zone. After the establishment of the republic, the São Paulo government took over the imperial colonies and continued with its own program. Twenty-five government-sponsored nucleos were established in São Paulo from 1885 through 1911, including fifteen in the western coffee zone and six along the Paraiba valley.[44]

With the nucleos of the 1880s and 1890s a pattern was set, which the state followed well into the twentieth century. The government acquired marginal land, often with poor soil or in valley bottoms not suitable for coffee, that insolvent or overextended planters were anxious to sell. The Department of Agriculture surveyed the area and staked off plots considered large enough to support immigrant families. Depending on the type of terrain and quality of the soil the farmsteads ranged in size from ten to perhaps forty hectares. The state appointed an administrator who was to help new arrivals get established, keep records of the payments colonists made on their plots, supervise such common labor as road maintenance, and see that numerous paternalistic regulations were enforced. Residents paid for their plots under a variety of payment plans, with five to ten years being the usual time limit.

In 1892 the secretary of agriculture lowered the price of nucleo lots to twenty milreis per hectare. He claimed the reduced prices would allow many people to pay off their remaining debts immediately and speed the "emancipation" of the colonies. "Emancipation" came when all or most of the inhabitants paid their debts and received clear title to the land, at which time the administrator departed and the ex-nucleo became a normal part of the municipio in which it was located. An executive decree in December 1893 declared eight state-sponsored nucleos "emancipated," with five such colonies continuing under state tutelage.[45]

By the turn of century the viveiro solution had become part of São Paulo's official immigration and labor policy. Candido Rodrigues, the secretary of agriculture, asserted that "if our system of immigration has a defect, it consists in not facilitating the long-term permanency of the laborers sent to the plantations," because the natural effect of the colono contract system was for the worker to leave as soon as he had accumulated savings. Rodrigues noted that in 1899 the Public Works Committee of the São Paulo senate, of which he had been a member, recommended that more colonial nucleos be established "so that they might become viveiros of workers for the plantations." He reiterated that suggestion as secretary of agriculture and saw the nucleo program as a veritable panacea for the plantation labor problem. More such colonies, he said, could help:

> (1) Fix the immigrant on the land, at the disposition of the coffee plantations; (2) Relieve the coffee planter of the need to open new groves every year to provide his colonos with land for the cultivation of cereals; (3) Relieve the planter of the need to build colono houses at his own expense and to fence off pasture land for the colonos' livestock; (4) Make it possible to experiment with the use of wage laborers [*camaradas*] to reduce coffee production costs; (5) Relieve the state treasury of the expense of bringing in new immigrants, through the stabilization of immigrants in such a way that they form viveiros of workers for the coffee industry; and (6) Create and develop many auxiliary industries in the state that can only be advantageously engaged in by small farmers, thus lowering the cost of foodstuffs and ultimately contributing to a reduction of wages.[46]

Ernesto Kuhlman, one of the administrators of the ill-fated nucleos set up near the city of São Paulo in 1878, wrote in 1901 of the vast expanse of unused land within the settled area of the São Paulo plateau. Such land was still ideal for food products that could be produced by small farmers, allowing the larger plantations to concentrate on coffee. He pointed out that the normal harvest period for cereals in São Paulo was March and April and that preparation of the ground for the September planting began in August. Thus, during the peak of the coffee harvest in May, June, and July, the independent farmer, "accompanied by his wife and children, could go pick coffee. This extra income would be to his great benefit." Also in 1901, the state governor, Rodrigues Alves, said that it was "necessary to tie the immigrant to the land, but this must be done in such a way that he remains available to plantation agriculture when his labor is needed." He advocated the establishment of colonial nucleos "near or within the centers of plantation agriculture of the state, where they could constitute viveiros of rural workers."[47]

Despite such expressions of official favor, the government concentrated on importing plantation colonos. Between 1892 and 1905, the Department of Agriculture opened only the Campos Salles nucleo in an area of sandy and mixed soils that would not support coffee well. In 1898, a year after the colony was founded, a railroad spur was completed from Campinas, forty kilometers to the south, and the resulting access to Campinas markets helped Campos Salles prosper. In 1903 the total population was 892, including 390 Brazilians, 164 Germans, 129 Austrians, 66 Italians, 49 Swiss, 46 Swedes, 30 Russians, and 18 of other nationalities. In 1906 the area of the colony was expanded onto land donated by Arthur Nogueira, an important planter in the area.[48]

During the term of Carlos Botelho as secretary of agriculture from 1904 to 1908, the concrete results of the nucleo program began to keep pace with the statements of official policy. Early in his administration Botelho reiterated the desired relationship between small farm colonies and the coffee plantations. "By creating nucleos directly or by assisting private initiative," he declared, "the state will establish the necessary viveiros of workers, from which will come the manpower for the plantations during the coffee harvest." Botelho said that in considering land for nucleos the state should give priority to land near railroads, to give the colonists access to regional markets for their produce, and to land "situated within the zones where the coffee plantations are located," so that the colonies "could become sources of agricultural workers for the plantations." The secretary recognized that much of the good land near railroads was already in private hands, and for that reason the state should work together with local landowners in the establishment of small farm colonies. The private capitalist would provide the land and profit from its eventual sale, and the government would provide management, surveys, administration, and immigrants. Such a system, according to Botelho,

> would contribute considerably toward the establishment of viveiros of workers and the stabilization of the immigrants, permitting the transformation of the system of plantation labor, thus reducing the burdens of high costs resulting from the need to sustain colonos throughout the entire year. These high labor costs, furthermore, do not relieve the coffee planter of the need to seek laborers constantly to replace those who, after working a few years and receiving their earnings, leave in order to realize the natural and just aspiration of the farm worker: possessing, for himself and his own, a plot where tilling and sowing produces for him alone.[49]

Small farm, with young coffee with interrow corn, fruit trees, main house, drying yards, colono houses, stock pens, corn

A nucleo was established in 1905 as just such a joint effort. A land speculator had bought up a tract of land near Rio Claro in a foreclosure sale. He formed the Small Property Company (Companhia Pequena Propriedade) and subdivided the 4,250 hectares into farm plots, but he had trouble financing the venture. The state paid one hundred thousand milreis for a half-interest and assumed administrative control. Half the plots, in an alternating pattern, were designated state property, with the Small Property Company retaining the remainder. It became the Jorge Tibiriçá nucleo, named after the current state governor. Also in 1905 the state opened the Nova Odessa nucleo in the municipio of Campinas, to accommodate 380 Russian Jews who emigrated to Brazil via England.[50] In January 1909 Nova Odessa was opened to other nationalities as well, with the result that "the remaining unoccupied lots were filled as if by magic."[51]

São Paulo's next three nucleos also came into existence as a result of

Immigrant schoolchildren with teacher, Campos Salles nucleo

joint public and private activity. Bernardo Avelino Gavião Peixoto, an important political figure of the late empire, had inherited a colonial sesmaria known as the Cambui estates, which stretched west from Araraquara for an expanse of nearly thirty thousand alqueires. Gavião Peixoto had little capital to invest in improvements, and his colonos were obliged to live in houses of mud and wattle. He had more than the normal difficulty in attracting workers because most large plantations offered brick houses. In an attempt to solve his labor problem, Gavião Peixoto got a large subsidy from the government to put the viveiro concept into practice.

In 1904 Gavião Peixoto agreed to donate three thousand alqueires to the state, and the government agreed to buy an additional three thousand alqueires from him. The land, all unused and in marginal areas of the estate, was divided into three separate nucleos that opened in 1907, each with about 190 rural lots of twenty-five hectares. The desire to attract newly arrived im-

Immigrant family, Nova Europa nucleo (note Department of Agriculture official at right center and mestizo and black at right)

migrants rather than colonos already on plantations was evident in the terms of payment. New immigrants from Europe were to pay one-tenth down, whereas current residents of Brazil were to pay two-thirds down. It proved difficult to fill the colonies under those conditions, and in December 1907 the down payment for current residents was dropped to one-fifth. In April 1908 the government lowered the price of lots in the Cambui nucleos to the same level as in the Nova Odessa and Jorge Tibiriçá settlements: 100 to 120 milreis per hectare, or 2,500 to 3,000 milreis per lot. In September 1908 land prices in all nucleos were further reduced, to a range of 40 to 60 milreis per hectare. That was equivalent to 100 to 150 milreis per alqueire, well below the reported value of good coffee land at the time. By 1912 the population of the three Cambui nucleos was 3,199, growing to 5,405 in 1918, including 1,040 aged fourteen and above.[52] It is doubtful that the nucleos became a significant source of manpower for the Cambui estates. Later owners retained the

Immigrant family and house nearing completion, Gavião Peixoto nucleo

colono system and occasionally experimented with other schemes to attract and retain workers. Still, it was good business for Gavião Peixoto, who profited from the sale of three thousand alqueires of otherwise unproductive land. With thirty thousand alqueires at his disposal, he was hardly breaking up his patrimony. It was good publicity for the state government as well, as the existence of the nucleos was used in immigration propaganda.

In 1910–11 the Department of Agriculture made a last effort to establish nucleos. Nova Veneza was created in the municipio of Campinas on 1,400 alqueires the state bought from three local planters. The state subdivided the property into lots measured in hectares, replacing the old alqueire units planters still used, and fixed the price of lots at 40–60 milreis per hectare. Soon after Nova Veneza was set up, Elyseu de Queiroz Telles, a member of one of São Paulo's most influential landholding families, offered to sell his adjacent plantation to the state for addition to the nucleo. Finally, the

Visconde de Indaiatuba, Conde de Parnaiba, and Martinho Prado Júnior nucleos—all named after pioneers of immigration in São Paulo—were established in March 1911 on the southern edge of the Mogiana zone.[53]

By 1913 the impetus Carlos Botelho gave the nucleos had faded, and Paulo de Morais Barros, the new secretary of agriculture, was disillusioned with the results. The system, according to Barros, was based on the assumption that new arrivals who wanted to become farmers needed special protection and state aid. But rather than benefiting new immigrants, "experience has demonstrated that the nucleos have been populated almost exclusively by colonos who already have savings and experience acquired through work on the large plantations." Barros reiterated that " 'manpower for the plantations' must be the government's motto, since only after the needs of the plantations are provided for will we be able to count on the development of a solid contingent of small farms. . . . The accumulation of savings on the plantations, on the part of the colono, is the most suitable means of breaking up the great rural properties, the path to the extinction of the *latifundios*." Barros recommended that no more nucleos be established, but that legal and administrative measures ought to be used to make public lands in the expanding frontier areas available to ex-colonos. He was specifically referring to the newly opened territory along the Noroeste railroad, where the state had more than three hundred thousand hectares available to survey, subdivide, and put up for sale.[54]

The state declared three of the existing nucleos free of official tutelage in 1920, and the remaining ones were "emancipated" in 1923. On the latter occasion the secretary of agriculture reiterated Barros's criticism of a decade earlier: "Contrary to the spirit of the law [of their establishment], the official nucleos have been filled almost exclusively by families of farmers who have been colonos on the large plantations for more or less extended periods, rather than being settled by immigrants." The secretary repeated the claim that the settlement of western São Paulo did not take place through the establishment of newly arrived immigrants on small farms, but rather through the process of ex-colonos buying up land with their savings from work on the plantations. "This can be observed in the constant loss of workers the plantations suffer, requiring that the government maintain the subsidized immigrant stream, and in the incessant breaking up of landholdings in the areas of the state where adequate land is still to be found." He went on to say that the annual exodus of coffee workers was natural and impossible to avoid because colonos who accumulated savings would naturally want to establish themselves as independent farmers. The secretary of agriculture phrased his recommended solution in 1923 in terms reminiscent of the proposals of the 1890s: "The government should take care that lands be made available where they might form viveiros of agricultural workers who could be made use of during the coffee harvest."[55] In place of the paternalistic nucleo system the secretary recommended land distribution through free market forces, whereby the state would survey land in the public domain or land acquired from private owners and divide it into small farms for sale to all comers.

By any standard of measurement, the official nucleos never represented more than a small part of São Paulo's agricultural complex. Planters at a meeting held in Amparo in 1911 voiced the suspicion that rather than developing into sources of seasonal labor, state-sponsored settlements competed with the coffee industry by absorbing new immigrants and attracting colonos away from the plantations. A committee appointed to investigate the matter reported that the ten nucleos existing in 1910 had a total population of 8,251, and that during the same year the state immigration service had sent 631 persons to the nucleos, comprising eighty-six families and ninety-five adults without families. The committee contrasted those figures with the estimate that São Paulo's coffee industry currently employed a total of about 400,000 workers, and with the fact that the immigration service had sent 28,475 persons, including workers and their families, to jobs in the interior of the state in the course of 1910. Faced with such comparisons, the committee concluded that the competition of the nucleos for manpower was insignificant. Although the report asserted that "the planters justly complain because the labor shortage disturbs the organization of work and raises the cost of production," the group recommended that the regional planters' meetings go no further with petitions for or against the nucleos.[56]

In 1918, near the peak of their development, the total population of the nucleos in São Paulo was 20,763, including 9,771 persons age fourteen or older. Even in the unlikely event that all working-age nucleo residents hired out their labor during the coffee harvest, their impact in the plantation labor force would have remained localized. In 1918 the total land area of the state nucleos was roughly 43,400 alqueires, less than 1 percent of the land claimed in private property in São Paulo. Nearly 12,000 alqueires were in cultivation in the nucleos, about 1.4 percent of São Paulo's cultivated land.[57]

Some coffee planters were willing to experiment with seasonal labor from nucleos and other schemes, but despite the attractiveness of the viveiro solution in theory, the idea had several drawbacks in practice. A 1907 analysis of the rural labor problem listed the following disadvantages of reliance on nucleos for seasonal manpower, from the planters' point of view: first, their location was seldom ideal—i.e., among and equidistant from the plantations that might need harvest labor; second, the initial cost of housing, access roads, and other improvements was high compared to the expense of establishing colonos on existing plantations. But most importantly, the nucleo residents were under no contractual obligation to hire out their labor for the coffee harvest. There was no assurance that farmers in nucleos would not be occupied with their own home industries during the coffee harvest or that the planters would be able to offer wages high enough to attract seasonal workers from the surrounding area. An even worse prospect would be for the nucleo residents to develop a collective monopoly on the local labor supply and dictate the conditions under which they would agree to harvest coffee.[58]

There were drawbacks from the workers' perspective as well. All the colonies established in western São Paulo from 1897 to 1911 were in marginal lands that the previous owners were anxious to sell to the state, and most were in areas where coffee did not do well or where the coffee cycle was past its peak. A worker who bought a plot took on a five- to ten-year debt with uncertain return. The low purchase price and easy time payments may have looked like a bargain to some, but there were risks and limitations involved in nucleo farming that the plantation colono did not have. It may well be, as some planters and consuls claimed, that colono work was often preferable to the uncertainties of working a piece of low-quality land in a state colony.

São Paulo kept its nucleo program alive partly for propaganda purposes, to provide a visible alternative to colono work. But the colonies were justified primarily as part of the larger effort to resolve the perennial problem of the geographical mobility of the plantation labor force. The continuation of such land policies as the nucleos and private viveiro plans, together with the weak and diffuse legal institutions of tenure, indicates that the planter elite did not intend to monopolize ownership of the land. The Paulistas literally had more good coffee land available than they could use, and the good coffee land was only a small part of the total area of the western plateau. Furthermore, there was no incentive to take control of the land in order to force unincorporated peasants into the plantation labor force, because the immigration system continued to bring in workers from abroad. Thus land policy and the rural labor question became closely related. As with the relatively favorable provisions of the colono contract itself, the liberal aspects of land policy resulted not from magnanimity or goodwill, but from the rational calculation of self-interest on the part of the planter elite. Such decisions had long-term effects on the structure of agrarian society that few native planters or politicians envisioned at the time.

IMMIGRANTS
AS LANDOWNERS

Travel writers arriving in the state of São Paulo in the early twentieth century had a mandatory itinerary. After the spectacular trip up the coastal escarpment from Santos, or from Rio de Janeiro via the Central Railway, such visitors remarked on the "European" atmosphere of the bustling state capital. São Paulo was a cosmopolitan city with many languages mingling with Portuguese, up-to-date architecture, wide boulevards, and imposing public buildings. The business of São Paulo was coffee, yet there was not a coffee tree in sight, much less a plantation. The visit was not complete without a trip to the interior, beyond the foggy wooded hills of the coastal range and into the western plateau. On the journey a cloud of red dust settled on everything, and soon the coffee trees began to appear. Hour after hour the train clacked through an apparently endless expanse of coffee groves.[1]

In Campinas, just one hundred kilometers from the capital, Baron Geraldo de Rezende often hosted foreign visitors, proudly showing off his flower gardens, stables of fine horses, and coffee groves totaling almost half a million trees. A more frequent goal was Ribeirão Preto, a full day out from the city of São Paulo. There travelers might visit the plantation of Martinho Prado Júnior and see two million trees in one vast block, worked by sixteen hundred immigrant field hands and about fifty native Brazilian laborers. Alternatively, the visitor took a narrow-gauge train to the English-owned Dumont fazenda. The statistics were as impressive as the view: four million coffee trees, three thousand resident laborers, of whom some four-fifths were immigrants. Not far away was the Monte Alegre plantation, headquarters of the coffee empire of Francisco Schmidt. This illiterate German had arrived in São Paulo as a child of six in 1856, and by the early twentieth century owned six million coffee trees. His thirty-five plantations in the Ribeirão Preto area, covering twenty-four thousand hectares, employed nearly three thousand immigrants and eight hundred native Brazilians.[2]

In the minds of these visitors an illusion was implanted: coffee production in São Paulo seemed characterized by huge plantations owned by native Brazilian "coffee barons," with some participation by foreign investors and a few fantastically successful immigrants. The image is one of a small entrepreneurial-minded planter class presiding over large estates producing a single crop for export, worked by a mass of immigrant field hands and some native Brazilian casual laborers. The perception was shared by the planters themselves. In the state legislature, in the press, and at periodic conventions, they continued to congratulate themselves for making the successful transition to free labor, for making expansion possible by importing immigrant workers, and for maintaining control over the economic lifeblood of the republic. There was enough truth in the perceptions of the planters and foreign visitors with itineraries arranged by the planters that the image of control and permanence could be maintained through the decades from abolition to the onset of the Great Depression. But while the Paulista elite's view remained complacently static, the socioeconomic complex over which they presided was inherently dynamic.

The tremendous growth of the coffee economy was apparent to the most casual observer. Less obvious was a qualitative change that is central to understanding the immigrant experience in western São Paulo. Beneath the Brazilian owners of large plantations in the rural social structure, an increasing number of small and medium-sized farms were acquired by first-generation immigrants. Some resident foreigners successful in commerce or industry acquired rural property, but many of the immigrants who became owner-operators of family-sized farms probably began as coffee colonos. Plantation work was the most readily available rural employment, and while those immigrants who acquired capital in urban pursuits may have subsequently invested in coffee production, it is less likely that many of them turned to farming as an occupation.

There is no doubt that the native planters considered the move from colono to independent farmer to be upward mobility. The assumption of the various viveiro plans was that immigrant workers generally wanted to become landowners themselves. Italian observers also assumed the colono would rather work his own plot. Zettiry, for example, called unfounded the Paulistas' fear that immigrants with savings would return to Europe. Rather than see their earnings evaporate in travel and living expenses, colonos "who have acquired some savings look for small property in the same country where they made the accumulation." An Italian journalist who worked in São Paulo for many years wrote: "The desire for property is instinctive in the European agriculturist, the Italian in particular. The greatest aspiration of the peasant family is to possess a plot of land." And in 1902 Rossi called the acquisition of a small farm "the dream of the peasant."[3] The degree to which the workers themselves shared these values can only be inferred from the historical record of their achievement. In examining the movement of immigrants from plantation work to independent farming, it is important to emphasize several aspects of the colono's condition, and the characteristics of the people who occupied that position.

First, the people who went to São Paulo tended to be from the low economic levels of the groups who emigrated to the New World. The Paulistas organized the subsidy program with the explicit goal of importing workers so destitute they would have no choice but to work on the plantations. As late as the 1920s state officials justified the continuation of subsidies on the grounds that the cost of steerage passage was beyond the means of the large families needed on the plantations. Especially in the early years, the subsidies attracted the poorest of the poor. Filippo Ugolotti, who lived in Brazil from 1893 to 1896, wrote: "Italian emigration to Brazil has been made up only of elements from the lowest social strata. . . . The great majority of the emigrants come from the poorest part of our peasantry, who bring the pitiful spectacle of their illiteracy and their poverty." Robert Foerster, a North American analyst of Italian emigration, concluded: "Whoever would understand the life of the Italians in Brazil, and particularly the shadow of failure that has tinged the careers of so many, both on the fazendas and elsewhere, should recollect the melancholy condition in which they arrived. They brought into the country little of capital or of personal accomplishment."[4]

Second, immigrant workers acquired a reputation for hard work, low levels of consumption, and frugality. Speaking of the Italian emigrant generally, Foerster noted: "Not cardinally the passion to earn but the passion to save is the form which the economic motive assumes. . . . This passion colors the details of the Italians' lives." Zettiry observed in São Paulo that "only the thrift of the Portuguese colono exceeds that of the Italian," and "the parsimony of the Italian farmer goes hand in hand with his love of saving." He added that there was no way of knowing how much colonos saved since they mistrusted banks, preferred to keep their money in their mattresses, and were very reluctant to discuss the subject with strangers. Discussing consumption patterns, he claimed the native Brazilian plantation workers spent twice as much on food as the Italians, and three times as much as the Portuguese. "Several times I was told," Zettiry went on, "that the amount of salt pork a Brazilian family consumes in one week would easily suffice for an Italian family of the same size for two weeks." A French visitor reported in 1911 that the Italian workers were remarkable "for their endurance, their frugality, their spirit of economy."[5] Other observers agreed that the immigrant colono's primary goal was the accumulation of savings, that he virtually ignored activities that did not directly contribute to reaching that goal, and that he avoided expenditures on amenities that might reduce his ability to save.[6]

Third, family cooperation was an essential prerequisite for coffee colonos to stay out of debt and get ahead financially. As seen in chapter 3, many immigrants arrived in family units, a pattern influenced by the eligibility requirements for transportation subsidies. In 1901 an Italian consul saw that the policy of subsidizing only families was in the immigrants' own interest. "Only under the most ideal conditions," he wrote, "can a single colono make enough to live on." A family with children who could help in the coffee harvest and with the livestock and food plots, on the other hand, "is in a much more advantageous position, and can even accumulate some savings. If the family has several older children able to work, things go much better."[7]

An extreme example of family size and solidarity was the case of Tommaso Peruzzolo, who presided over an extended family of twenty members, eighteen of whom were able to contribute to the labor pool. The clan contracted for the care of some nineteen thousand coffee trees, and they owned seven horses, twenty hogs, and four goats. They harvested enough corn from their food plots to feed fifty people, selling the excess in local markets. The family had worked as colonos for only two and one-half years when they were interviewed in 1891, but Peruzzolo "confessed" to having accumulated some savings in that period. This group was larger than most, but it illustrates the tendency for immigrant families to join in coordinated economic units. As the French journalist Pierre Denis commented in 1908, the Italian families stayed together "in regular tribes, one of which would take charge of 10,000 coffee trees."[8] For a broader sample, in 1903 an Italian consul studied the records of one large plantation in Santa Cruz das Palmeiras, in the Paulista zone, and reported that the 108 colono families comprised 734 persons, for an average of 6.8 members each. Each family contracted to care for an average of seven thousand trees, but one extended family unit had thirty members of all ages and contracted for the care of eighteen thousand trees. From the number of livestock owned by colonos, he calculated that the average family had one horse, one cow, two goats, and nine hogs. Thirteen of the families owned their own carts for transporting food products to local markets.[9]

Fourth, the importance of the food crop and pasture provisions of the work contract should again be emphasized; it was the mechanism through which personal saving became possible for some colonos. The Italian consul general wrote in 1901 that colonos in favorable circumstances, on plantations with access to local markets, could save the wages they received for the annual care of the coffee trees and subsist on "the wages for the harvest and the proceeds from the sale of poultry, hogs, corn, beans, etc." Reversing the order of the calculation, the vice-consul in Campinas reported in 1903 that the colono "can live off the wages for the care and harvest of coffee, and can save the proceeds from the sale of his own produce." Silvio Coletti said in a 1907 report that "better than in Italy, [the colono] can abundantly supply himself with corn flour, beans, milk, eggs, chickens, and pork—all of which he produces for himself in relative abundance, and which also constitute a source of profit."[10] All these reports were submitted during the relative depression of the first decade of this century, by officials who were often sharply critical of the negative aspects of the colono's existence.

In attempting to evaluate the immigrant experience, it is difficult to separate the harsh realities of plantation life from the longer-range prospects for accumulating a nest egg and becoming an independent farmer. Even in the best of times the work of a coffee colono was menial drudgery. Planters maintained strict control over the workers' daily routine. Medical care was lacking or prohibitively expensive. Schools were practically nonexistent in the early years, although the Patronato Agricola established a few plantation schools after 1912.[11] In worse conditions, colonos lost back wages when marginal plantations went bankrupt, had their pay reduced by fines, were charged exorbitant prices for essential supplies by plantation stores or local merchants, or suffered physical abuse. The immigrants were imported so that their labor could be used for the benefit of the planters, and for many colonos the experience on the plantation was negative. The tales of misery and degradation are there to be told, but there is clear evidence that many first-generation immigrants were able to make the move from coffee colono to independent farmer.

The evidence may be classified as descriptive and quantitative. An example of the first type comes from a 1903 report of an Italian consular official. He said the recent development of food crop and sugar cane cultivation in the municipio of Pirassununga, in the Paulista zone, was "due to the Italian farmers, of whom more than thirty . . . own small farms acquired with savings accumulated while they were colonos."[12]

A more detailed example is the story of the Marchetti family, Italians who arrived in São Paulo in 1888, worked as colonos near the town of Jaú in the Araraquarense zone until 1895, and in those seven years saved the considerable sum of twelve thousand milreis. The family was made up of the parents, three sons, and one daughter, all of whom were able to contribute to the family labor pool. In 1895 they used eight thousand milreis of their savings to buy thirty alqueires (seventy-three hectares) of virgin land on a large plantation being broken up by the heirs of the former owner. With the remainder of their funds they paid for clearing the ground and bought seeds, breeding stock, tools, and other supplies. The going was hard at first, but by 1898 they were beginning to prosper. They had ten alqueires planted in corn, from which they expected to harvest more than one hundred cartloads of grain, and two alqueires of manioc. They fed a mixture of corn and manioc to their herd of eighty hogs and to their flock of laying hens, which produced from two to eight dozen eggs per day. The Marchettis also had a large potato field, and a coffee grove and vineyard had been planted but were not yet in production.[13] This case is informative regarding the preconditions and the specific mechanisms for movement from colono work to independent farming, but such career descriptions are rarely available.

Only a few fabulously successful immigrants have been the subject of biographical reporting. They include such coffee planters as Francisco Schmidt and Geremia Lunardelli. Each of these men labored in the fields for a time during his youth, and each eventually acquired the unofficial title "King of

Coffee'' for owning more coffee trees than anyone else in Brazil. But neither
based his great wealth, of course, on savings accumulated while working
as a colono. Schmidt was able to establish financial and political ties with
the native planter elite in time to expand his holdings during the coffee boom
of the early 1890s. Lunardelli's parents emigrated from northern Italy to São
Paulo in 1886 when Geremia was one year old. The family worked as colonos
on the Dumont fazenda while Geremia was growing up, and he bought his
first farm at age nineteen in 1904 in partnership with his brother and several
other relatives. But Lundardelli built his principal financial base during the
second decade of this century as a coffee middleman. He bought small lots
from the many immigrants who had by that time become coffee producers in
the Mogiana zone but who had no traditional link with the established bro-
kerage houses in Santos. He then acquired his most important rural properties
after the frost of 1918 and during the expansion of the 1920s, becoming
''King of Coffee'' in 1927.[14] These careers stand out because they were
exceptional; they cannot be considered typical of the thousands of immigrants who became rural property owners or small farmers.

Schmidt, Lundardelli, and some other upwardly mobile immigrants owned
large fazendas concentrating on coffee for export that were worked by immigrant colonos in the familiar pattern. An example of this type of property
is the plantation of 200 alqueires (484 hectares) that Miguel Rinaldi bought
from José Paulo César in the municipio of Rio Claro in April 1900. For an
investment of ninety thousand milreis Rinaldi got a fully equipped establishment with crop land, pastures, one hundred thousand coffee trees, a
residence for the owner, houses for colono laborers, and other improvements
and equipment. Still in the range of investment property was the smaller
plantation of eighty alqueires in the municipio of Taquaritinga acquired by
Angelino and Joannini Martucci from Antonio Raphael de Souza in 1914.
The property had pastures and some woodland, fifty-five thousand coffee
trees, a house for the owner, three duplex and two single colono houses, and
coffee-processing machinery, along with a full complement of outbuildings
and equipment. The value of the transaction was sixty-six thousand milreis,
but the Martuccis gave Souza three lots with houses in the city of Taquaritinga
instead of paying cash.[15] Such dealings reflect the activities of a mobile and
ambitious middle class of immigrant origins, mingling with Brazilians,
moving between urban and rural activities, active in finance, commerce,
real estate speculation, local industry, and agriculture.

Many immigrants who joined the middle class had personal or family
origins in plantation work, and their story is part of the complex expansion
of the network of regional urban centers in western São Paulo during the
coffee boom.[16] For some, an initial step away from colono labor came with
the acquisition of a small farm of a type that would be of little interest to
urban-based investors. Representative of the property an ex–plantation

worker might hope to buy was the plot of five and one-half alqueires (thirteen hectares) in the municipio of Ribeirão Preto that Vicente Prette bought from Felisberto Ferreira Gandra in April 1905. It had five thousand coffee trees, two hundred banana plants, an orchard of three hundred fruit trees, a house for the owner and another for hired help, a storage shed, pigsty, wire-fenced pastures, and other improvements. On such a diversified small farm a family could satisfy most of its subsistence needs and produce coffee, fruit, and livestock for cash income. The value of the sale contract was four thousand milreis, an amount a colono family might accumulate in several years under favorable conditions. Another example is the farm of fourteen and one-half alqueires near Taquaritinga that Angelo Genare bought from João Martins da Cunha in June 1914. There were nine thousand coffee trees just two years old on the land, along with two wooden houses with tile roofs, pastures, and other minor improvements, at a purchase price of five thousand milreis.[17]

At times immigrants pooled their resources to acquire property. In January 1900, for example, Antonio, Valentino, and Giuseppe Camonato bought a farm in Rio Claro from Antonio Maciel. For thirty-nine hundred milreis the three Camonatos got ten alqueires of land, a house, two smaller houses with thatch roofs, an old sugar mill, fenced pasture, a small coffee grove, and other improvements. In December 1904 three men identified as colonos named Pedro Hespanhol, Alexandre Hespanhol, and Giuseppe Zavanetti bought twenty-seven alqueires from José Pinheiro de Azevedo in Cravinhos, near Ribeirão Preto. There were twenty-three hundred coffee trees, some wire-fenced pasture, and two small houses of mud and wattle construction with thatch roofs. The value of the sale was nine thousand milreis, and more investment and labor were needed to make it a viable farm. In September 1909 João and Annibal Greggi, colonos in Ribeirão Preto, contributed equal shares of one thousand milreis each to buy a farm of twenty alqueires from Miguel Tripoli. The property was nearly all fenced, and had a house, orchard, some planted crops, pastures, and other improvements, but no coffee. On occasion farming was combined with other economic activities, as on the property comprising eleven alqueires that a colono named Giuseppe Visoni bought from Alexandre Albertini near Ribeirão Preto in 1907. The value of the sale was thirty-five hundred milreis, which included machinery and a kiln for making brick and tile from a clay deposit, along with a house, fenced fields, a plot of sugar cane, an old-style cane mill, and other improvements.[18]

Immigrants also bought land at lower value levels. Some lesser purchases may have reflected speculative investment in odd lots, but others could have provided a family with subsistence income. In January 1905 in the municipio of Sertãozinho, for example, Francisco Menighetti bought four alqueires of unimproved but arable land, some of which was fenced, from Marinho José de Silva. A wooden house in poor condition was included. If Menighetti planned to make a living off his acquisition he faced considerable work, but at two hundred milreis the price was right. Domingos and José Charma, colonos in Ribeirão Preto, bought fifteen alqueires of land from Francisco José Ferreira in October 1907. The property had two small wooden houses roofed with tile, some fences, and not much else. Of the total price of one thousand milreis, the Charmas paid four hundred at the time of purchase and agreed not to dispose of the property until the remaining six hundred milreis were paid.[19]

These individual cases illustrate the range and variety of immigrant-owned rural property in western São Paulo. The examples should be kept in mind through the following discussion of aggregate data on landholding by nationality group on a statewide and regional basis. In the earliest attempt to enumerate the agricultural property owned by immigrants, the Italian consul general studied 40 municipios of the approximately 160 existing in São Paulo in 1901. Of the 40 municipios studied, 36 were in the western plateau. Without explaining the criteria used for size divisions, he reported that Italians owned 351 "large plantations," 1,237 "small rural properties," and 907 properties not discriminated by size, for a total of 2,495. Recognizing that the data were only partial and approximate, the consul considered the results remarkable, since "a dozen years ago [i.e., in 1889] there were only some twenty Italian planters in the state of São Paulo."[20]

The first systematic statewide survey to include land ownership by national origin of owner was the census of 1905. The timing was fortuitous, coming about twenty years after the beginning of mass immigration. Many people who entered after the mid-1880s were thus still economically active, yet enough time had elapsed for some accumulation and acquisition to begin to take place. Tables 7 and 8 show the number of properties and declared values for the major nationality groups in 1905, putting the western plateau (zones 4–9) in the statewide context by presenting data for the Paraiba valley and the noncoffee areas in the southern part of the state. The 8,484 properties owned by foreigners comprised 14.8 percent of the total, with Italians alone holding 9.2 percent. The contrast between the western plateau and the rest of the state is clear: it contained 55 percent of the property units but 88 percent of the declared value of all properties. And while the plateau contained 50 percent of the Brazilian-owned properties, 80 percent of the foreign-owned properties were located there.

When zones 4 through 9 are examined in more detail, the position of immigrant property owners is more impressive. The 6,840 foreign-owned properties in the western plateau comprised nearly 22 percent of the total, and Italians alone held 14.3 percent. Spanish immigrants, who were relatively important in the immigrant stream only after 1903, had not become a significant landholding group by 1905. Although foreigners, especially Italians, had made considerable inroads throughout western São Paulo, the breakdown by zone gives an indication of the paths of least resistance to the movement of immigrants into the landholding group. In both absolute and relative terms Italians were most important in the older zone 4 (Central), and in zone 7 (Araraquarense), which prior to 1905 was an area of frontier expansion. In the intermediate zone 5 (Mogiana), where native planters had settled during the boom of the 1880s and 1890s, Brazilians retained a relatively greater degree of control over the land than in the older area around Campinas and on the frontier. In zone 6 (Paulista), Brazilians owned only two-thirds of the rural properties, and foreign landowners were of more diverse origins, with sizable contingents of Portuguese and Germans along with Italians. There had been experiments with German and Portuguese immigrant laborers in the Paulista zone since the mid-nineteenth century, and it seems likely that many property owners of these nationalities had been in São Paulo for most of their working lives by 1905. Zone 8 (Noroeste), with just one municipio (Baurú) and 341 farms in 1905, does not provide a large enough unit for generalization, except to indicate that perhaps native Brazilian pioneers remained in the forefront during the earliest stage of frontier development.

Foreign landownership in 1905 was less significant by value than in numbers of property units. For example, Italians, Spaniards, and Portuguese together owned 19 percent of the properties in the western plateau but only 8.1 percent of the declared value. The details of the value data are more easily summarized in terms of average (mean) value per property unit, as shown in part B of table 8. The contrast between the western plateau and the less dynamic areas of the state is again apparent. In the Paraiba valley (zone 2) the average Brazilian property owner was no better off than his immigrant counterpart, although here, as throughout this discussion, averages obscure the unequal distribution between the small group of large plantations and the mass of small farms. In the west there were marked contrasts among nationalities. As would be expected from the immigrant origins of the Italians and Spaniards, the average farms of these nationality groups were consistently much less valuable than the average property owned by native Brazilians.

Again the Araraquarense zone stands out in these averages. Not only did that frontier area have more Italian-owned farms in both absolute and relative terms than any other zone of the state, but the average Italian-owned farm in zone 7 was more valuable than in other areas. At 12,500 milreis it was nearly twice as valuable as the average Italian-owned farm in the older Central zone. This reflects the greater abundance of land and easier access to it on the frontier relative to the older zones where unoccupied land was of poorer quality and where the subdivision of declining coffee plantations was an important mechanism through which immigrants acquired farms.

Some of the Italian- and Spanish-owned properties were probably medium-sized or large coffee plantations, including a few owned by investors based in urban areas. But the average values suggest that most were probably smaller

TABLE 7
Rural Properties in São Paulo, 1905

A. National Origin of Owner

Zone	Total	Brazil	Italy	Portugal	Spain	Germany	Other
1	2,524	2,028	257	144	18	55	22
2	14,252	13,535	303	255	89	20	50
3	2,570	2,439	62	26	8	23	12
4	7,680	6,200	1,020	137	92	121	110
5	8,087	6,884	826	236	16	63	62
6	4,563	3,042	799	366	67	251	38
7	5,597	3,938	1,188	227	102	90	52
8	341	274	35	16	8	6	2
9	5,050	4,140	626	159	63	28	34
10	4,078	4,000	56	9	0	4	9
11	2,442	2,220	67	46	13	13	83
São Paulo Total	57,184	48,700	5,239	1,621	476	674	474
western plateau (zones 4–9)	31,318	24,478	4,494	1,141	348	559	298

a. Percentages may not total 100 due to rounding.
  Source: Calculated from São Paulo, Secretaria de Agricultura, *Estatística agrícola e zootéchnica, 1904–1905.*

subsistence and cash crop farms of the type an ex-colono family with some savings might be able to acquire. The wide variation in average values of the Portuguese, German, and "other" properties is an indication that relatively more of the plantations owned by those groups were large commercial operations, skewing the averages in some zones and for the western plateau as a whole. That is certainly the case in the Mogiana zone, where Francisco Schmidt, of German birth, owned many large properties. The data on "other nationalities" are skewed in the Mogiana zone, and to a lesser extent in some other areas, by the few properties owned by British companies. The twelve plantations owned by British interests in the western plateau were among the largest, averaging perhaps one million trees each. Along with a large sugar refinery with adjacent cane fields owned by a French company

B. Proportional Distribution by Origin of Owner (Percent per Category)[a]

Zone	Total	Brazil	Italy	Portugal	Spain	Germany	Other
1	100	80.3	10.2	5.7	0.7	2.2	0.9
2	100	95.0	2.1	1.8	0.6	0.1	0.4
3	100	95.0	2.4	1.0	0.3	0.9	0.5
4	100	80.7	13.3	1.8	1.2	1.6	1.4
5	100	85.1	10.2	2.9	0.2	0.8	0.8
6	100	66.7	17.5	8.0	1.5	5.5	0.8
7	100	70.4	21.2	4.1	1.8	1.6	0.9
8	100	80.4	10.3	4.7	2.3	1.8	0.6
9	100	82.0	12.4	3.1	1.2	0.6	0.7
10	100	98.1	1.4	0.2	0.0	0.1	0.2
11	100	90.9	2.7	1.9	0.5	0.5	3.4
ʌo Paulo ʌtal	100	85.2	9.2	2.8	0.8	1.2	0.8
ʌstern plateau ʌnes 4–9)	100	78.2	14.3	3.6	1.1	1.8	1.0

in Capivari in the Central zone, the twelve British-owned plantations comprised most of the properties owned by nonresident foreign investors in the western plateau as of 1905.

These regional totals and averages obscure the extent to which immigrants had become important as rural property owners in some local areas. In thirty-seven of the ninety-seven municipios in the western plateau, immigrants owned 30 percent or more of the rural properties enumerated in 1905. In five municipios foreign owners were in a majority, with 50 percent or more of all properties. The most extreme case of foreign penetration was the municipio of Taquaritinga, located northwest of Araraquara in what was still a frontier area in 1905. Of the total 352 rural properties in Taquaritinga, 171 (49 percent) were owned by Italians. The average declared value of the Italian properties was 19,544 milreis. Brazilians owned 141 properties (41 percent), with an average value of 64,653 milreis. Other nationalities owned 37 properties, with an average value of 33,324 milreis.[21] Taquaritinga was an area

TABLE 8

Declared Value of Rural Properties in São Paulo, 1905 (In Thousands of Milreis)

A. National Origin of Owner

Zone	Total	Brazil	Italy	Portugal	Spain	Germany	Other
1	18,614	15,650	1,442	781	40	564	137
2	69,429	63,717	1,406	3,561	69	209	467
3	16,978	16,180	317	115	31	228	107
4	127,580	114,243	6,516	2,252	211	1,114	3,244
5	331,541	280,682	10,292	6,870	165	19,383	14,149
6	202,843	178,655	6,844	7,319	874	6,524	2,627
7	141,542	116,634	14,838	6,241	1,262	781	1,786
8	7,977	7,547	103	152	19	154	2
9	117,906	104,986	5,772	5,506	294	690	658
10	15,386	14,918	236	86	0	130	16
11	4,246	2,351	217	566	36	14	1,062
São Paulo Total	1,054,042	915,563	47,983	33,449	3,001	29,791	24,255
western plateau (zones 4–9)	929,389	802,747	44,365	28,340	2,825	28,646	22,460

Sources: Part A: same as table 7. Part B: calculated from data in part A of tables 7 and 8.

of Italian-owned small properties par excellence, with immigrant-owned farms characteristically interspersed with larger Brazilian-owned plantations in the frontier of the coffee zone.

Fifteen years after the 1905 agricultural census the Brazilian government carried out the first economic census of the entire nation. The resulting data on São Paulo's rural sector provide a progress report independent of the state Department of Agriculture's own periodic surveys. Information on landholding by nationality from the 1920 census for the state of São Paulo as a whole is shown in table 9.

The data show a clear improvement in the position of the main immigrant groups over 1905, in both absolute and relative terms. While the number of Brazilian-owned rural properties had increased by only 11 percent, the number of Italian-owned properties had increased by 126 percent to almost

B. Average Value by National Origin of Owner

Zone	Total	Brazil	Italy	Portugal	Spain	Germany	Other
1	7.4	7.7	5.6	5.4	2.2	10.3	6.2
2	4.9	4.7	4.6	14.0	0.8	10.5	9.3
3	6.6	6.6	5.1	4.4	3.9	9.9	8.9
4	16.1	18.4	6.4	16.4	2.3	9.2	29.5
5	40.1	40.8	12.5	29.1	10.3	307.7	228.2
6	44.5	58.7	8.6	20.0	13.0	26.0	69.1
7	25.3	29.6	12.5	27.5	12.4	8.7	34.3
8	23.4	27.5	2.9	9.5	2.4	25.7	1.0
9	23.3	25.4	9.2	34.6	4.7	24.6	19.4
10	3.8	3.7	4.2	9.6	—	32.5	1.8
11	1.7	1.1	3.2	12.3	2.8	1.1	12.8
São Paulo Total	18.4	18.8	9.2	20.6	6.3	44.2	51.2
Western plateau (zones 4–9)	29.7	32.8	9.9	24.8	8.1	51.2	75.4

12,000. Portuguese-owned properties increased by 139 percent, and the number of properties owned by the late-arriving Spaniards increased by 642 percent over 1905, from 476 to 3,530. These three nationality groups together nearly doubled their share of all rural properties, from 12.8 percent in 1905 to 25.2 percent in 1920. The Japanese, who began arriving in small numbers in 1908, owned more than 1,000 rural properties by 1920. Many of the relatively small Japanese-owned farms were probably in the agricultural colony established during World War I in the coastal lowlands southwest of Santos.

The average value of the farms owned by immigrants also improved markedly between 1905 and 1920, while Brazilian-owned properties showed virtually no improvement in this regard. The average value of Italian-owned farms for the state as a whole went from 9,200 milreis (part B of table 8) to 21,800 milreis. The Spanish-owned farms went from an average value of

TABLE 9
Rural Landownership in São Paulo, by Country of Birth of Owner, 1920

Country	Properties		Area			Value		
	No.	% of Total	Hectares	% of Total	Average Area per Property	Thousands of Milreis	% of Total	Average Value per Property
Brazil	54,245	71.1	9,824,482	83.7	181	1,834,402	78.5	33.8
Italy	11,825	15.5	916,487	7.8	78	257,547	11.0	21.8
Portugal	3,875	5.1	437,308	3.7	113	121,299	5.2	31.3
Spain	3,530	4.6	208,418	1.8	59	53,209	2.3	15.1
Japan	1,151	1.5	37,912	0.3	33	4,779	0.2	4.2
Germany	502	0.7	81,831	0.7	163	20,482	0.9	40.8
Austria	398	0.5	43,745	0.4	110	9,536	0.4	24.0
England	21	0.0[a]	45,946	0.4	2,188	6,132	0.3	292.0
France	40	0.1	17,908	0.2	448	3,443	0.1	86.1
U.S.A.	42	0.1	17,501	0.1	417	2,012	0.1	47.9
Other	681	0.9	107,402	0.9	158	24,701	1.1	36.3
Total	76,310[b]	100.0	11,738,940	100.0	154	2,337,542	100.0	30.6

a. Percentages of 0.0 indicate less than 0.05. Percentages may not total 100 due to rounding.
b. In addition to total shown, owners of unknown or multiple nationalities and governmental agencies owned 4,611 properties in São Paulo in 1920.

Source: Brazil, Directoria Geral de Estatistica, *Recenseamento do Brazil*, 3, 2: xxxv.

6,300 milreis to 15,100 milreis. The data in table 9 on landownership by natives of England, France, and the United States show that the properties owned by those groups, especially the English investment interests, were much larger and more valuable than the statewide average. But they comprised a very small share of the total number of properties, area, and value.

The 1920 census does not include a nationality division at the municipio level, making it impossible to discriminate the data in table 9 by zone. Municipio-level data were published, however, separating foreign-born from native Brazilian landowners, as summarized in table 10. The concentration of non-Brazilian property owners in the western plateau is striking. Only 56 percent of the Brazilian-owned farms were in zones 4 through 9, versus 89 percent of the foreign-owned farms. For the plateau as a whole, nearly four of every ten properties were owned by foreign-born in 1920, and the statewide totals shown in table 9 indicate that most of those foreign-born property owners were from Italy, Portugal, and Spain, the countries that supplied most of the immigrants in the preceding thirty-five years.

Again, the regional breakdown is indicative of where immigrants found it easiest to acquire land. The Mogiana zone was still dominated relatively more by native Brazilians, as was zone 9 (Alta Sorocabana), which had not yet experienced marked frontier expansion along the new railroad line by 1920. In absolute numbers, far more immigrants had become landowners in zone 7 (Araraquarense) than in any other single region. The most drastic transformation between 1905 and 1920 took place in zone 8, the newly opening frontier along the Noroeste railroad. The total number of properties there increased nearly tenfold in those fifteen years, from 341 to 3,239. While non-Brazilians owned only 67 properties in zone 8 in 1905, less than one-fifth of the total, they had acquired 2,141 properties along the Noroeste railroad by 1920, two-thirds of all the agricultural properties in the zone.

In the fiscal system of the old republic, a major source of revenue for the municipios of São Paulo was a tax on coffee trees, commonly at a rate of two milreis per year per thousand trees in production. In 1923 the Department of Agriculture conducted a survey of the coffee tax records that indicates the extent of immigrant ownership in São Paulo's most important economic sector. Of the 209 municipios existing in that year, 158 taxed trees and were included in the survey. But because 95 percent of São Paulo's coffee was grown in the western plateau in 1923, I have discriminated the results of the survey only for that part of the state in tables 11 and 12. These data clearly show that immigrants assumed a significant position as landowners and coffee producers, before the expansion of the late 1920s and well before the economic dislocation and breakup of older plantations during the Great Depression. The farms in this survey were by definition commercially oriented, producing for the export market. The smaller units probably supplied subsistence for owner-operators as well, whether native or immigrant.

TABLE 10

Rural Properties in São Paulo, by National Origin of Owner and Zone, 1920

Zone	Total Properties	Brazilian		Foreign	
		No.	% of Total	No.	% of Total
1	2,211	1,900	86	311	14
2	11,045	10,105	91	940	9
3	6,702	6,375	95	327	5
4	6,501	4,049	62	2,452	38
5	10,149	7,301	72	2,848	28
6	7,586	4,141	55	3,445	45
7	13,395	7,163	53	6,232	47
8	3,239	1,098	34	2,141	66
9	9,265	6,837	74	2,428	26
10	3,781	3,715	98	66	2
11	2,436	1,561	64	875	36
São Paulo Total	76,310	54,245	71	22,065	29
western plateau (zones 4–9)	50,135	30,589	61	19,546	39

Source: Brazil, Directoria Geral de Estatistica, *Recenseamento do Brazil*, 3, 1: 280–95.

For the western plateau as a whole, natives of Italy owned nearly one-third of the coffee farms in 1923. The more than twelve thousand farms belonging to Italians, Spaniards, and Portuguese comprised 40 percent of the coffee producing properties. In zones 6 and 7 native Brazilians were in the minority, and in zone 7 the Italians alone outnumbered Brazilian owners. The data for zone 8 (Noroeste) are deficient because two of the seven municipios existing there in 1923, containing some 24 percent of the coffee trees in the zone, were not included in this survey.[22] In the older Central zone there were 2,452 foreign-owned properties in 1920, but only 1,627 foreign-owned coffee farms counted in 1923. There is less divergence between the two surveys for the other zones for which data are reasonably complete. Thus it appears that relatively more immigrant landowners grew coffee in the newer areas of the plateau, whereas in the older zones they more often acquired exhausted coffee

TABLE 11
Coffee Farms in Western São Paulo, 1923

A. National Origin of Owner

Zone	Total	Brazil	Italy	Portugal	Spain	Germany	Other
4	5,338	3,711	1,271	59	89	141	67
5	7,004	4,687	1,743	307	134	73	60
6	5,258	2,523	1,805	417	195	269	49
7	7,632	3,187	3,395	348	524	94	84
8	536	355	90	44	31	9	7
9	4,323	2,649	1,327	107	150	46	44
Total	30,091	17,112	9,631	1,282	1,123	632	311

B. Proportional Distribution by National Origin of Owner[a]

Zone	Total	Brazil	Italy	Portugal	Spain	Germany	Other
4	100	69.5	23.8	1.1	1.7	2.6	1.3
5	100	66.9	24.9	4.4	1.9	1.0	0.9
6	100	48.0	34.3	7.9	3.7	5.1	0.9
7	100	41.8	44.5	4.6	6.9	1.2	1.1
8	100	66.2	16.8	8.2	5.8	1.7	1.3
9	100	61.3	30.7	2.5	3.5	1.1	1.0
Total	100	56.9	32.0	4.3	3.7	2.1	1.0

a. Percentages may not total 100 due to rounding.
Source: Calculated from *Boletim do departamento estadual de trabalho*, nos. 50–51, pp. 23–28.

land, which they converted to other crops. An examination of individual municipio units reveals the preponderance of immigrant-owned coffee farms in many local areas, which these regional totals gloss over. In 51 of the 126 municipios in the western plateau, foreigners owned 50 percent or more of the farms counted. In 32 municipios foreigners owned 60 percent or more. In 11 municipios foreigners owned 70 percent or more. And in 4 municipios foreigners owned 80 percent or more of the coffee farms.[23]

The data in part A of table 12, giving the number of trees owned by the major nationalities, reveal the expected pattern: The 188,666,000 coffee trees owned by Italians, Spaniards, and Portuguese comprised only 25 percent of the trees in the west, while 40 percent of the coffee farms belonged to those

TABLE 12

Producing Coffee Trees in Western São Paulo, by National Origin of Owner, 1923
(In Thousands of Trees)

A. Number of Trees

Zone	Total	Brazil	Italy	Portugal	Spain	Germany	Other
4	77,254	57,380	13,861	1,253	499	2,171	2,090
5	226,174	174,937	22,588	5,315	1,489	10,606	11,239
6	166,315	111,422	31,486	10,885	4,971	5,057	2,494
7	178,125	99,045	57,021	6,455	8,815	2,034	4,755
8	27,353	19,672	1,973	1,401	3,287	814	206
9	87,619	67,637	12,996	3,031	1,340	1,366	1,249
Total	762,840	530,093	139,925	28,340	20,401	22,048	22,033

B. Average Trees per Farm

Zone	Total	Brazil	Italy	Portugal	Spain	Germany	Other
4	14	15	11	21	6	15	31
5	32	37	13	17	11	145	187
6	32	44	17	26	25	19	51
7	23	31	17	19	17	22	57
8	51	55	22	32	9	90	29
9	20	26	10	28	9	30	28
Total	25	31	15	22	18	35	71

Source: Same as table 11.

groups. Due to the inadequacy of surveys and the uncertainty of property claims, the Paulistas commonly used the number of coffee trees rather than the surface area as the measure of farm size. The comparison of trees to number of farms is facilitated by the averages shown in part B of table 12.

For the western plateau as a whole, the average Italian-owned coffee farm was only half as large as the average Brazilian-owned farm. This survey indicates, somewhat surprisingly, that the coffee farms owned by Spaniards were larger on the average than those owned by Italians in 1923. In the breakdown by zone, the subdivision of coffee properties in the older zone 4 is revealed by the small size of the average unit for all nationalities. The average size of the Italian-owned farms increases from zone 4 through intermediate zones 5 and 6, to the frontier zones 7 and 8. Here again these averages tell little about the distribution of property into the few large plantations and the many small farms in all zone and nationality categories. Still, the average of fifteen thousand coffee trees on Italian-owned properties would be considered large for a family farm, yet small for an urban-based investor in coffee properties.

A report on coffee farms by national origin of owner in 1932 provides a point of comparison with the coffee tax survey of nine years earlier. According to the 1932 data, 91 percent of all coffee farms in São Paulo, including 97 percent of the foreign-owned farms and 86 percent of the Brazilian-owned, were located in the western plateau. Some 96 percent of the producing coffee trees, including 98 percent of the foreign-owned and 95 percent of the Brazilian-owned, were in the western plateau. Thus I have excluded from tables 13 and 14 the Paraiba valley and the southern parts of the state. The data in these tables continue the trends appearing in the 1920 census and the 1923 coffee tax report. By 1932 Brazilians owned only 51.5 percent of the coffee-producing farms in western São Paulo, although their average size was still greater than the averages for coffee farms owned by immigrant nationalities. The few plantations owned by British and French interests were on the average much larger than those of other nationality groups, as reflected in the "Other" column of table 14. Although the 1932 report is not strictly comparable with the 1923 survey, the most notable development in the interim was the general expansion of the coffee industry and the decrease in the size of the average farm. During the growth of the later 1920s, followed by subdivisions and sales with the onset of the Depression, the number of coffee farms increased by more than 150 percent from 1923 to 1932. The increase for Brazilian-owned properties was 130 percent, while the number held by foreign-born owners nearly tripled, from 12,979 to 38,308.

The regional division by nationality also continued expected trends. The Italian-owned farms were spread more evenly than those of other immigrant groups. While natives of Italy owned more properties in absolute numbers in zone 7 than in other areas, they were more important in relative terms in zone 6 (Paulista), which along with zone 5 could by 1932 be considered an older coffee area. The Spaniards and Portuguese, who succeeded the Italians in the immigrant stream earlier in the twentieth century, apparently found it easier to acquire land in the expanding frontiers of zones 7, 8, and 9. The Japanese were by 1932 the most recent of the major immigrant groups, having arrived in large numbers during the 1920s. Very few Japanese became coffee farmers in the older zones. In the Noroeste, however, Japanese immigrants owned more than 16 percent of the coffee farms and nearly 13 percent of the producing trees. Some 93 percent of the Japanese-owned coffee farms were concentrated in the frontier zones 8 and 9. The average sizes shown in part B of table 14 indicate that the major immigrant groups were remarkably

TABLE I3
Coffee Farms in Western São Paulo, 1932

A. National Origin of Owner

Zone	Total	Brazil	Italy	Portugal	Spain	Japan	Other
4	8,067	5,222	2,293	162	160	3	227
5	10,848	7,321	2,544	472	306	12	193
6	9,842	4,960	3,356	616	583	61	266
7	21,333	10,177	6,510	1,301	2,783	191	371
8	17,434	7,670	3,561	1,083	1,929	2,868	323
9	11,477	5,343	3,892	608	933	427	274
Total	79,001	40,693	22,156	4,242	6,694	3,562	1,654

B. Proportional Distribution by National Origin of Owner

Zone	Total	Brazil	Italy	Portugal	Spain	Japan	Other
4	100	64.7	28.4	2.0	2.0	0.0	2.8
5	100	67.5	23.5	4.4	2.8	0.1	1.8
6	100	50.4	34.1	6.3	5.9	0.6	2.7
7	100	47.7	30.5	6.1	13.0	0.9	1.7
8	100	44.0	20.4	6.2	11.1	16.5	1.9
9	100	46.6	33.9	5.3	8.1	3.7	2.4
Total	100	51.5	28.0	5.4	8.5	4.5	2.1

a. Percentages may not total 100 due to rounding.
Source: São Paulo, Secretaria de Agricultura, *Lavoura cafeeira paulista e sua distribuição por nacionalidade, 1932–33*, pp. 8–23.

similar in this regard for the western plateau as a whole, although the farms owned by Japanese tended to be smaller than those of other nationalities.

Included in the 1934 census of São Paulo were statewide aggregate data on coffee farms that show little change from 1932 in the number of farms, number of trees, or average size by nationality group. The returns of the 1934 agricultural census were not published for each municipio, making it impossible to discriminate the data by zone. Data were published, however, dividing coffee farms into size units by national origin of owner. This information helps put the average size data of earlier surveys in a more specific context. It clearly illustrates two important related points. First, immigrants predominated over native Brazilians in the ownership of small and medium-

TABLE 14

Producing Coffee Trees in Western São Paulo, by National Origin of Owner,
1932 (In Thousands of Trees)

A. Number of Trees

Zone	Total	Brazil	Italy	Portugal	Spain	Japan	Other
4	97,803	63,428	27,713	1,191	882	254	4,335
5	286,915	224,915	41,416	6,880	3,369	118	10,217
6	207,293	133,158	46,840	10,499	10,316	608	5,872
7	414,590	219,855	112,840	22,203	42,561	1,840	15,291
8	274,655	144,091	50,189	14,812	21,493	34,562	9,508
9	168,149	97,180	40,413	10,439	9,993	4,888	5,236
Total	1,449,405	882,627	319,411	66,024	88,614	42,270	50,459

B. Average Trees per Farm

Zone	Total	Brazil	Italy	Portugal	Spain	Japan	Other
4	12	12	12	7	6	85	19
5	29	31	16	15	11	10	53
6	21	27	14	17	18	10	22
7	19	22	17	17	15	10	41
8	16	19	14	14	11	12	29
9	15	18	10	17	11	11	19
Total	18	22	14	16	13	12	31

Source: Same as table 13.

sized farms. Second, most of the coffee properties owned by foreigners
were small and medium-sized family farms.

Table 15 gives the 1934 census totals for each category and the proportions
of ownership by nationality in each size division. The smallest units, of less
than five alqueires, were necessarily subsistence oriented.[24] The average of
2,600 coffee trees on each such small plot would hardly provide more than
supplementary income to help support a family in the money economy. Native
Brazilians owned nearly two-thirds of the farms in that size group. Farms in
the next two size divisions, between five and ten alqueires and between ten
and twenty-five alqueires, were economically more viable, with sufficient
area to provide a family with food crops and livestock for subsistence and

TABLE 15

Coffee Farms in São Paulo, by Size Category and National Origin of Owner, 1934

Size Category (Alqueires)[a]	Total		Brazilian			
			Coffee Farms		Producing Trees	
	Coffee Farms	Producing Trees	No.	% of Size Cat.	No. (1000's)	% of Size Cat.
up to 4.9	14,304	36,598	9,089	64	19,100	52
5– 9.9	23,905	135,190	10,941	46	48,934	36
10– 24.9	21,689	227,137	9,615	44	78,881	35
25– 49.9	10,460	193,764	5,368	51	83,509	43
50–199.9	8,697	383,418	5,541	64	241,857	63
200–499.9	2,415	230,031	1,817	75	180,863	79
500 and up	835	179,873	669	80	149,574	83
Total	82,305	1,386,011	43,040	52	802,718	58

a. The alqueire in São Paulo was equivalent to 2.42 hectares or 5.98 acres.

Source: São Paulo, Secretaria de Agricultura, *Recenseamento agricola-zootechnico realizado em 1934*, pp. 35–198.

sale. In these two size groups, foreign-born owners were in a clear majority, with 55 percent of the coffee farms and nearly two-thirds of the coffee trees. The foreign-owned farms in these two categories had an average of 6,700 and 12,300 coffee trees respectively, sufficient to provide a family with considerable cash income, particularly if the owner-operator provided necessary labor and avoided paying wages to nonfamily workers.

In the next size division, between twenty-five and fifty alqueires, ownership of coffee farms was nearly evenly divided between Brazilians and foreigners, but the foreigners owned 57 percent of the coffee trees. The average of 21,700 coffee trees per foreign-owned farm in this category could be cared for by a large extended family with occasional outside help, such as during the harvest. In the three size categories that could be considered economically viable family-operated coffee farms, between five and fifty alqueires in area, foreigners owned 30,130 properties, compared to 25,924 Brazilian-owned. Of all foreign-owned coffee farms, 77 percent were concentrated in those three size divisions. The size division between fifty and two hundred alqueires must be considered intermediate. Such properties had an average of 44,100 coffee trees each, too large for a family farm without

	Foreign		
Coffee Farms		Producing Trees	
No.	% of Size Cat.	No. (1000's)	% of Size Cat.
5,215	36	17,498	48
2,964	54	86,256	64
2,074	56	148,256	65
5,092	49	110,254	57
3,156	36	141,561	37
598	25	49,168	21
166	20	30,299	17
,265	48	583,292	42

additional resident laborers, yet too small to be very attractive for foreign investors residing outside Brazil. Here again native Brazilians predominated, with two-thirds of the farms in this size category. The two largest size groups, between two and five hundred alqueires and over five hundred alqueires, were large commercially oriented coffee plantations. Included in the large foreign-owned plantations were the few owned by British and French investors, along with those of immigrant entrepreneurs resident in Brazil.

In 1934 there were still nearly twenty-five hundred Brazilian-owned coffee plantations with two hundred alqueires of land or more, averaging 133,000 trees each. They accounted for just 3 percent of the coffee-producing units but had 24 percent of the coffee trees. Thus a visitor might come away from a quick tour of the western plateau with the impression that the large plantations of his Paulista acquaintances still dominated São Paulo's coffee industry. But at the same time there were more than thirty thousand coffee farms owned by first generation immigrants ranging between five and fifty alqueires and averaging 11,400 coffee trees each. They comprised 36 percent of the coffee-producing units and accounted for 25 percent of the trees in production. In 1934, as much coffee production was in the hands of immigrants with small and medium-sized farms as was retained by the native elite. This situation was not envisioned by the Paulistas who promoted immigration as a solution to the labor problem in the 1880s, and its origins were hardly perceived by the native planters who rode the crest of the "green wave" into the expanding frontier in subsequent decades.

The general results of the 1934 agricultural census, including all other types of rural establishments along with the coffee farms just discussed, are summarized in table 16. They show that while the relative position of immigrants was less impressive in noncoffee pursuits, coffee production was by no means the only activity immigrant farmers engaged in. Non-Brazilians owned 48 percent of all coffee farms in São Paulo in 1934, but there were 43,723 additional foreign-owned rural properties that did not produce coffee. Thus the 82,978 foreign-owned farms of all types shown in table 16 comprised just 30 percent of the rural properties included in the census for the entire state.

Of all farms owned by foreigners, 51,824 (62 percent) were in the size groups between five and fifty alqueires. There were, of course, some cases of more than one property belonging to a single owner; but if we assume for purposes of extrapolation that each farm in this size range supported a family of five, then more than a quarter of a million first-generation immigrants and their descendants might have been living on economically viable farms in São Paulo as of 1934. This is without considering the 6,379 foreign-owned properties of more than fifty alqueires or the 24,775 foreign-owned farms smaller than five alqueires.[25] It is questionable whether the acquisition of a plot in the smallest size group could be considered an upward shift for a coffee colono, but a truck or poultry farm near urban markets could still provide subsistence and some cash income on such a small area.

By 1934 most of the Italians who were in the economically active age group when they emigrated in the last years of the nineteenth century were either past their prime or dead. Those who were children when they entered, however, still comprised an important part of the economically active population. Also, significant numbers of Italians continued to arrive throughout the first three decades of the twentieth century. Portuguese, Spaniards, and later Japanese became more important in the immigrant stream, and by 1934 those groups were also important as landholders. The number of rural properties owned by the natives of Italy increased by 184 percent between 1920 and 1934, from 11,825 to 33,590, but the share of Italian-owned farms fell from 15.5 to 12.2 percent. In that same period the number of Portuguese-owned farms increased by 205 percent, Spanish-owned by 308 percent, and Japanese-owned by 1,112 percent.

Very few immigrants ever became naturalized Brazilian citizens, so few passed into the "Brazilian" nationality group in these statistics.[26] For the 1920 census the classification criterion was explicitly foreign birth. Thus the censuses and surveys refer to the landholdings of people who were born in another country, emigrated to São Paulo, and acquired property within their

TABLE 16

Rural Landownership in São Paulo, by National Origin of Owner, 1934

	Properties		Area			Value		
Country	No.	% of Total	Hectares	% of Total	Average Area per Prop.	1000's of Milreis	% of Total	Average Value per Prop.
Brazil	191,762	69.8	15,300,353	72.5	80	3,684,185	65.5	19.2
Italy	33,590	12.2	2,339,520	11.1	70	886,607	15.8	26.4
Portugal	11,801	4.3	763,954	3.6	65	276,936	4.9	23.5
Spain	14,410	5.2	648,356	3.1	45	261,915	4.7	18.2
Japan	13,945	5.1	518,232	2.5	37	160,335	2.8	11.5
Germany	2,546	0.9	271,636	1.3	107	42,460	0.8	16.7
Austria	848	0.3	39,364	0.2	46	13,919	0.2	16.4
Syria	1,597	0.6	257,225	1.2	161	78,832	1.4	49.4
Russia	451	0.2	11,731	0.1	26	3,662	0.1	8.1
England	310	0.1	277,415	1.3	895	64,249	1.1	207.3
France	202	0.1	35,658	0.2	177	11,140	0.2	55.1
Other	3,278 [a]	1.2	654,287	3.1	200	142,924	2.5	43.6
Total	274,740	100.0	21,117,731	100.0	77	5,627,164	100.0	20.5

a. Including 874 of undeclared nationality. Percentages may not total 100 due to rounding.
Source: Same as table 15.

lifetimes. By the time of the 1920 census and later, an unknown number of property owners were second-generation immigrants, the children of foreigners born in Brazil after the beginning of mass immigration. It is not possible to trace such intergenerational movement through these data. But in view of the large proportion of foreigners in the population of the western coffee zone by the early twentieth century, the number of second-generation immigrants in the Brazilian landholding group in later censuses may have been large.[27]

Nor is it possible to follow in detail the movement of native Brazilian migrants who entered São Paulo to work in agriculture and subsequently acquired rural property. Migration of working people from other parts of Brazil became increasingly important during the 1920s, but the data available on total numbers and the state of origin are only suggestive of the complete picture. Not until the 1934 census were Brazilian landowners listed by their state of birth, and even then only ten of the twenty states of Brazil were discriminated in published reports. In 1934, natives of Bahia, Ceará, and Pernambuco—northern states supplying many of the migrants—owned a total of 3,445 rural properties in São Paulo, less than 2 percent of all properties owned by Brazilians. Of those 3,445 properties, 48 percent were in the smallest size category of less than five alqueires, and another 24 percent contained between five and ten alqueires.[28] Thus the few farms internal migrants acquired by 1934 were concentrated in the smallest size categories. These fragmentary data conform to the expected pattern: at any given census date the major identifiable groups that had been in São Paulo the longest owned more rural properties of larger average size than more recent arrivals.

By the first decade of this century there were foreign-owned farms scattered throughout western São Paulo, and their numbers increased in the following years. Immigrant landowners eventually predominated numerically in many local areas, especially on the frontier and especially as coffee producers. Others continued to arrive to work as colonos, and the many farms owned by immigrants who came earlier were present for all to see. For the new arrivals there was increasing evidence that it was possible for workers to become landowners. Thus there was a "demonstration effect," an illusion of opportunity and upward mobility perhaps as significant in the collective attitudes of plantation workers as the already impressive reality.

As the agrarian society grew in size and complexity from the abolition of slavery to the Great Depression, Paulista planters were supplemented rather than replaced by the entry of immigrants into the lower levels of the landholding group. Only a few rural entrepreneurs of immigrant origins joined the native planter elite. To the extent that the acquisition of rural property by immigrants can be considered social mobility, then, it was structural mobility

Native caipira *family and typical native thatched hut (Department of Agriculture officials in jackets)*

rather than exchange mobility. There was no revolutionary destruction of the old order, but rather a process of accretion and evolutionary change taking place over several decades.

The native planters adopted the colono system and developed a program for importing workers, which facilitated the transition to free labor and the subsequent growth of the coffee industry. In doing so they helped ensure their own survival as an economic group and maintained political hegemony for several more decades. But as the twentieth century wore on, many immigrants moved into the proliferating niches in the rural socioeconomic system. Much of that system was out of the hands of the old elite by the time the Depression hit, despite the continuing political dominance of the native Brazilians. The Paulista planters found themselves presiding over a transformation of agrarian society that few would have envisioned in the 1880s.

The essential human element in that change was the group of immigrant workers. They were imported to replace slaves, and they established for themselves a place as landowners and independent farmers in São Paulo's western plateau.

7

CONCLUSION

The onset of the Great Depression signaled the end of an era for western São Paulo no less than for the rest of the world economy. Coffee prices fell, expansion slowed, and the colono system changed as planters adjusted to new economic conditions. Immigration was already declining when the Depression sharply cut the inflow of laborers from abroad; the reliance on the resident population and internal migrants accelerated. Coffee trees planted on the frontier during the boom of 1885–96 were ending their productive life during the 1920s, so that the external crisis was little more than a final blow for areas that by 1930 were considered older zones.

In less than half a century prior to the Depression, western São Paulo had become a different place. A special and in some ways unique relationship between Brazil and the world economy had formed in the São Paulo periphery in the 1880s. Agrarian society and the accompanying institutional structures expanded into the virgin resource base of the western plateau over the following decades, fed by demand for coffee in Europe and North America and by the excess workers of Europe and later Japan, until the general collapse of the 1930s. One way of summarizing the historical legacy of the era is by examining the results for the three major groups involved: the native coffee planters, the immigrant workers, and the native Brazilian workers.

The Brazilian planters, heirs of a long tradition, remained dominant throughout this period. Their economic decisions, their government and its policies, continued to affect the lives of other social groups. As a ruling class, albeit dependent on the world economy, they continued to rule. The self-contained plantation as an economic and social institution was a continuation of earlier patterns that brought together factors of production in units large enough to make successive moves into the western frontier attractive for the native coffee capitalists and their foreign allies. Only the income potential of the large-scale agricultural enterprise could attract the initial investment and transport infrastructure without which the productive capacity of the São Paulo hinterland would have remained only potential. The plantation, then, led the way into the frontier, occupied the best land, and remained. It persisted because it served the interests of individual planters in generating profits. Its continued viability contributed to the sense of hegemony that the Paulista elite retained.

Unlike the sugar plantation from which it was historically derived, however, the coffee plantation did not persist because of an inherent technical requirement for large units. The proof of this is not only in the small coffee farm characteristic of Colombia or the Brazilian state of Paraná today; it is also in the interstitial small farms of western São Paulo in 1905, 1923, and 1932. Nor did the plantation persist because of a desire on the part of the native elite to monopolize the available coffee land. Again, the proof is in the small and medium-sized farms, many of which belonged to immigrants who were not members of the native elite. These were not marginal *minifundia* barely providing foodstuffs for the occupant. The small farms were also viable, producing coffee for the external market as well as cereals and livestock for local markets and subsistence. Rather than diminishing in importance as plantations expanded, the small farms grew in number and in proportional share of the coffee industry. The eventual emergence of a significant stratum of immigrant-owned farms was an accretion, a complementary activity posing no direct challenge to the large plantations. Indeed, planters in older areas encouraged the transition to smaller units as a way of turning fixed but declining assets into liquid capital, which they could reinvest on the frontier or in other economic sectors. These other sectors—commerce, construction, and food processing and other light industry—all grew as a function of coffee expansion, as urban centers, internal demand, and local markets grew. They were the historical antecedents of the diversified economic structure of modern São Paulo.[1]

With the rapid expansion into the west and the growing complexity of the agrarian structure, it was possible for the old elite to lose control in relative terms while still gaining absolutely. It was in this sense that the hegemony of the native planter class eventually became something of an illusion. One indication that the political power of the planters was no longer total was the state government's unilateral decision in 1927 to eliminate transportation subsidies—the key to the immigration program. This and other signs, notably the growing influence of the urban-industrial sector of the regional economy, point to a relative weakening of São Paulo's traditional plantocracy before the international crisis. It is worth suggesting that the difficulty of maintaining Paulista influence in national politics in 1930 and in the ensuing move toward national political centralization under Getúlio Vargas was related to the planters' relative loss of control over the agricultural resources of São Paulo in the preceding period.[2] Economic change altered political relationships. The planters, looking complacently out over their verandas at the vast domains they had been able to preserve, were slow to adjust to the new realities.

From the sixteenth-century beginnings of the Brazilian plantation system to the eve of the Paulista coffee boom, despite some halting experimentation, the dominant form of labor organization had been slavery. At the very time rising demand at the center of the world economy and the installation of a railroad network made expansion possible, it was no longer possible to retain slavery. The slaves themselves would no longer tolerate their servile condition, and international and internal political pressure forced the planters' hand. There ensued a radical break with the past, as the Paulistas developed the unique colono system virtually from whole cloth and created their immigration program. Between the planters at the top and the native peasants and ex-slaves at the bottom of the rural social structure there emerged a new social category—the immigrant workers. In retrospect, it is clear that the coffee planters' solution to their labor needs, at the time of abolition and in the following decades, brought to São Paulo an immense inflow of human capital. As an agricultural and then industrial labor force, as producers for local markets and for export, as consumers of goods and services, as the parents of new Brazilian generations, the immigrants provided the social basis for São Paulo's rise to preeminence among the regions of Brazil.

Unlike the transfer of workers from Africa in the earlier era, the mass foreign migration to São Paulo after 1886 was voluntary. That is not to say it was spontaneous or random. It was induced and controlled by the planter elite, particularly in the initial stages. First through semipublic agencies and then through the state government, the planters moved decisively to tap the pool of foreign manpower. The Paulistas determined how many would come through the regulation of subsidized passage. They influenced the origin of the workers initially by sending recruiters to northern Italy and later by maintaining contractual arrangements with shippers who operated between specified ports and Santos. They influenced the composition of the immigrant stream by specific restrictions on eligibility for subsidized passage and access to the facilities of the immigrant hostel. They influenced the eventual destination of the immigrants by controlling egress from the hostel and arranging free passage to the interior, and by determining which employers could hire through state facilities. Thus the planters were able to ensure an abundant and continuing supply of poor people in family units. Given the yearly cycle of labor demand and the technical aspects of coffee production, the colono system functioned well only when whole families worked together. The planters, acting in their short-run interest in solving the labor problem, brought to São Paulo the type of workers who had the best chance of survival and even success on the plantations.

In this incident in the history of the modern world economy there was some respite from the exploitation, degradation, and institutionalized coercion that have characterized plantation labor systems in other areas. Compared to the chattel slave of earlier times, the indentured laborer of the postabolition Caribbean, the debt peon of Mexico or Guatemala, or the semiserf of the Andean highlands or central Chile, the São Paulo coffee colono had an enviable existence.[3] His standard of living, relative freedom of action, and life chances compared favorably with those of workers in other plantation systems, as with the migrant field hand in São Paulo today.

The explanation of this apparent anomaly lies not in any imputation of altruism on the part of the planters. There is no reason to suppose the São Paulo coffee capitalist was less rational in the pursuit of profits than his counterpart in other plantation complexes. Planters were not under attack from an urban-based populist government inimical to their goals, as in other areas in more recent times. Nor did colonos organize themselves into unions through which they could defend their own interests on a group basis. There was some activity by the governments of the labor-supplying countries to protect their citizens. Negative publicity, occasional restrictions on emigration, and consular intervention in specific incidents demanded responses that sometimes operated in the workers' favor. But such external pressure hardly counterbalanced the overwhelming power of the São Paulo government and the planters on their individual domains.

The origins of the coffee workers' relatively advantageous condition are to be found primarily in the conjuncture of economic forces during the era of mass immigration. The continued existence of the frontier and the abundance of land were central to the system. Planters did not need to institutionalize coercion to keep money wages low and profits high. The heart of the colono system was partial payment in usufruct of plantation land. Throughout the plateau the food crop and pasture portions of the work contract provided some cushion from fluctuations in the local wage-price structure and was a mechanism that made saving possible for some families. Those who accumulated enough to set themselves up as farmers found land available, both on the frontier and in the older areas where the decline of coffee left room for other activities.

If colonos generally remained free and could live relatively well, it was not due to a conscious policy of income distribution for purposes of promoting a more egalitarian society. On the contrary, planters repeatedly showed they would rather be rid of the colono system and the occasional benefits and opportunities it gave to some workers. Planters preferred to reduce their wage bill even further, reduce the constant need to provide for interrow cropping or separate subsistence plots, and reduce the geographical mobility of the labor force. But over the long term, immigrants refused to submit to an exploitative labor regime. A system of positive incentives was necessary, and the specific elements of the colono contract were possible. Given the abundance of land and the characteristic topography of the plateau, with ridges for coffee and valley bottoms for cereals and pasture, it was possible to offer workers an incentive package without a direct distribution of coffee income away from the planters. One important result was that colonos could usually feed themselves and sometimes sell surplus. As part of the price they received for their labor power, they gained access to the means of production, albeit on a partial and temporary basis. This is the crucial difference between the colono's lot and the historical condition of an urban proletariat. It is a key to understanding the experience of the immigration plantation workers.

The immigrants had no traditional attachment to any given locality or activity. Beyond their first contract many were able to go into those areas and occupations where they thought their interests could best be fulfilled. With the continuing attraction of more land, and thus more advantageous contracts on the frontier, plantation workers continued to move. Others left agriculture to work in the growing urban centers or to return to their homelands. Planters in the older zones and marginal areas sometimes resorted to restrictive measures and negative sanctions. But without the police power of the state to bolster their control over workers, in competition with thousands of other planters for the services of people from a mobile labor pool, planters maintained the package of positive incentives. When the coffee growers in declining areas could no longer compete successfully, the decline was accelerated. The ensuing geographical mobility of the planters, like that of the workers, was facilitated by the existence of the frontier. Seeing the denuded hills and the abandoned great houses of the Mogiana zone today, one might be led to conclude that the land was used wastefully—that the land paid in the long run. But at the time, from the short-run perspective of the Paulistas, extensive use of the land was a rational allocation of resources.

Huge areas of natural forest were eliminated as coffee advanced; this loss evoked some concern by the 1920s. To facilitate hoe cultivation, coffee was planted in burned-over ground in rows running vertically up slopes. The surface of the soil was then kept bare to ensure the coffee shrubs a monopoly on nutrients and water and to facilitate the harvest. As a result, rivers that once ran clear turned mud-red as erosion became chronic.[4] In some areas the destructive results of this extensive, transient agriculture persist, but the incorporation of the São Paulo west into the world economy was not an unmitigated process of devastation and abandonment. Some older zones have been reclaimed for coffee through conservation techniques. Other hilly areas were replanted in eucalyptus to save the soil and provide fuel and cellulose. Dairy cattle now graze over broken terrain where coffee trees once stood in endless rows. On the rolling flatlands of the plateau, sugar cane, cotton, citrus, soy beans, and a variety of other crops give São Paulo economic strength in agriculture, which complements its preeminent position as the industrial heartland of Brazil. Historically, coffee was the leading sector that brought in capital, a transport infrastructure unrivaled in the nation, entrepreneurial activity, the regional market system and urban centers, and the human resources that make rural São Paulo what it is today. That the people who work the land no longer share in the bounty as they once did is the result of historical forces since the watershed of the Great Depression.

The chronic attrition of the immigrant work force through geographical mobility must be seen in the context of an increase in the total labor needs of the coffee industry during several decades of growth. The planters responded to this situation by maintaining the immigration program, thus ensuring an abundant labor supply to replace those lost and provide for expansion. Voluntary immigration became more important over the years, reducing the need for transport subsidies, and in the 1920s internal migration began to provide another source of workers. This was another reason for the relatively advantageous condition of the coffee colono: there was little incentive for the planters to extract even more surplus from those already on the plantations because additional workers continued to enter from outside São Paulo. It was a system open at both ends.

If the São Paulo coffee frontier constituted a safety valve for labor in the Turnerian sense, it can only be seen as such in the context of the world economy. It may well have been a safety valve for the areas providing the bulk of the labor force—Italy, Spain, Portugal, Japan. For the long-run development of São Paulo, relief of demographic pressure in those areas meant the injection of an invaluable supply of human resources. Local working people—the free peasantry and ex-slaves—were relegated to a marginal role in the process.

Maintenance of external labor sources also meant that the precoffee population of the plateau was not coerced or induced into participating in the plantation sector. While the nomadic Indians were killed off and forced to retreat further into the interior, the native peasant population was pushed aside and passed by during the incorporation of the area into the world economy. The traditional backwoodsmen, or *caipiras*, often of mixed Portuguese, Indian, and African racial stock, had lived in scattered areas of the São Paulo hinterland since the colonial era. The caipira's world view was circumscribed by his condition of isolation, illiteracy, and hand-to-mouth economic level. He normally had only tenuous legal claim to the plot of land on which he subsisted, and as the coffee zone expanded he was no match for planters, grileiros, and their political allies in land offices.

The caipiras were not normally absorbed into the plantation labor force, for two related reasons. On the one hand, the Paulista elite generally thought that compared to the disciplined and industrious immigrant, the native rural population was shiftless, lazy, ignorant, and generally undesirable. Even those planters who urged more rational use of local sources of manpower reflected such attitudes. Augusto Ramos, one of the more perceptive contemporary observers, wrote in 1902 that the caipiras of the interior were "the victims of foreign progress, those conquered by modern agriculture, besieged by their competitors like a flock of pigeons besieged by a pair of hawks." While the immigrant colonos made up the labor force, he continued, "that reserve of old Paulistas vegetates, without hope and without horizon."[5]

Such self-serving social Darwinism became self-fulfilling as the planters continued to import hundreds of thousands of immigrant workers.

From the point of view of the caipira, on the other hand, submission to the regimen of plantation life was undesirable; he valued personal autonomy over a marginal existence in the commercial sector. According to an authoritative study of caipiras in the municipio of Bofete in the Alta Sorocabana zone, the caipira was "master of his own destiny, due to the precarious independence of poverty. He rejected the discipline of employer and wage as they were offered, in patterns developed under slavery. The slave and the European colono were called, in succession, to fill the role that the caipira could not fill, did not know how to fill, or did not want to fill."[6] As planters complained of labor shortages over the years, they eventually suggested tapping the pool of surplus workers in the Brazilian northeast. But rarely did the Paulistas discuss the possibility of recruiting their own peasantry. In any case, even a total mobilization of local labor sources would have supplied only part of the labor needs of the coffee industry.

Similar conclusions may be reached regarding the ex-slaves. There is no doubt that the freedmen and their descendants continued to suffer racist rejection by elite and immigrant alike, the heritage of generations in bondage. But that same heritage identified field labor on plantations with slave status, which the freedmen themselves rejected. It is not surprising that ex-slaves, a social group considered by the Brazilian upper class to be a superfluous embarrassment, largely disappeared from the historical record after abolition. But it does not follow that they disappeared from the historical reality. Their "disappearance" must be seen relative to the massive influx of white Europeans.

Many freedmen remained on the plantations performing a variety of tasks outside the coffee groves, particularly as camaradas in a patron-client relationship with the landowner. An 1899 survey of the municipio of São Carlos, in the Paulista zone, reported a total of 15,688 plantation workers. Of that number, only 2,270 (14 percent) were Brazilians, but 1,242, more than half of the Brazilians and 8 percent of the total labor force, were listed as black. There were just 68,400 slaves in the rural areas of western São Paulo in 1887, and less than twenty years later there were 338,275 agricultural workers counted in the same area. Of that total, 116,888 (35 percent) were Brazilian natives—many of whom must have been ex-slaves and their descendants.[7] Some freedmen joined the caipiras in isolated pockets of subsistence farming; others migrated to the cities where they were also at a disadvantage in competition with the immigrant proletariat. Many others remained as an identifiable—if marginal—group in commercial agriculture.

Because the open lands of the São Paulo west are fundamental to this analysis, another aspect of the Turnerian hypothesis deserves mention: the democratizing effect of the frontier. Compared to other plantation systems, there was a degree of distribution of economic resources in favor of immigrant workers. This took place through the allocation of abundant land, but it was essentially a mechanism by which the Paulista elite could attract an outside labor force, maintain profits through concentration on coffee for export to the center of the world economy, and preserve their hegemonic position on the periphery. Similarly, the eventual rise of immigrant-owned small farms was possible partly because of the availability of land, but this development took place despite the original intentions of the native planters and posed no threat to their political control. Deliberate democratization was the furthest thing from the thinking of the Paulista ruling class. The small farmers never became a political force based either on their economic status or on an appeal to common immigrant origins. Nor did an ideology based on values imputed to the farmer of the frontier achieve currency. If some immigrants and their descendants eventually participated in the formal political system, it was through collaboration rather than through the development of an independent interest group.

The immigrants on the land were part of an agrarian world that no longer exists. It was a complex that emerged from the convergence of an abundant resource base and an economic and social matrix that came together in the 1880s, matured in the following decades, and grew old by the time the world crisis of the 1930s broke it apart. In that span of a lifetime this case of expansion on the periphery of the capitalist world economy affected the lives of millions of people. Just as the colono labor system itself was a transitory phase in São Paulo's agrarian history, so was the predominance of immigrants in the labor force transitional between black slaves earlier and native Brazilians later. Children of foreigners, internal migrants, and a local population much larger and more complex than before the arrival of immigrants continued to labor on the land in another era.

APPENDIXES

1. World Coffee Production, by Region, 1880–1937
(In Thousands of Sixty-Kilogram Bags)

Year[a]	Brazil[b]				Other Countries[c]	World Total
	Rio	Santos	Other Ports	Total		
1880	4,521	1,126	136	5,783	4,192	9,975
1881	3,841	1,723	126	5,691	4,113	9,804
1882	4,737	1,968	147	6,852	4,944	11,796
1883	3,186	1,872	108	5,166	3,979	9,145
1884	4,276	2,095	121	6,492	4,149	10,641
1885	3,870	1,665	235	5,770	3,900	9,670
1886	3,510	2,620	190	6,320	4,145	10,465
1887	1,805	1,115	155	3,165	3,760	6,925
1888	4,125	2,610	190	6,925	4,090	11,015
1889	2,350	1,870	185	4,405	4,015	8,420
1890	2,395	2,915	215	5,525	3,760	9,285
1891	3,720	3,655	320	7,695	4,245	11,940
1892	2,980	3,215	340	6,535	4,740	11,275
1893	2,590	1,720	730	5,040	4,360	9,400
1894	2,710	3,985	540	7,235	4,530	11,765
1895	2,400	3,090	515	6,005	4,390	10,395
1896	3,580	5,100	635	9,315	4,600	13,915
1897	4,300	6,160	750	11,210	4,840	16,050
1898	3,190	5,580	550	9,320	4,405	13,725
1899	3,265	5,705	455	9,425	4,380	13,805
1900	2,930	7,970	385	11,285	3,785	15,070
1901	5,330	10,165	650	16,145	3,645	19,790
1902	3,975	8,350	620	12,945	3,720	16,665
1903	4,020	6,395	686	11,101	4,891	15,992
1904	2,542	7,426	555	10,523	3,923	14,446
1905	3,244	6,983	617	10,844	3,948	14,792

1. *continued*

Brazil[b]

Year[a]	Rio	Santos	Other Ports	Total	Other Countries[c]	World Total
1906	4,234	15,392	564	20,190	3,596	23,786
1907	3,108	7,203	690	11,001	3,861	14,862
1908	2,883	9,533	496	12,912	4,003	16,915
1909	3,449	11,495	380	15,324	3,801	19,125
1910	2,438	8,110	300	10,848	3,676	14,524
1911	2,484	9,972	581	13,037	4,337	17,374
1912	2,906	8,585	640	12,131	4,275	16,406
1913	2,960	10,855	642	14,547	5,154	19,611
1914	3,349	9,497	625	13,471	4,394	17,865
1915	3,250	11,747	963	15,960	4,801	20,761
1916	2,310	9,803	628	12,741	3,951	16,692
1917	2,958	12,169	709	15,836	3,001	18,847
1918	1,768	7,369	575	9,712	4,500	14,212
1919	2,549	4,169	782	7,500	7,681	15,181
1920	3,305	10,511	680	14,496	5,787	20,283
1921	3,672	8,179	1,011	12,862	6,926	19,788
1922	2,669	6,759	766	10,194	5,705	15,899
1923	3,798	10,195	871	14,864	6,868	21,732
1924	3,082	9,402	1,237	13,721	6,762	20,483
1925	3,939	9,082	1,093	14,114	7,052	21,166
1926	3,634	9,476	1,074	14,184	7,068	21,252
1927	3,793	10,321	2,306	16,420	8,003	24,423
1928	2,993	8,874	1,754	13,621	8,660	22,281
1929	3,013	9,721	2,785	15,519	8,273	23,792
1930	4,800	9,793	2,676	17,269	8,633	25,902
1931	3,990	9,732	2,032	15,754	8,287	24,041
1932	3,973	7,055	2,380	13,408	9,239	22,647
1933	3,132	12,333	2,080	17,545	8,931	26,476
1934	2,817	9,034	2,146	13,997	7,699	21,696
1935	3,117	10,670	2,619	16,406	10,028	26,434
1936	2,067	8,790	3,041	13,898	10,889	24,787
1937	2,371	9,486	3,060	14,917	10,011	24,928

a. Fiscal years (i.e., 1880 is 1880–81 crop year).
b. Data are for quantities received in ports listed, not exports.
c. Data are for quantities exported.
Sources: 1880–84: *Brazilian Yearbook, 1909*, pp. 632–33. 1885–1937: Brazil, Departamento Nacional do Café, *Anuário estatístico, 1938*, p. 264.

2. Coffee Prices in Santos and U.S. Dollar Equivalents, 1885–1933

Year[a]	Milreis per 10 Kilograms[b]	Dollars per 10 Kilograms[c]	Year	Milreis per 10 Kilograms[b]	Dollars per 10 Kilograms[c]
1885	3$950	1.50	1910	5$850	1.93
1886	5$650	2.15	1911	7$550	2.42
1887	6$450	2.97	1912	6$900	2.21
1888	5$400	2.75	1913	5$000	1.60
1889	6$650	3.59	1914	4$300	1.25
1890	8$150	3.75	1915	4$850	1.21
1891	10$100	3.03	1916	5$500	1.27
1892	12$200	2.93	1917	4$150	1.04
1893	15$800	3.79	1918	10$750	2.69
1894	14$700	2.94	1919	14$000	3.64
1895	14$200	2.84	1920	8$000	1.68
1896	10$700	1.93	1921	14$750	1.92
1897	8$550	1.37	1922	20$200	2.63
1898	7$300	1.10	1923	23$500	2.35
1899	7$800	1.17	1924	37$000	4.07
1900	5$850	1.11	1925	26$000	3.12
1901	4$650	1.07	1926	22$800	3.19
1902	4$200	1.01	1927	27$000	3.24
1903	4$900	1.18	1928	30$500	3.66
1904	5$150	1.29	1929	22$000	2.64
1905	4$250	1.36	1930	16$250	1.79
1906	3$900	1.29	1931	13$900	.97
1907	3$450	1.07	1932	13$100	.92
1908	3$400	1.05	1933	13$000	1.04
1909	3$800	1.18			

a. Fiscal years (i.e., 1885 is 1885–86 crop year).

b. Annual average. Standard grade was New York "good average" up to 1906. Santos grade 7 for 1907–33 period.

c. Calculated at average annual exchange rates from appendix table 6.

Source: Brazil, Departamento Nacional do Café, *Anuário estatístico, 1938*, p. 264.

3. Producing Coffee Trees in Western São Paulo, by Zone, 1886–1932 (In Thousands of Trees)

Year	Central	Mogiana	Paulista	Arara-quarense	Noroeste	Alta Soro-cabana	Total
1886	37,325	57,380	47,827	6,864	0	4,896	154,292
1900	84,983	202,174	135,306	97,463	2,623	49,065	571,614
1905	97,645	218,871	146,352	93,541	2,652	54,625	613,686
1910	94,809	217,150	146,968	101,790	2,652	56,390	619,759
1915	99,955	255,303	158,032	130,424	10,326	78,233	732,273
1920	99,502	261,659	176,468	169,890	27,524	86,387	821,430
1925	95,210	269,478	182,938	228,804	45,440	100,456	922,326
1928	100,427	276,031	202,420	299,107	106,088	120,481	1,104,554
1932	97,794	286,907	207,273	416,084	274,647	168,002	1,450,707

Sources: 1886: Calculated from F. W. Dafert, *Colleção dos trabalhos agricolas estrahidos dos relatorios annuaes de 1888–1893*, pp. 171–77. 1900: *Boletim de Agricultura*, 1904, pp. 46–49. 1905: São Paulo, Secretaria de Agricultura, *Relatório*, 1907, between pp. 46 and 47. 1910–28: São Paulo, Secretaria de Agricultura, *Estatísticas de produção e commercio do café*, various years. 1932: Brazil, Departamento Nacional do Café, *Anuário estatístico, 1935*, pp. 170–73.

4. Immigration to São Paulo, 1882–1934, and Steerage Departures from Santos, 1892–1934

Year	Immigration	Santos Departures	Year	Immigration	Santos Departures
1882	2,743		1909	38,308	34,512
1883	4,912		1910	39,486	30,761
1884	4,868		1911	61,508	27,331
1885	6,500		1912	98,640	37,440
1886	9,534		1913	116,640	41,154
1887	32,110		1914	46,624	41,834
1888	91,826		1915	15,614	26,183
1889	27,664		1916	17,011	12,776
1890	38,291		1917	23,407	9,397
1891	108,688		1918	11,447	6,542
1892	42,061	16,555	1919	16,205	14,509
1893	81,755	11,814	1920	31,854	16,748
1894	44,740	18,192	1921	32,678	16,796
1895	136,142	18,916	1922	31,281	20,612
1896	94,987	23,157	1923	45,240	20,697
1897	94,540	24,608	1924	56,085	24,085
1898	42,674	23,007	1925	57,429	26,304
1899	28,367	24,182	1926	76,796	26,425
1900	21,038	27,917	1927	61,607	26,591
1901	70,348	36,099	1928	40,847	26,591
1902	37,831	31,437	1929	53,262	29,493
1903	16,553	36,410	1930	30,924	32,263
1904	23,761	32,679	1931	16,216	20,486
1905	45,839	34,819	1932	17,420	12,174
1906	46,214	41,349	1933	33,680	13,992
1907	28,900	36,269	1934	30,757	14,557
1908	37,278	30,750	Total	2,321,130	1,078,413

Sources: Immigration: *Anuario estatístico de São Paulo* and São Paulo, Secretaria de Agricultura, *Relatório*, various years. Santos departures: 1892–1907, from São Paulo Secretaria de Agricultura, *Relatório*, various years; 1908–1934, from *Boletim da Directoria de Terras, Colonisação e Immigração*, no. 1 (1937), p. 46.

5. People Leaving the São Paulo Immigrant Hostel for the Western Plateau, by Zone, 1893–1929

Year	Central	Mogiana	Paulista	Arara-quarense	Noroeste	Alta Soro-cabana	Total
1893	6,003	12,461	11,494	4,424	0	2,449	36,831
1894	3,578	8,611	7,563	2,245	0	1,557	23,554
1895	10,499	24,624	18,502	6,544	0	3,755	63,924
1896[a]	11,867	25,960	22,250	7,417	0	4,450	71,944
1897	10,380	17,034	17,195	5,392	0	3,205	53,206
1898	3,458	8,726	6,692	2,782	0	1,626	23,284
1899	1,735	3,920	4,814	1,890	0	1,630	13,989
1900	1,102	4,366	2,471	1,923	123	2,087	12,072
1901	5,160	18,678	16,359	6,165	0	5,952	52,314
1902	2,580	9,354	7,020	2,437	0	1,674	23,065
1903	1,013	2,172	1,174	725	0	737	5,821
1904	1,567	6,268	2,373	1,768	0	2,903	14,879
1905	3,335	12,287	6,513	5,205	457	5,823	33,620
1906	4,629	11,398	6,603	5,504	349	3,865	32,348
1907	2,100	5,629	3,259	3,347	238	2,408	16,981
1908	2,057	8,486	5,803	3,933	1,306	2,144	23,729
1909	2,204	8,538	5,713	4,771	2,272	2,895	26,393
1910	2,190	9,793	5,180	5,055	1,877	4,057	28,152
1911	3,008	10,735	7,186	6,514	1,477	7,445	36,365
1912	4,646	16,104	9,572	10,799	1,506	8,243	50,870
1913	5,434	24,379	13,302	11,338	1,840	8,854	65,147
1914	4,283	15,997	9,301	6,456	1,304	5,714	43,055
1915	1,571	5,574	4,073	4,059	1,032	4,153	20,462
1916	1,501	5,387	3,912	4,179	1,479	3,597	20,055
1917	2,196	7,616	4,908	6,782	1,846	4,515	27,863
1918	1,005	4,756	2,619	2,972	1,775	3,428	16,555
1919	660	4,113	2,259	3,633	1,877	3,723	16,265
1920	804	6,881	5,084	6,224	4,018	5,696	28,707
1921	1,135	7,723	4,870	5,704	4,249	4,860	28,541
1922	1,039	5,165	2,871	3,769	3,550	5,592	21,986
1923	1,008	5,882	5,363	7,162	6,258	8,962	34,635
1924	1,113	9,920	4,939	7,622	5,544	8,517	37,655
1925	842	10,537	4,816	4,862	7,365	10,173	38,595
1926	2,018	7,518	6,841	5,340	4,520	10,312	36,549
1927	293	13,857	5,699	5,227	16,888	8,249	50,213

5. *continued*

Year	Central	Mogiana	Paulista	Arara-quarense	Noroeste	Alta Soro-cabana	Total
1928	970	12,472	9,022	10,887	33,690	15,519	82,560
1929	938	18,778	10,436	9,303	31,397	26,606	97,458

a. Specific destination data for 1896 are not available. These interpolations are based on distribution of those entering the hostel in 1896 by zone in proportions equal to the average for the 1893–95 period. Data for all other years are recorded destinations.

Sources: 1893–99: São Paulo, Repartição de Estatística, *Relatório*, various years. 1900–29: *Anuario estatístico de São Paulo*, various years.

6. Average Annual Exchange Rate of Brazilian Milreis in Current U.S. Dollars, 1880–1940

Year	Dollar	Year	Dollar	Year	Dollar	Year	Dollar
1880	.45	1896	.18	1912	.32	1928	.12
1881	.44	1897	.16	1913	.32	1929	.12
1882	.43	1898	.15	1914	.29	1930	.11
1883	.44	1899	.15	1915	.25	1931	.07
1884	.42	1900	.19	1916	.23	1932	.07
1885	.38	1901	.23	1917	.25	1933	.08
1886	.38	1902	.24	1918	.25	1934	.08
1887	.46	1903	.24	1919	.26	1935	.08
1888	.51	1904	.25	1920	.21	1936	.09
1889	.54	1905	.32	1921	.13	1937	.09
1890	.46	1906	.33	1922	.13	1938	.06
1891	.30	1907	.31	1923	.10	1939	.06
1892	.24	1908	.31	1924	.11	1940	.06
1893	.24	1909	.31	1925	.12		
1894	.20	1910	.33	1926	.14		
1895	.20	1911	.32	1927	.12		

Sources: 1880–1930: Julian S. Duncan, *Public and Private Operation of Railways in Brazil*, p. 183. 1931–1940: Vernon Dale Wickizer, *The World Coffee Economy*, pp. 248–49.

NOTES

Abbreviations Used in Notes

AESP	*Annuario estatístico de São Paulo*
BDET	*Boletim do Departamento Estadual de Trabalho*
Bol. Ag.	*Boletim de Agricultura*
CPORI	Cartório do Primeiro Ofício, Registro de Imóveis
-C	Campinas
-RC	Rio Claro
-RP	Ribeirão Preto
-S	Sertãozinho
-T	Taquaritinga
LDESP	*Leis e Decretos do Estado de São Paulo*
-PE	Poder Executivo
-PL	Poder Legislativo
O Faz.	*O Fazendeiro*
R. dos F.	*Revista dos Fazendeiros*
RSRB	*Revista da Sociedade Rural Brasileira*
SAR	São Paulo, Secretaria de Agricultura, *Relatório*

Chapter 1

1. One approach to the evolution of the world economy and its components is summarized in Immanuel Wallerstein, "The Rise and Future Demise of the World Capitalist System." 'An elaboration on the conceptual framework is given in Immanuel Wallerstein, *The Modern World-System.* For a friendly critique see Sidney Mintz, "The So-called World System."

2. For an overview of the goals, patterns, and effects of Iberian colonization in the new world, see Stanley J. Stein and Barbara H. Stein, *The Colonial Heritage of Latin America.* On Brazilian economic cycles, see J. F. Normano, *Brazil*, pp. 18–56. On Brazil's colonial era and the master-slave leitmotiv, see Caio Prado, Jr., *The Colonial Background of Modern Brazil*, pp. 313–46, and Gilberto Freyre, *The Masters and the Slaves.*

3. This central fact has been noted by Ralph Della Cava, ''The Italian Immigrant Experience,'' p. 188.

4. Quoted in Stein and Stein, *Colonial Heritage*, p. 12.

5. Allen K. Manchester, *British Preeminence in Brazil*, and Richard Graham, *Britain and the Onset of Modernization in Brazil*.

6. Robert Conrad, *The Destruction of Brazilian Slavery, 1850–1888*, and Robert Brent Toplin, *The Abolition of Slavery in Brazil*.

7. Shepard B. Clough, *Economic History of Modern Italy*, pp. 120–21.

8. Odilon Nogueira de Matos, *Café e ferrovias*, 2nd ed., p. 72.

9. Peter L. Eisenberg, *The Sugar Industry in Pernambuco*, pp. 8–9.

10. The classic monograph on the Paraiba valley era is Stanley Stein, *Vassouras*.

11. Stein and Stein, *Colonial Heritage*, pp. 39–44. A useful typology and discussion of the origins of the plantation is given in Leo Waibel, ''The Tropical Plantation System.'' See also Eric Wolf and Sidney Mintz, ''Haciendas and Plantations in Middle America and the Antilles,'' and Kenneth Duncan and Ian Rutledge, eds., *Land and Labour in Latin America*, pp. 1–20.

12. On the early development of export agriculture in western São Paulo see Warren Dean, *Rio Claro*, pp. 1–87.

13. These commercial manipulations and their effect on the world coffee market are discussed in Thomas H. Holloway, *The Brazilian Coffee Valorization of 1906*, pp. 69–75.

14. See, for example, George Rogers Taylor, ed., *The Turner Thesis*. An excellent comparative essay is Alistair Hennessy, *The Frontier in Latin American History*.

Chapter 2

1. An indispensable tool for tracing the development of the municipio network is São Paulo, Departamento Estadual de Estatística, *Ensaio de um quadro do desmembramento dos municípios*.

2. On the development of the city of São Paulo see Gerald M. Greenfield, ''The Challenge of Growth,'' and Richard M. Morse, *From Community to Metropolis*.

3. Pierre Deffontaines, ''As feiras de burro de Sorocaba.''

4. Alice Pifer Cannabrava, *O desenvolvimento da cultura do algodão na provincia de São Paulo, 1861–1875*.

5. Maria Thereza Schorer Petrone, *A lavoura canavieira em São Paulo*, pp. 41–53.

6. On the interprovincial slave traffic, see Robert Slenes, ''The Demography and Economics of Brazilian Slavery,'' pp. 120–78, 594–686, and Conrad, *Destruction*, pp. 20–29, 47–69.

7. In the 1909–18 decade annual receipts of Minas coffee averaged 5.7 percent of all Santos receipts. See São Paulo, Secretaria de Agricultura, *O café, estatísticas de produção e exportação*, 1920, p. 8. In the 1919–29 period the figure was 11.9 per-

cent. See São Paulo, Secretaria de Agricultura, *Estatísticas de produção e commércio do café, 1921–1930*, p. 16.

8. Frederick V. Gifun, "Ribeirão Prêto, 1880–1914."

9. Robert H. Mattoon, Jr., "Railroads, Coffee, and the Growth of Big Business in São Paulo, Brazil."

10. Alfredo Ellis, Jr., *Tenente Coronel Francisco da Cunha Bueno*, pp. 23, 94, 105, 123.

11. Examples of such maps are in Adolpho A. Pinto, *História da viação pública de São Paulo*, pp. 230–31, and São Paulo, Secretaria de Agricultura, *Lo stato di S. Paolo (Brasile) agli emigranti*, pp. 84–85.

12. SAR, 1905, pp. 207–9; SAR, 1906, p. 271. See also São Paulo, Commissão Geográphica e Geológica, *Exploração dos rios Feio e Aguapehy* and *Exploração do rio Peixe*.

13. "Bandeirantes do café," p. 364. On the Kaingang, see Jules Henry, *Jungle People*. The history of the Noroeste is in Fernando de Azevedo, *Um trem corre para o oeste*. All translations from Portuguese, Italian, and French are the author's.

14. Reports of the boom in the Noroeste are in *O Faz.*, 1914, pp. 371–72; 1915, pp. 202–4, 222. On the 1920s see Pierre Monbeig, "Algumas observações sobre Marília."

15. In the prerailroad era the Alta Sorocabana was called the Sertão do Parana-panema. For the early history of the area see Amador Nogueira Cobra, *Em um recanto do sertão paulista*. A report of the opening of the rail line is in "O oeste do estado de São Paulo," pp. 202–3.

16. Jorge Setzer, *Os solos do estado de São Paulo*, p. 352 and passim, and Preston James, "The Coffee Lands of Southeastern Brazil."

17. This regionalization scheme is adapted from those used by Sérgio Milliet, *Roteiro do café e outros ensaios*, and José Francisco de Camargo, *Crescimento da população do estado de São Paulo e seus aspectos econômicos*, 1:27–49. For a more detailed discussion of this territorial division and a list of the municipios in each zone, see Thomas H. Holloway, "Migration and Mobility," pp. 442–53.

18. *The Brazilian Yearbook, 1909*, pp. 622, 629.

19. Dias Martins, "A escolha do sitio para café," 1:350, and Pierre Deffontaines, "Regiões e paisagens do estado de São Paulo," p. 25.

20. Although state property was often measured in hectares from the early twentieth century, private lands continued to be measured in the pre-metric alqueire until the post–World War II era. The alqueire in São Paulo was equal to 2.42 hectares or 5.98 acres.

21. *Bol. Ag.*, 1904, pp. 46–49.

22. The most elaborate treatment of this theme is the essay by the Paulista writer José Bento Monteiro Lobato, *A onda verde*.

23. On the early experiments see Emília Viotti da Costa, *Da senzala à colônia*, p. 187.

24. São Paulo law 1,029 of 12 December 1906 authorized cash prizes for the successful development of coffee implements; see *Bol. Ag.*, 1906, pp. 553–54. On the "Planet Junior," see *Bol. Ag.*, 1904, p. 528. On the Deere cultivator, see "Nova 'carpideira' de cafesal," pp. 558–60. Local manufacturers are listed in Antonio Gomes Carmo, *Considerações históricas sôbre a agricultura no Brasil*, pp. 11–12.

25. *Bol. Ag.*, 1908, p. 121.

26. "Questões agricolas," p. 130.

27. Dario Leite de Barros, "A cultura mechanica dos cafezais," and Carlos Botelho, "Emprego das carpideiras na lavoura de café."

28. João do Amaral Castro, "Um novo sistema de cultura e colheita do café," p. 607.

29. On interrow cropping, see Mario Maldonado, "A cultura mechanica dos cafeeiros," pp. 302–3. Germano Vert mentions the strike threat in "O café barato," p. 127.

30. Olavo Baptista Filho, *A fazenda de café em São Paulo*, p. 21. Workers can be observed today cultivating coffee in São Paulo by essentially similar techniques.

31. Sociedade Paulista de Agricultura, *Relatório referente ao ano de 1908*, pp. 25–27; João do Amaral Castro, *A colheita natural*.

32. Augusto Ramos, *O café no Brasil e no estrangeiro*, p. 116.

33. C. F. Van Delden Laerne, *Brazil and Java*, p. 317. A list of machines introduced by 1885 is in Costa, *Da senzala*, p. 184. The story of Conrado Engelberg is in Warren Dean, *The Industrialization of São Paulo, 1880–1945*, pp. 11–12. Technical descriptions of later machines are in Amour Lalière, *Le Café dans l'état de Saint Paul*, pp. 161–263.

34. On the stability of the worker-tree ratio through time, see the following: Elias Antonio Pacheco e Chaves et al., *Relatório apresentado ao Exmo. Sr. Presidente da Província de São Paulo pela Commissão Central de Estatística*, p. 247; "Estatística agrícola do município de São Carlos do Pinhal organizada pelo Club da Lavoura, 1899," p. 1020; Gherardo Pio di Savoia, "Lo stato di San Paolo (Brasile) e l'emigrazione italiana," p. 42; "Contractos de trabalho nas fazendas"; Flavio M. de Toledo Piza, "Colonos."

Chapter 3

1. See Leslie Bethell, *The Abolition of the Brazilian Slave Trade*; Conrad, *Destruction*; Toplin, *Abolition*; Stein, *Vassouras*, pp. 250–76; Dean, *Rio Claro*, pp. 124–25; Eisenberg, "Abolishing Slavery"; Slenes, "Demography."

2. Eugenio Egas, *Galeria dos presidentes de São Paulo*, 1:445, 459, 469, and Paula Beiguelman, *Pequenos estudos de ciência política*, 2:43.

3. Egas, *Galeria*, 1:472, 489–90, 505, and "Movimento migratório no estado de São Paulo," p. 46.

4. Egas, *Galeria*, 1:572, 898, and SAR, various years.

5. SAR, 1893, Annex 2, p. 37, and Lucy Maffei Hutter, "Imigração italiana em São Paulo, 1880–1889," pp. 69–70, and Adelino Riccardi, "Parnaíba, o pioneiro da imigração," p. 147. The sum spent was equal to U.S. $244,557 at the average exchange rate for 1888.

6. Louis Couty, *Le Brésil en 1884*, pp. 333–37.

7. Couty, *Le Brésil*, pp. 336, 337–38.

8. Egas, *Galeria*, 1:642.

9. Riccardi, "Parnaíba," p. 154. On the activities of the Prado brothers see Darrell Levi, *A família Prado*.

10. *A Provincia de São Paulo no Brasil, emigrante*, pp. 18, 50–55, 57. The imperial government grant is mentioned in *In Memoriam, Martinho Prado Júnior*, p. 356.

11. SAR, 1893, pp. 12–13; SAR, 1895, p. 38.

12. SAR, 1892, p. 31.

13. For details on the quantitative aspects of the transition and the political maneuvering involved, see Thomas H. Holloway, "Immigration and Abolition." For annual data on the proportion of immigrants to Brazil who entered São Paulo, 1882–1934, and the proportion subsidized, 1889–1934, see Thomas H. Holloway, "Creating the Reserve Army?", pp. 207–9.

14. Robert F. Foerster, *The Italian Emigration of Our Times*, p. 289, and Italy, Istituto Centrale di Statistica, *Sommario di statistiche storiche italiane*, p. 66. For quantitative data on the nationality breakdown of immigration to São Paulo, see Holloway, "Migration and Mobility," pp. 185–98.

15. Clough, *Economic History*, pp. 120–21. See also Alexander Gerschenkron, "Notes on the Role of Industrial Growth in Italy, 1881–1913," pp. 360–75.

16. José Arthur Rios, *Aspectos políticos da assimilação do italiano no Brasil*, pp. 28–29; Franco Cenni, *Italianos no Brasil*, p. 187; and Vincenzo Grossi, *Storia della colonizzazione europea al Brasile e della emigrazione italiana nello stato di S. Paulo*, pp. 505–9.

17. Alfredo Cusano, *Italia d'oltre mare*, pp. 20–21; Foerster, *Italian Emigration*, pp. 293–95; and Grossi, *Storia*, pp. 519–28.

18. On Portuguese immigration see Ann Pescatello, "Both Ends of the Journey." On the Japanese see Hiroshi Saito, *O japonês no Brasil*; Arlinda Rocha Nogueira, *A imigração japonesa para a lavoura cafeeira paulista, 1909–1922*; and Takashi Maeyama, "Familialization of the Unfamiliar World." On Syrio-Lebanese, see Clark Knowlton, *Sírios e libaneses*. Spanish immigration to Brazil remains to be studied in detail. On internal migration in historical perspective, see Thomas Merrick and Douglas Graham, *Population and Economic Development in Brazil*, pp. 118–32.

19. Paula Beiguelman, *A formação do povo no complexo cafeeiro*, p. 104.

20. SAR, 1896, Annex, p. 84.

21. Silvio Coletti, "Lo stato di S. Paolo e l'emigrazione italiana," 3:374.

22. The data for 1881–82 through 1891 are in Holloway, "Immigration and Abolition," p. 166.

23. See, for example, SAR, 1896, Annex, p. 83.

24. The text of the Fiorita contract is in SAR, 1894, Annex 1, pp. 38–45.

25. See, for example, SAR, 1895, p. 41.

26. SAR, 1893, p. 16.

27. SAR, 1895, pp. 40–41.

28. On the Canadian venture see SAR, 1896, p. 58. Some five hundred Canadians arrived in Santos during 1896, but most were eventually repatriated by the British consul. See Alice R. Humphrey, *A Summer Journey in Brazil*, pp. 70–71. On the system of commissioners and inspection officers see SAR, 1897, p. 90; 1905, p. 114; 1912–13, pp. 114–17; and 1919, p. 64.

29. SAR, 1896, Annex, pp. 92–103, 160.

30. SAR, 1896, p. 59; 1897, pp. 104–13.

31. SAR, 1898, pp. 57–71; 1899, pp. 77–78.

32. SAR, 1902, pp. 168, 173. See also São Paulo, Secretaria de Agricultura, *Lo stato*.

33. The original legislation is São Paulo law 673 of 9 September 1899, implemented by decree 823 of 20 September 1900. The details of a later contract are in SAR, 1904, p. 348.

34. Santos entry data are in SAR, various years.

35. SAR, 1899, p. 76. See also John A. Blount, "The Public Health Movement in São Paulo, Brazil," pp. 60–62.

36. São Paulo, Secretaria de Agricultura, *Lo stato*, pp. 159–70.

37. SAR, 1893, p. 37.

38. Adolfo Rossi, "Condizioni dei coloni italiani nello stato di San Paolo," pp. 7–15. On hostel deaths, see SAR, 1906, p. 174; 1907, p. 132; and 1908, p. 120.

39. Filippo Ugolotti, *Italia e italiani in Brasile*, pp. 98–99.

40. SAR, 1896, Annex, p. 166.

41. Silvio Coletti, "Lo stato di S. Paolo e l'emigrazione italiana," pp. 61–62.

42. SAR, 1905, p. 115; and Pierre Denis, *Brazil*, pp. 196–99.

43. These data are from AESP, various years. They are collected in Holloway, "Migration and Mobility," pp. 239–40.

44. Data on Santos entries are collected in Holloway, "Migration and Mobility," p. 221.

45. SAR, 1920, pp. 39–40.

46. Jorge Seckler, comp., *Almanach da Provincia de São Paulo*, 5:676–78, and Paul Walle, *Au pays de l'or rouge*, pp. 340–42.

47. The slave registry data for São Paulo in March 1886 are in Chaves et al., *Relatório*, pp. 59–64.

48. São Paulo, Secretaria de Agricultura, *Estatística agrícola e zootéchnica, 1904–1905*.

49. See Dean, *Rio Claro*, pp. 170–74 on the role of native Brazilian workers in one municipio in the early twentieth century.

50. SAR, 1927, p. 183, and RSRB, 8:234–35.

51. RSRB, 8:331–32.

Chapter 4

1. Analytical confusion has resulted from the multiplicity of terms for rural workers and labor systems in Latin America. *Colono* is one of the more common of such terms, and in Brazil alone it has been applied to immigrant farmers in general, to inhabitants of semiautonomous farm colonies, and to plantation workers under the system discussed here. By the same token, the coffee plantation system called the *contrato de colono* or *colonato* has been confused with the task-rate jobbing contract (*empreitada*), sharecropping (*parceria*), and wage labor (*trabalho assalariado*). There are fundamental differences in the historical development, incentive patterns, and social effects of these systems. In the present study, *colono* is used to refer only to coffee workers remunerated under the complex and unique contract arrangement discussed in this chapter. For a comparative framework see Duncan and Rutledge, *Land and Labour*.

2. The best account in English of this incident is Dean, *Rio Claro*, pp. 83–123. See also Thomas Davatz, *Memórias de um colono no Brasil*.

3. Costa, *Da senzala*, pp. 78–109.

4. José Vergueiro, *Memorial acêrca de colonisação e cultivo de café*, p. 5.

5. Louis Couty, *Pequena propriedade e immigração europea*, p. 36, and Laerne, *Brazil and Java*, p. 138.

6. Vergueiro, *Memorial*, p. 6; Balthazar da Silva Carneiro, "O trabalho e a locação de serviços," p. 12; and Dean, *Rio Claro*, pp. 115–16.

7. João Pedro Carvalho de Morais, *Relatório apresentado ao Ministro da Agricultura*, pp. 20–21.

8. Ibid., p. 64.

9. Sérgio Buarque de Hollanda, "As colônias de parceria," II, 3:257, and Laerne, *Brazil and Java*, p. 139.

10. Laerne, *Brazil and Java*, p. 140. See also *A provincia de São Paulo*, pp. 52–55, and Francisco de Paula Lazaro Gonçalves, *Relatório apresentado à Associação Promotora de Immigração em Minas*, pp. 22–81.

11. A colono account book for 1905–7 is reproduced in Lalière, *Le Café*, pp. 270–73.

12. Morais, *Relatório*, p. 73.

13. Pio di Savoia, "Lo stato," p. 43.

14. Denis, *Brazil*, pp. 202–3.

15. Santos Werneck, "Despeza e receita do café." See also Denis, *Brazil*, pp.

198–216, and Deffontaines, "Regiões e paisagens," p. 25.

16. For an estimate of *formador* incomes see Júlio Brandão Sobrinho, *Apreciação da situação agricola, zootechnica, industrial, e commercial do 3° districto agronomico do estado de S. Paulo com sede em Ribeirão Preto*, p. 32.

17. Horace B. Davis and Marian Rubins Davis, "Scale of Living of the Working Class in São Paulo, Brazil," pp. 245–53. The U.S. surveys are summarized in the U.S. Bureau of Census, *Historical Statistics of the United States*, pp. 180–81.

18. Pio di Savoia, "Lo stato," p. 51.

19. "Estatística agrícola," p. 1019.

20. For 1886 see *A provincia de São Paulo*, p. 52; for 1888 see Gonçalves, *Relatório*, pp. 20–81; and for 1895 see SAR, 1895, pp. 44–45.

21. *Boletim do Departamento Estadual do Trabalho*, 1912–29.

22. SAR, 1897, p. 43.

23. SAR, 1895, pp. 44–45.

24. Income data from Mortari's report are reproduced in Pio di Savoia, "Lo stato," pp. 36–37.

25. Ibid., p. 39.

26. Brandão Sobrinho, *Apreciação*, p. 32.

27. Antonio Gomes Carmo, "A lavoura brasileira e os colonos italianos," pp. 105–9.

28. Werneck, "Despeza," pp. 63–67.

29. Augusto Ramos, "Questões agricolas," pp. 26–28.

30. Brandão Sobrinho, *Apreciação*, pp. 31–32.

31. Gil Vidal, "A politica," p. 1.

32. Carlos Botelho, "Exodo de colonos," pp. 351–52.

33. Eduardo da Silva Prado to Rui Barbosa, 23 April 1901, in the archive of Luis da Silva Prado. I am indebted to Darrell Levi for the use of this source. An Italian analyst confirmed that wage reductions during the "crisis" caused an increase in repatriation to Italy. See Antonio Franceschini, *L'Emigrazione italiana nell'America del Sud*, p. 48.

34. SAR, 1896, p. 80.

35. SAR, 1898, p. 9.

36. SAR, 1900, pp. 99–107.

37. *Bol. Ag.*, 1900, pp. 279, 423.

38. Ibid., 1901, pp. 42, 43, 99, 379, 527.

39. Ibid., 1902, pp. 269, 481, and 1903, pp. 191, 274, 443.

40. Ibid., 1908, pp. 366–68.

41. *Rev. Ag.*, 1902, pp. 370–74. For another detailed justification for planting restrictions, see Carlos Botelho, "Colonização e limitação da plantação cafeeira," pp. 378–83.

42. LDESP-PE, 1903, pp. 7–8.

43. *Bol. Ag.*, 1903, p. 103.

44. *Rev. Ag.*, 1903, pp. 93–96.

45. São Paulo, Secretaria de Agricultura, *O café*, various years.

46. For an analysis of the 1906 crop and the price support scheme it prompted, see Holloway, *Brazilian Coffee*.

47. *Bol. Ag.*, 1907, pp. 366, 467.

48. "O trabalho agrícola," p. 231. See also André Betim Paes Leme, "A fixação de um salario minimo."

49. *R. dos F.*, vol. 2, no. 16; vol. 5, no. 62; and vol. 6, no. 68. See also Sociedade Paulista de Agricultura, *Relatório da directoria*, p. 8.

50. The borer was the same insect that virtually eliminated Ceylon as a coffee exporter in the 1880s. See Laerne, *Brazil and Java*, p. 432. On the borer (*broca*) in São Paulo see the following: SAR, 1925, p. 32; *Bol. Ag.*, 1925, pp. 49–51; RSRB, 1925, pp. 183–84; and RSRB, 1928, p. 291. Data on coffee productivity are from São Paulo, Secretaria de Agricultura, *Estatística agrícola e zootéchnica, 1904–1905*, and São Paulo, Secretaria de Agricultura, *O café*, various years.

51. Varro Neto, "O nomadismo dos colonos," p. 126. See also Antonio dos Santos Figueiredo, "Nomadismo agricola," p. 442.

52. J. Marcondes, *A lavoura de café e o braço agrícola*, pp. 9–10.

53. See, for example, the 1887 reports of the suspicious deaths of two immigrants, miserable living conditions, whippings, and other punishment on the plantations of Henrique Dumont (father of the aviator Santos Dumont), Martinho Prado Júnior, and other planters in the Mogiana zone, in Pedro Brasil Bandecchi, "Documento sobre a imigração italiana em Ribeirão Preto," pp. 601–5. Other reported examples of mistreatment of colonos, most taken from Italian consular reports, are in Michael M. Hall, "The Origins of Mass Immigration in Brazil, 1871–1914," pp. 121–40.

54. SAR, 1896, p. 80.

55. Rossi, "Condizioni," pp. 33–34.

56. Coletti, "Lo stato," p. 42.

57. Gonçalves reported in 1888 that excessive indebtedness was the most important reason colonos abandoned plantations, and for that reason fazendeiros tried to keep their colonos from going into debt. See Gonçalves, *Relatório*, p. 22. When the Department of Agriculture sent Augusto Ramos on an inspection tour of the coffee-producing countries of Spanish America in 1904–5, he reported on the blatant and widespread debt peonage system used to ensure the availability of manpower in the coffee areas of Guatemala and southern Mexico, with an apparent sense of curiosity and discovery. See SAR, 1906, pp. 109, 113. Ramos's report of the trip is reproduced in his *O café*, pp. 287–362.

58. Coletti, "Lo stato," p. 42.

59. See, for example, *Protesto dos lavradores paulistas reunidos na cidade de Amparo*, p. 10, Rossi, "Condizioni," p. 5, and Coletti, "Lo stato," 3:383, 385.

60. Arrigo de Zettiry, "I coloni italiani dello stato di S. Paulo," p. 89.

61. The original law was federal decree 1,150 of 5 January 1904, amended by decree 1,607 of 29 December 1906, and given legal effect by federal executive decree 6,427 of 27 March 1907. The mechanism by which the wage debt guarantee could be

circumvented is discussed in a 1910 Italian consular report, reproduced in *Protesto dos lavradores paulistas*, pp. 10–11.

62. *Bol. Ag.*, 1903, p. 242.

63. *Bol. Ag.*, 1903, p. 297. Meetings in São Carlos and Rio Claro at which planters agreed to attempt these wage ceilings are also reported in *Rev. Ag.*, 1903, pp. 277–78.

64. Carlos Leôncio de Magalhães, "A colonisação das fazendas," pp. 462–63. Higher wages alone were no sure solution to worker mobility. To the extent that immigrants considered colono work a temporary occupation, improved wages would allow them to accumulate savings more rapidly, shortening the time necessary to achieve economic independence, thus contributing to colono transience.

65. *Rev. Ag.*, 1905, p. 116.

66. Pedro Gordilho Paes Leme, "Meios de fazer crescer a produção," pp. 458–62. Leme quoted at length from the Código Rural of the Argentine province of Santa Fé, which, among other measures, provided for the forced induction of "vagabonds" into the army for a three-year period.

67. "O Sr. Ministro da Italia em S. Paulo," p. 1.

68. Antonio de Queiroz Teles, "Lavoura e Imigração," p. 334.

69. Sociedade Paulista de Agricultura, *Sétimo Congresso Agrícola realizado na cidade de Jahu*, pp. 152, 175.

70. *O Faz.*, 1914, pp. 262–63.

71. Article 1,230 of the civil code did not require the new employer to demand an affidavit declaring that the colono had no outstanding contractual obligation to the previous employer. Thus a planter could circumvent the law by claiming ignorance as to his workers' prior activities. See *Anais da Sociedade Rural Brasileira*, 15:918–22.

72. See, for example, Ugolotti, *Italia*, p. 101; Attilio Monaco, "L'immigrazione italiana nello stato di San Paolo del Brasile," p. 47; Rossi, "Condizioni," pp. 20–23; Coletti, "Lo stato," pp. 42, 54, 71.

73. Sociedade Paulista de Agricultura, *Sétimo Congresso Agrícola*, p. 167, and Coletti, "Lo stato," p. 42. For other examples see Dean, *Rio Claro*, p. 171.

74. *Sexto Congresso Agrícola*, pp. 9, 17.

75. Sheldon Maram, "The Immigrant and the Brazilian Labor Movement, 1890–1920." See also J. W. F. Dulles, *Anarchists and Communists in Brazil, 1900–1935*.

76. Rossi, "Condizioni," p. 41, and L. A. Gaffré, *Visions du Brésil*, p. 220.

77. Coletti, "Lo stato," p. 67.

78. Zettiry, "I coloni italiani," pp. 73, 81.

79. Sociedade Paulista de Agricultura, *Sétimo Congresso Agrícola*, p. 165, and Gifun, "Ribeirão Preto," pp. 177–80.

80. "Lo sciopero dei coloni," p. 12, and *Correio Paulistano*, 8 May 1913, p. 2, 23 May 1913, p. 1. Correspondence between Baroli and the Patronato Agricola is reproduced in SAR, 1912–13, pp. 200–205.

81. *Anais da Assembleia Legislativa de São Paulo*, p. 592. The Patronato was created by state law 1299-A of 27 December 1911, and implemented by decree 2214 of 15 March 1912.

82. SAR, 1912–29.

83. SAR, 1914, pp. 171–72.

84. Luiz Pereira Barreto, "A colonisação," pp. 260–64. See also Candido F. de Lacerda, *A crise da lavoura*, pp. 4–5; Vert, "O café barato," pp. 125–28; Marcello Piza, *O trabalho na lavoura de café*, pp. 15–17.

85. Piza, "Colonos." See also Paulo Cuba, "Um apoio firme para o principal alavanca da produção agricola"; Carlos Borges Schmidt, "Systems of Land Tenure in São Paulo"; Baptista Filho, *A fazenda*; "Tipos de trabalhadores rurais no Brasil"; and Pierre Monbeig, *Novos estudos de geografía humana brasileira*.

86. On the coffee complex of northern Paraná see Maxine Margolis, *The Moving Frontier*.

87. Maria Conceição d'Incao e Mello, *O "bóia-fria."*

Chapter 5

1. Dwight B. Heath, "Land Tenure and Social Organization," p. 66. For a general discussion of the problem of rural social structure see Arthur Stinchcombe, "Agricultural Enterprise and Rural Class Relations."

2. See the following: *Bol. Ag.*, 1904, pp. 46–49; SAR, 1907, pp. 46–47; Brazil, Directoria Geral de Estatística, *Recenseamento do Brazil, realizado em 1 de setembro de 1920*, 3,2:ix; São Paulo, Secretaria de Agricultura, *Recenseamento agrícola-zootechnico realizado em 1934*, p. 29.

3. Warren Dean, "Latifundia and Land Policy in Nineteenth-Century Brazil," pp. 607–8, 621–23, and Alberto Passos Guimarães, *Quatro séculos de latifundio*, pp. 41–59.

4. On one such occupation near São Carlos in 1874, see Ellis, *Tenente Coronel*, pp. 252–78. On the subsistence *caipira* see Antonio Cândido, *Os parceiros do Rio Bonito*.

5. Cobra, *Em um recanto*, pp. 10–14.

6. SAR, 1892, pp. 4–5; 1893, pp. 11–13.

7. SAR, 1892, p. 4; 1893, p. 30.

8. SAR, 1897, pp. 29–30.

9. SAR, 1896, pp. 25–28, and Gregorio de Castro Mascarenhas, *Terras devolutas e particulares no estado de S. Paulo*.

10. LDESP-PE, 1900, p. 29.

11. SAR, 1901, pp. 74–97.

12. SAR, 1900, pp. 95–99.

13. SAR, 1901, pp. 99–109.

14. SAR, 1903, pp. 57–60.

15. SAR, 1904, pp. 109–12, and LDESP-PL, 1905, p. 87. See also São Paulo law 2,400 of 9 July 1913.

16. SAR, 1908, p. xxix; 1909, p. 111.

17. SAR, 1909, p. 115; 1912–13, pp. 170, 175.

18. SAR, 1915–16, pp. 283–84; 1917, p. 211.

19. BDET, 12:141.

20. SAR, 1924, p. 93.

21. SAR, 1926, p. 142, and 1930.

22. CPORI-C, No. 21, 4 February 1867, and CPORI-RP, No. 16,432, 30 November 1925.

23. CPORI-C, No. 5,704, 16 April 1900, and No. 11,092, 27 June 1914.

24. CPORI-C, No. 90, 9 December 1868, and CPORI-RP, No. 5,278, 5 May 1904.

25. Francisco Jose Oliveira Vianna, "O povo brasileiro e a sua evolução," p. 309, and Lobato, *A onda verde*, pp. 9–16.

26. SAR, 1893, Annex 2, p. 61.

27. SAR, 1895, pp. 35–36.

28. *O Estado de São Paulo*, 2 September 1896, p. 1, and 6 October 1896, p. 1.

29. SAR, 1897, pp. 30–31, 67.

30. *Rev. Ag.*, 1898, p. 98.

31. Ricardo Fereira de Carvalho, "Parcelamento da grande lavoura," pp. 321–22. Emphasis in original.

32. *Bol. Ag.*, 1901, p. 590, and 1902, p. 50.

33. *Bol. Ag.*, 1907, p. 366.

34. *Bol. Ag.*, 1906, pp. 169–71.

35. Dario Leite de Barros, "Nucleos coloniaes particulares," and Everardo de Sousa, "Nucleos coloniaes."

36. See *Bol. Ag.*, 1908, p. 291, and "Um bom exemplo de colonização."

37. CPORI-C, 1906–12; *O Faz.*, 1908, p. 127; Brazil, Ministério da Agricultura, *Questionário sobre as condições da agricultura*.

38. São Paulo, Secretaria de Agricultura, *Brevi notizie sulla colonizzazione e immigrazione nello stato di San Paolo*, p. 16.

39. See, for example, São Paulo law 2,400 of 9 July 1913, the list of "private" colonies in BDET, 12:140, and the advertisements of the Marcondes Colonization Company for land along the Alta Sorocabana inside the front cover of RSRB, nos. 8, 9, and 10.

40. "O oeste," p. 203.

41. Carlos Mendes, "O operario agricola," p. 163.

42. "As nossas forças productivas."

43. For a sociological study of these early colonies see José de Souza Martins, *A imigração e a crise do Brasil agrário*.

44. Chaves et al., *Relatório*, p. 249. Two of the later colonies were projects of the Federal Repartição do Povoamento do Solo, established in 1907.

45. SAR, 1892, p. 12; 1895, p. 31; and LDESP-PE, 1900, pp. 73–85.

46. SAR, 1900, pp. 111–12.

47. Ernesto Kuhlman, "Imigração," and *Bol. Ag.*, 1901, pp. 691, 695.

48. SAR, 1906, pp. 179–80. The urban center of Campos Salles is now the city of Cosmópolis.

49. SAR, 1904, pp. 119, 132–34.

50. Denis, *Brazil*, pp. 229–31; Dean, *Rio Claro*, pp. 186–87.

51. SAR, 1909, p. 163.

52. See *Bol. Ag.*, 1904, pp. 434–37; SAR, 1907, p. 154; 1908, pp. 171–73; AESP, 1912, 1:22; 1918, 1:20; George F. G. Little, "Fazenda Cambuhy," pp. 62–70.

53. *O Faz.*, 1910, p. 308, and SAR, 1910–11, pp. 145–50.

54. SAR, 1912–13, pp. xlii–xlvi, and *O Faz.*, 1914, pp. 332–33. For a later critique of the nucleo program see *R. dos F.*, 2:16.

55. SAR, 1923, pp. 127–29.

56. *Exposição de motivos da commissão nomeada no III Congresso Agricola reunido em Amparo*, pp. 3–7.

57. AESP, 1918, 1:19–20. On later nucleo schemes in São Paulo see Pierre Monbeig, "The Colonial Nucleus of Barão de Antonina, São Paulo," and João Baptista Borges Pereira, *Italianos no mundo rural paulista*.

58. Barros, "A cultura mechanica," pp. 393–94.

Chapter 6

1. Variations on this itinerary are found in the following: Alessandro d'Atri, *Uomini e cose del Brasile*, pp. 230–38; Marie R. Wright, *The New Brazil*, pp. 203–18, 253–64; Nevin O. Winter, *Brazil and Her People of Today*, pp. 109–32; Charles Domville-Fife, *The United States of Brazil*, pp. 191–210; Clayton S. Cooper, *The Brazilians and Their Country*, pp. 195–212; Frank G. Carpenter, *Along the Paraná and the Amazon*, pp. 128–71.

2. Plantation data are from São Paulo, Secretaria de Agricultura, *Estatística agrícola e zootéchnica, 1904–1905*.

3. Zettiry, "Coloni italiani," p. 76; L. V. Giovannetti, *O Rei do Café*, p. 34; and Rossi, "Condizioni," p. 32.

4. Ugolotti, *Italia*, p. 16, and Foerster, *Italian Emigration*, p. 316.

5. Foerster, *Italian Emigration*, pp. 422–23; Zettiry, "Coloni italiani," pp. 74, 91–94; Gaffré, *Visions*, p. 286.

6. See, for example, Pio de Savoia, "Lo stato," p. 41, and the remarks by Fernando Santos Werneck in *O Estado de São Paulo*, 6 October 1896, p. 1.

7. Monaco, "L'immigrazione," pp. 46–48.

8. Zettiry, "I coloni italiani," p. 84, and Denis, *Brazil*, p. 216.

9. Pio de Savoia, "Lo stato," p. 46.

10. Monaco, "L'immigrazione," p. 42; Pio de Savoia, "Lo stato," p. 51; Coletti, "Lo stato," 3:377.

11. When the rural schools were transferred from the Patronato Agricola to the state

secretary of the interior in 1920 they totaled eighty-seven, including thirty-seven on state-sponsored nucleos and forty-seven on private fazendas, with a total enrollment of 3,958 students. See SAR, 1920, p. 45.

12. Pio de Savoia, "Lo stato," p. 46.

13. Antonio Gomes Carmo, "Uma familia de antigos colonos italianos."

14. On Schmidt see RSRB, vol. 6, no. 60, pp. 207–9. Lunardelli's biography is L. V. Giovannetti, *O Rei do Café*.

15. CPORI-RC, No. 2,676, 24 April 1900, and CPORI-T, Nos. 1,536 and 1,537, 2 July 1914.

16. On the development of urban centers in western São Paulo see the following: Dean, *Rio Claro*, pp. 156–93; Monbeig, "Algumas observações," pp. 609–14; Gifun, "Ribeirão Preto." On Descalvado, see Eunice Ribeiro Durham, *Assimilação e mobilidade*. On São José do Rio Preto, see A. Tavares de Almeida, *O oeste paulista*. On Campos Novos do Paranapanema, see Cobra, *Em um recanto*.

17. CPORI-RP, No. 5,540, 1 April 1905, and CPORI-T, No. 1,513, 24 June 1914.

18. CPORI-RC, No. 2,598, 13 January 1900, and CPORI-RP, No. 5,456, 5 December 1904, No. 6,884, 10 September 1909, No. 6,240, 15 May 1907. Land buyers were only occasionally identified by profession in notarial records. Such surnames as "Hespanhol" or "Alemão" were at times entered into the record when true surnames were not known.

19. CPORI-RP, No. 5,491, 25 January 1905, and No. 6,372, 1 October 1907.

20. Monaco, "L'immigrazione," pp. 52, 54–55.

21. São Paulo, Secretaria de Agricultura, *Estatística agrícola e zootéchnica, 1904–1905*, folder "Ribeirãozinho." The name was changed to Taquaritinga in 1907.

22. Five of the 131 municipios in the western plateau did not tax trees in 1923 and are not included in this survey. The missing units are Piracicaba (zone 4), Socorro (zone 5), Birigui and Lins (zone 8), and Espirito Santo do Turvo (zone 9). These municipios contained 23,346,000 trees, less than 3 percent of the 786,200,000 coffee trees in the western plateau in 1923. See São Paulo, Secretaria de Agricultura, *Estatísticas de produção e commércio do café*, pp. 8–15.

23. The four municipios with 80 percent or more foreign ownership were Rio das Pedras (zone 4), Barra Bonita and Taquaritinga (zone 7), and Conchas (zone 9). See BDET, No. 50–51, 1924, pp. 23–28.

24. The size in hectares corresponding to the size in alqueires for each category is as follows: less than 5 alqueires, less than 12 hectares; 5 to 10 alqueires, 12 to 24 hectares; 10 to 25 alqueires, 24 to 60 hectares; 25 to 50 alqueires, 60 to 121 hectares; 50 to 200 alqueires, 121 to 484 hectares; 200 to 500 alqueires, 484 to 1,210 hectares; more than 500 alqueires, more than 1,210 hectares.

25. São Paulo, Secretaria de Agricultura, *Recenseamento agrícola-zootéchnico*, pp. 29–198.

26. From 1889 through 1907 a total of 4,663 persons became naturalized citizens in all of Brazil. See *Brazilian Yearbook, 1909*, p. 37. That figure is less than 0.3 percent of the 1,740,833 immigrants entering Brazil in the 1889–1907 period. Another

study reported that between 1871 and 1918 a total of 8,962 foreigners were naturalized, including 5,101 Portuguese, 1,388 Italians, 638 Spaniards, 454 Germans, and 1,381 from other countries. See Joaquim da Silva Rocha, *História da colonisação do Brasil*, 3:91–93. The 1920 census counted 9,284 naturalized citizens in São Paulo, 1.1 percent of the 829,851 foreign-born persons in the state in that year. See Brazil, Directoria Geral de Estatística, *Recenseamento do Brazil*, 4:466–67. The "Great Naturalization" of the 1891 constitution, by which all foreigners in Brazil automatically became citizens on 15 November 1889, unless they declared otherwise, became a dead letter for practical purposes. In any case, most immigrants arrived after the date of that law.

27. Of the total population of 6,433,327 in 1934, there were 1,999,271 native Brazilians age twenty-two and older in São Paulo. Of that number, both the parents of 508,000 (25.4 percent) were non-Brazilian. Another 79,989 (4.0 percent) had a non-Brazilian father and a Brazilian mother. Only 29,078 (1.5 percent) had a Brazilian father and a non-Brazilian mother. See *Boletim do Departamento Estadual de Estatística*, 1939, 1:101.

28. São Paulo, Secretaria de Agricultura, *Recenseamento agrícola-zootéchnico*, p. 25.

Chapter 7

1. On the role of coffee in the more general development of São Paulo see Fernando Henrique Cardoso, "O café e a industrialização da cidade de São Paulo"; Wilson Cano, *Raizes da concentração industrial em São Paulo*; Sérgio Silva, *Expansão cafeeira e origens da indústria no Brasil*; Dean, *Industrialization of São Paulo*; and Joseph Love, *São Paulo in the Brazilian Federation, 1889–1937*.

2. For analyses of the 1930 revolution see Boris Fausto, *A revolução de 1930*, and Thomas E. Skidmore, *Politics in Brazil, 1930–1964*, pp. 3–21.

3. A good review of recent research on rural labor in Latin America is Arnold J. Bauer, "Rural Workers in Spanish America." See also Alain de Janvry, "The Political Economy of Rural Development in Latin America."

4. On climatic changes resulting from deforestation see Pierre Monbeig, *Pionniers et planteurs de São Paulo*.

5. Osorio Rezende Mierelles, "Pela lavoura," p. 165, and Ramos, "Questões agricolas," pp. 78–79.

6. Cândido, *Os parceiros*, p. 82.

7. "Estatística agrícola," p. 1020, and São Paulo, Secretaria de Agricultura, *Estatística agrícola e zootéchnica, 1904–1905*. On the problems of native workers in competition with immigrants see Jorge Balán, "Migrações e desenvolvimento capitalista no Brasil," pp. 123–24, 128–29. On the fate of the free blacks in the urban context see Florestan Fernandes, *The Negro in Brazilian Society*.

BIBLIOGRAPHY

Alden, Dauril, and Dean, Warren, eds. *Essays Concerning the Socioeconomic History of Brazil and Portuguese India*. Gainesville, 1977.

Almeida, A. Tavares de. *O oeste paulista; a experiencia etnográfica e cultural*. Rio de Janeiro, 1943.

Amaral, Aristides do. *Aspectos Rurais de São Paulo*. São Paulo, 1929.

Amaral, Luís. *História geral da agricultura brasileira*. São Paulo, 1958.

Anais da II Reunião Brasileira de Antropologia. Bahia, 1957.

Anais da Assembleia Legislativa de São Paulo, 58ª Sessão Ordinaria em 6 de dezembro de 1910. São Paulo, 1911.

Anais da Sociedade Rural Brasileira. no. 15 (1929).

Anais do V Simposio Nacional dos Professôres Universitários de História. Campinas, 1971.

Anais do IX Congresso Brasileiro de Geografia. 5 vols. Rio de Janeiro, 1941–44.

"As nossas forças productivas." *Revista dos Fazendeiros* 3, no. 20 (1920): n.p.

Atri, Alessandro d'. *Uomini e cose del Brasile*. 2d ed. Naples, 1895–96.

Azevedo, Fernando de. *Um trem corre para o oeste*. São Paulo, 1950.

Balán, Jorge, ed. *Centro e periferia no desenvolvimento brasileiro*. São Paulo, 1974.

———. "Migrações e desenvolvimento capitalista no Brasil." In *Centro e periferia no desenvolvimento brasileiro*, edited by Jorge Balán. São Paulo, 1974.

Bandecchi, Pedro Brasil. "Documento sobre a imigração italiana em Ribeirão Preto." *Revista de História*, no. 72 (October–December 1967): 601–12.

Bandeira, Antonio Francisco, Jr. *A industria no estado de São Paulo em 1901*. São Paulo, 1901.

"Bandeirantes do café." *Revista da Sociedade Rural Brasiliera* 4, no. 37 (July 1923): n.p.

Baptista Filho, Olavo. *A fazenda de café em São Paulo*. Rio de Janeiro, 1952.

Barreto, Luiz Pereira. "A colonisação." *Revista Agrícola de São Paulo* (1901): 260–64.

Barros, Dario Leite de. "A cultura mechanica dos cafezais." *Revista Agrícola de São Paulo* (1907): 392–95.

———. "Nucleos coloniaes particulares." *Revista Agrícola de São Paulo* (1907): 535–37.

Barros, Gilberto Leite de. *A cidade e o planalto, processo de dominância da cidade de São Paulo*. 2 vols. São Paulo, 1967.

Bauer, Arnold J. "Rural Workers in Spanish America: Problems of Peonage and Oppression." *Hispanic American Historical Review* 59, no. 1 (February 1979): 34–63.

Beiguelman, Paula. *A formação do povo no complexo cafeeiro; aspectos políticos.* São Paulo, 1968.

―――. *Pequenos estudos de ciência política.* 2 vols. São Paulo, 1968.

Bertarelli, Ernesto. *Il Brasile Meridionale; ricordi e impressione.* Rome, 1914.

Bethell, Leslie. *The Abolition of the Brazilian Slave Trade.* Cambridge, England, 1970.

Blount, John A. "The Public Health Movement in São Paulo, Brazil: A History of the Sanitary Service, 1892–1918." Ph.D. dissertation, Tulane University, 1971.

Boletim da Directoria de Terras, Colonisação e immigração, no. 1 (October 1937).

Boletim do Departamento Estadual de Estatística 1, no. 1 (January 1939).

Boletim do Departamento Estadual do Trabalho. São Paulo, 1912–30.

Boletim do Departamento do Trabalho Agrícola. São Paulo, 1930–34.

Botelho, Carlos. "Colonização e limitação da plantação cafeeira." *Revista Agrícola de São Paulo* (1902): 378–83.

―――. "Emprego das carpideiras na lavoura de café." *Revista Agrícola de São Paulo* (1899): 43–50.

―――. "Exodo de colonos." *Revista Agrícola de São Paulo* (1899): 350–52.

Braga, Cincinato. *Magnos Problemas Economicos de São Paulo.* São Paulo, 1924.

Brandão Sobrinho, Júlio. *Apreciação da situação agricola, zootechnica, industrial, e commercial do 3° districto agronomico do estado de S. Paulo com sede em Ribeirão Preto.* São Paulo, 1903.

Brazil, Departamento Nacional do Café. *Anuário estatístico.* Rio de Janeiro, 1935, 1938.

―――. *O café no segundo centenário de sua introdução no Brasil.* 2 vols. Rio de Janeiro, 1934.

Brazil, Directoria Geral de Estatística. *Recenseamento do Brazil, realizado em 1 de setembro de 1920.* 40 vols. Rio de Janeiro, 1922–30.

Brazil, Ministério da Agricultura. *Questionário sobre as condições da agricultura dos 173 municípios do Estado de São Paulo de abril de 1910 a janeiro de 1912.* Rio de Janeiro, 1913.

The Brazilian Yearbook, 1909. Rio de Janeiro, n.d.

Camargo, José Francisco de. *Crescimento da população do estado de São Paulo e seus aspectos econômicos.* 3 vols. São Paulo, 1952.

Cândido, Antonio. *Os parceiros do Rio Bonito.* 2d ed. São Paulo, 1971.

Cannabrava, Alice Pifer. *O desenvolvimento da cultura do algodão na província de São Paulo, 1861–1875.* São Paulo, 1951.

Cano, Wilson. *Raizes da concentração industrial em São Paulo.* São Paulo, 1977.

Cardoso, Fernando Henrique. "O café e a industrialização da cidade de São Paulo." *Revista de História* 20, no. 42 (April–June 1960): 471–75.

Carmo, Antonio Gomes. "A lavoura brasileira e os colonos italianos." *Revista Agrícola de São Paulo* (1898): 105–9.

———. *Considerações históricas sôbre a agricultura no Brasil.* Rio de Janeiro, 1939.

———. "Uma familia de antigos colonos italianos." *Revista Agrícola de São Paulo* (1898): 113–14.

Carneiro, Balthazar da Silva. "O trabalho e a locação de serviços." *Jornal do Agricultor* 7, no. 14 (1886): 9–12.

Carone, Edgard. *A república velha, instituições e classes sociais.* São Paulo, 1970.

Carpenter, Frank G. *Along the Paraná and the Amazon.* Garden City, N.Y., 1926.

Carvalho, Augusto de. *Estudo sobre a colonisação e emigração para o Brazil.* Oporto, 1874.

Carvalho, C. M. Delgado de. *Le Brésil Méridional, étude économique.* Paris, 1910.

Carvalho, Péricles de Mello. "A legislação." *Revista de Imigração e Colonização* 1, no. 4 (October 1940): 719–36.

Carvalho, Ricardo Fereira de. "Parcelamento da grande lavoura." *Revista Agrícola de São Paulo* (1901): 319–24.

Castaldi, Carlo. "Considerações sobre o processo de ascensão social do imigrante italiano em São Paulo." *Anais da II Reunião Brasileira de Antropologia.* Bahia, 1957.

Castro, João do Amaral. *A colheita natural.* [São Paulo], 1924.

———. "Um novo sistema de cultura e colheita do café." *Anais da Sociedade Rural Brasileira,* no. 10 (April 1921): 607–11.

Cenni, Franco. *Italianos no Brasil.* São Paulo, [1959].

Chaves, Elias Antonio Pacheco e, et al. *Relatório apresentado ao Exmo. Sr. Presidente da Província de São Paulo pela Commissão Central de Estatística.* São Paulo, 1888.

Clough, Shepard B. *Economic History of Modern Italy.* New York, 1964.

Cobra, Amador Nogueira. *Em um recanto do sertão paulista.* São Paulo, 1923.

Coletti, Silvio. "Lo stato di S. Paolo e l'emigrazione italiana." *Bolletino dell'Emigrazione,* no. 14 (1908): 3–77; no. 15 (1908): 3–100.

———. "Lo stato di S. Paolo e l'emigrazione italiana." In *Emigrazione e Colonie,* vol. 3, Rome, 1908: 360–89.

Conrad, Robert. *The Destruction of Brazilian Slavery, 1850–1888.* Berkeley and Los Angeles, 1972.

"Contractos de trabalho nas fazendas." *Revista dos Fazendeiros* 3, nos. 30–31 (July 1920): n.p.

Cooper, Clayton S. *The Brazilians and Their Country.* New York, 1917.

Correio Paulistano [newspaper], 8 May 1913; 23 May 1913.

Costa, Emília Viotti da. *Da senzala à colônia.* São Paulo, 1966.

Couty, Louis. *Le Brésil en 1884.* Rio de Janeiro, 1884.

———. *Pequena propriedade e immigração europea.* Rio de Janeiro, 1887.

Cuba, Paulo. "Um apoio firme para o principal alavanca da produção agricola." *Revista de Agricultura* 14, nos. 1–2 (1939): 17–32.

Cusano, Alfredo. *Italia d'oltro mare: impressioni e ricordi dei miei cinque anni di Brasile*. Milan, 1911.

Dafert, F. W. *Colleção dos trabalhos agrícolas extrahidos dos relatórios annuaes de 1888–1893, do Instituto Agronômico do Estado de S. Paulo (Brazil) em Campinas*. São Paulo, 1895.

Davatz, Thomas. *Memórias de um colono no Brasil (1850)*. Translation and Preface by Sérgio Buarque de Hollanda. São Paulo, 1941.

Davis, Horace B., and Davis, Marian Rubins. "Scale of Living of the Working Class in São Paulo, Brazil." *Monthly Labor Review* 44, no. 1 (January 1937): 245–53.

Dean, Warren. *The Industrialization of São Paulo, 1880–1945*. Austin, 1969.

———. "Latifundia and Land Policy in Nineteenth-Century Brazil." *Hispanic American Historical Review* 51, no. 4 (November 1971): 606–25.

———. *Rio Claro, A Brazilian Plantation System, 1820–1920*. Stanford, 1976.

Deffontaines, Pierre. "As feiras de burro de Sorocaba." *Geografia* 1, no. 3 (1935): 263–70.

———. "Investigações sôbre os tipos de povoamento no estado de São Paulo." *Boletim Geográfico* 5, no. 51 (1948): 249.

———. "Regiões e paisagens do estado de São Paulo." *Boletim Geográfico* 2, no. 24 (March 1945): 1837–1850; 3, no. 25 (April 1945): 18–27.

Della Cava, Ralph. "The Italian Immigrant Experience: Views of a Latin-Americanist." In *Perspectives on Italian Immigration and Ethnicity*, edited by S. M. Tomasi. New York, 1977.

Denis, Pierre. *Brazil*. New York, 1911.

Diégues, Manuel, Jr. *Imigração, urbanização, industrialização*. Rio de Janeiro, 1964.

Diniz, José Alexandre F. "Evolução das propriedades agrícolas do município de Araras." *Anais do V Simposio Nacional dos Professôres Universitários de História*. Campinas, 1971.

Domville-Fife, Charles. *The United States of Brazil*. London, 1910.

Dore, Grazia. *Bibliografia per la storia dell'emigrazione italiana in America*. Rome, 1956.

Dulles, J. W. F. *Anarchists and Communists in Brazil, 1900–1935*. Austin, 1973.

Duncan, Julian S. *Public and Private Operation of Railroads in Brazil*. New York, 1932.

Duncan, Kenneth, and Rutledge, Ian, eds. *Land and Labour in Latin America*. Cambridge, England, 1977.

Durham, Eunice Ribeiro. "A mobilidade do imigrante italiano na zona rural." *Revista do Museu Paulista*, n.s. 14 (1963): 299–310.

———. *Assimilação e mobilidade; a história do imigrante italiano num município paulista*. São Paulo, 1966.

Egas, Eugenio. *Galeria dos presidentes de São Paulo*. 3 vols. São Paulo, 1927.

Eisenberg, Peter L. "Abolishing Slavery: The Process on Pernambuco's Sugar Planta-
tions." *Hispanic American Historical Review* 52, (November 1972): 580–97.
————. *The Sugar Industry in Pernambuco: Modernization Without Change, 1840–
1910*. Berkeley and Los Angeles, 1974.
Ellis, Alfredo, Jr. *Tenente Coronel Francisco da Cunha Bueno, pioneiro da cafei-
cultura no oeste paulista*. São Paulo, 1960.
O Estado de São Paulo [newspaper], 2 September 1896; 6 October 1896.
"Estatística agrícola do município de São Carlos do Pinhal organizada pelo Club da
Lavoura, 1899." *Revista do Instituto do Café* 27, no. 161 (1940): 1017–28.
*Exposição de motivos da commissão nomeada no III Congresso Agricola reunido em
Amparo para representar ao Governo do Estado sobre immigração e colonização
nos nucleos coloniaes*. São Paulo, [1911].
Fausto, Boris. *A revolução de 1930: historiografia e história*. São Paulo, 1972.
Fernandes, Florestan. "O café na evolução de São Paulo." *Revista de História* 19,
no. 40 (October–December 1959): 435–38.
————. *The Negro in Brazilian Society*. New York, 1969.
Figueiredo, Antonio dos Santos. "Nomadismo agricola." *Revista da Sociedade Rural
Brasileira*, no. 113 (October 1929): 442.
Foerster, Robert F. *The Italian Emigration of Our Times*. Cambridge, Mass., 1919.
Franceschini, Antonio. *L'Emigrazione italiana nell'America del Sud*. Rome, 1908.
Freitas, Affonso A. de. *Geographia do Estado de São Paulo*. São Paulo, 1906.
Freyre, Gilberto. *The Masters and the Slaves*. New York, 1946.
Furtado, Celso. *The Economic Growth of Brazil*. Berkeley and Los Angeles, 1965.
Gaffré, L. A. *Visions du Brésil*. Paris, 1912.
Gerschenkron, Alexander. "Notes on the Role of Industrial Growth in Italy, 1881–
1913." *Journal of Economic History* 15, no. 4 (December 1955): 360–75.
Ghinassi, P. "Per le nostre colonie." *L'Italia Coloniale* 2 (February 1901): 16–55.
Gifun, Frederick V. "Ribeirão Prêto, 1880–1914: The Rise of a Coffee County, or the
Transition to Coffee in São Paulo as Seen Through the Eyes of its Leading
Producer." Ph.D. dissertation, University of Florida, 1972.
Giovannetti, L. V. *O Rei do Café—Geremia Lunardelli*. São Paulo, 1951.
Gonçalves, Francisco de Paula Lázaro. *Relatório apresentado à Associação Promo-
tora de Immigração em Minas*. Juiz de Fora, 1888.
Graham, Douglas H. "Migração estrangeira e a questão da oferta de mão-de-obra no
crescimento econômico brasileiro, 1880–1930." *Estudos econômicos* 3, no. 1
(April 1973): 7–64.
Graham, Richard. *Britain and the Onset of Modernization in Brazil*. London, 1968.
Greenfield, Gerald M. "The Challenge of Growth: The Growth of Urban Public
Services in São Paulo, 1885–1913." Ph.D. dissertation, Indiana University,
1975.
Grossi, Vincenzo. *Storia della colonizzazione europea al Brasile e della emigrazione
italiana nello stato di S. Paulo*. Rome, 1905.
Guimarães, Alberto Passos. *Quatro séculos de latifúndio*. São Paulo, 1964.

Hall, Michael M. "The Origins of Mass Immigration in Brazil, 1871–1914." Ph.D. dissertation, Columbia University, 1969.

Heath, Dwight B. "Land Tenure and Social Organization: An Ethno-Historical Study from the Bolivian Oriente." *Inter-American Economic Affairs* 13, no. 4 (Spring 1960): 46–66.

Hennessy, Alistair. *The Frontier in Latin American History*. Albuquerque, 1978.

Henry, Jules. *Jungle People*. 2d ed. New York, 1964.

Hollanda, Sérgio Buarque de. "As colônias de parceria." In *História geral da civilização brasileira*, edited by Sérgio Buarque de Hollanda, tomo II, vol. 3. São Paulo, 1969.

―――, ed. *História geral da civilização brasileira*. Multivolume. São Paulo, 1960–.

Holloway, Thomas H. *The Brazilian Coffee Valorization of 1906: Regional Politics and Economic Dependence*. Madison, 1975.

―――. "Creating the Reserve Army? The Immigration Program of São Paulo, 1886–1930." *International Migration Review* 12, no. 2 (Summer 1978): 187–209.

―――. "Immigration and Abolition: The Transition from Slave to Free Labor in the São Paulo Coffee Zone." In *Essays Concerning the Socioeconomic History of Brazil and Portuguese India*, edited by Dauril Alden and Warren Dean. Gainesville, 1977.

―――. "Migration and Mobility: Immigrants as Laborers and Landowners in the Coffee Zone of São Paulo, Brazil, 1886–1934." Ph.D. dissertation, University of Wisconsin, 1974.

Humphrey, Alice R. *A Summer Journey in Brazil*. New York, 1900.

Hutchinson, Bertram A., et al. *Mobilidade e trabalho*. Rio de Janeiro, [1960].

Hutter, Lucy Maffei. "Imigração italiana em São Paulo, 1880–1889: os primeiros contactos do imigrante com o Brasil." Ph.D. dissertation, Universidade de São Paulo, 1971.

In Memoriam, Martinho Prado Júnior. São Paulo, 1944.

Italy, Istituto Centrale di Statistica. *Sommario di statistiche storiche italiane*, 1861–1955. Rome, 1958.

James, Preston. "The Coffee Lands of Southeastern Brazil." *Geographical Review* 22, no. 2, (April 1932): 225–41.

Janvry, Alain de. "The Political Economy of Rural Development in Latin America: An Interpretation." *American Journal of Agricultural Economics* 57 (1975): 490–99.

Knowlton, Clark S. *Sírios e libaneses, mobilidade social e espacial*. São Paulo, 1960.

Kuhlman, Ernesto. "Immigração." *Revista Agrícola de São Paulo*, supp. 69 (1901): 27–40.

Lacerda, Candido F. de. *A crise da lavoura; estudo das causas da crise do café e os meios de combate-la*. São Paulo, 1903.

Laerne, C. F. Van Delden. *Brazil and Java*. London, 1885.

Lalière, Amour. *Le Café dans l'état de Saint Paul.* Paris, 1909.

Leme, André Betim Paes. "A fixação de um salario minimo." *Revista dos Fazendeiros* 5, no. 56 (15 February 1922): n.p.

Leme, Pedro Gordilho Paes. "Meios de fazer crescer a produção." *Revista Agrícola de São Paulo* (1900): 458–62.

Levi, Darrell. *A família Prado.* São Paulo, 1977.

Little, George F. G. "Fazenda Cambuhy: A Case History of Social and Economic Development in the Interior of São Paulo, Brazil." Ph.D dissertation, University of Florida, 1960.

Lobato, José Bento Monteiro. *A onda verde.* São Paulo, 1920.

Love, Joseph. *São Paulo in the Brazilian Federation, 1889–1937.* Stanford, 1980.

Lowrie, Samuel Harman. *Imigração e crescimento da população no estado de São Paulo.* São Paulo, 1938.

Maeyama, Takashi. "Familialization of the Unfamiliar World: The Familia, Networks, and Groups in a Brazilian City." Ph.D dissertation, Cornell University, 1975.

Magalhães, Carlos Leôncio de. "A colonisação das fazendas." *Revista da Sociedade Rural Brasileira*, no. 38 (August 1923): 461–63.

Maldonado, Mario. "A cultura mechanica dos cafeerios." *O Fazendeiro* (1909): 302–3.

Manchester, Allen K. *British Preeminence in Brazil, Its Rise and Decline.* Chapel Hill, 1933.

Maram, Sheldon. "The Immigrant and the Brazilian Labor Movement, 1890–1920." In *Essays Concerning the Socioeconomic History of Brazil and Portuguese India*, edited by Dauril Alden and Warren Dean. Gainesville, 1977.

Marcondes, J. *A lavoura de café e o braço agrícola.* Rio de Janeiro, 1899.

Marcondes, J. V. Freitas, and Smith, T. Lynn. "The Caipira of the Paraitinga Valley." *Social Forces* 31, no. 1 (October 1952): 47–53.

Margolis, Maxine. *The Moving Frontier; Social and Economic Change in a Southern Brazilian Community.* Gainesville, 1973.

Martins, Dias. "A escolha do sitio para café." In *O café no segundo centenário de sua introdução no Brasil*, vol. 1, pp. 350–52. Rio de Janeiro, 1934.

Martins, José de Souza. *A imigração e a crise do Brasil agrário.* São Paulo, 1973.

Mascarenhas, Gregorio de Castro. *Terras devolutas e particulares no estado de S. Paulo.* 2d ed., rev. São Paulo, 1912.

Matos, Odilon Nogueira de. *Café e ferrovias.* 2d ed. São Paulo, 1974.

Mattoon, Robert H., Jr. "Railroads, Coffee, and the Growth of Big Business in São Paulo, Brazil." *Hispanic American Historical Review* 57, no. 2 (May 1977): 273–95.

Mello, Afonso Bandeira de. "A emigração italiana no Brasil." *Correio Paulistano* [newspaper], 15 May 1913, p. 1.

Mello, Jorge. *Pela lavoura.* São Paulo, 1918.

———. *A terra do café.* São Paulo, 1919.

Mello, Maria Conceição d'Incao e. *O "bóia-fria": acumulação e miséria*. 4th ed. Petrópolis, 1976.

Mendes, Carlos. "O operario agricola: a colheita do café." *Revista da Sociedade Rural Brasileira*, nos. 33–34 (March–April 1923): 159–63.

Mendes Sobrinho, Octavio Teixeira. "Tamanho da propriedade no estado de São Paulo," *São Paulo Agrícola* 2, no. 13 (1960): 54–59.

Merrick, Thomas, and Graham, Douglas. *Population and Economic Development in Brazil, 1800 to the Present*. Baltimore, 1979.

Mierelles, Osorio Rezende. "Pela lavoura." *Revista Agrícola de São Paulo* (1899): 123–69.

Milliet, Sérgio. *Roteiro do café e outros ensaios*. 3d ed. São Paulo, 1941.

Mintz, Sidney. "The So-called World System: Local Initiative and Local Response." *Dialectical Anthropology* 2 (1977): 253–70.

Monaco, Attilio. "L'immigrazione italiana nello stato di San Paolo del Brasile." *Bolletino dell'Emigrazione*, no. 8 (1902): 31–55.

Monbeig, Pierre. "Algumas observações sobre Marília, cidade pioneira do estado de São Paulo." *Anais do IX Congresso Brasileiro de Geografia* 3 (1941–44): 609–14.

———. "The Colonial Nucleus of Barão de Antonina, São Paulo." *Geographical Review* 30 (April 1940): 260–71.

———. *Novos estudos de geografia humana brasileira*. São Paulo, 1957.

———. *Pionniers et planteurs de São Paulo*. Paris, 1952.

Monteiro, Norma de Góes. "Esboço da política imigratória e colonizadora do govêrno de Minas Gerais; 1889 a 1930." *Revista Brasileira de Estudos Políticos* 29 (July 1970): 195–216.

Morais, João Pedro Carvalho de. *Relatório apresentado ao Ministro da Agricultura*. Rio de Janeiro, 1870.

Morse, Richard M. *From Community to Metropolis*. Gainesville, 1958.

Mortara, Giorgio. "Bibliografia sôbre a emigração italiana para o Brasil." *Revista Brasileira de Estatística* 17, no. 68 (October–December 1956): 308–23.

"Movimento migratório no estado de São Paulo." *Boletim da Diretoria de Terras, Colonização e Imigração*, no. 1 (October 1937): 46–50.

Nogueira, Arlinda Rocha. *A imigração japonesa para a lavoura cafeeira paulista, 1909–1922*. São Paulo, 1973.

Normano, J. F. *Brazil, A Study of Economic Types*. 2d ed. New York, 1968.

Nougués, Luiz. "Estudo sobre a lavoura cafeeira do estado de S. Paulo." *Revista do DNC* 1, no. 11 (May 1934): 673–718.

"Nova 'carpideira' de cafesal." *Revista Agrícola de São Paulo* (1907): 558–60.

O café no segundo centenário de sua introdução no Brasil. 2 vols. Rio de Janeiro, 1934.

"O oeste do estado de São Paulo." *O Fazendeiro* (1917): 202–3.

"O Sr. Ministro da Italia em S. Paulo." *Jornal do Commércio* [newspaper, Rio de Janeiro], 28 February 1898, p. 1.

Pereira, João Baptista Borges. *Italianos no mundo rural paulista.* São Paulo, 1974.

Pereira, Rubens Salomé. *The State of São Paulo, Brazil: Facts, Notes on Statistics, Useful Information.* São Paulo, 1933.

Pescatello, Ann. "Both Ends of the Journey: An Historical Study of Migration and Change in Brazil and Portugal, 1889–1914." Ph.D dissertation, University of California, Los Angeles, 1970.

Pestana, Paulo Rangel. *O café em São Paulo (notas históricas).* São Paulo, 1927.

Petrone, Maria Thereza Schorer. *A lavoura canavieira em São Paulo; expansão e declinio, 1765–1851.* São Paulo, 1968.

Piccarolo, Antonio. *L'Emigrazione italiana nello stato di S. Paulo.* São Paulo, 1911.

Pinto, Adolpho A. *História da viação pública de São Paulo, Brasil.* São Paulo, 1903.

Pio di Savoia, Gherardo. "Lo stato di San Paolo (Brasile) e l'emigrazione italiana." *Bolletino dell'Emigrazione,* no. 3 (1905): 3–119.

Piza, Flavio M. de Toledo. "Colonos." *Revista de Agricultura* 7, nos. 5–6 (1932): 207–11.

Piza, Marcello. *O trabalho na lavoura de café: novo rumo.* [São Paulo], 1929.

Platt, Robert S. "Coffee Plantations of Brazil, A Comparison of Occupance Patterns in Established and Frontier Areas." *Geographical Review* 25 (1939): 231–39.

Prado, Caio, Jr. *The Colonial Background of Modern Brazil.* Berkeley and Los Angeles, 1967.

———. "Distribuição da propriedade fundária rural no estado de São Paulo." *Boletim Geográfico,* no. 29 (August 1945): 692–700.

———. *História Econômica do Brasil.* 13th ed., rev. São Paulo, 1970.

Protesto dos lavradores paulistas reunidos na cidade de Amparo, estado de S. Paulo em 20 de junho de 1911, contra inverdades contidas no relatorio distribuido pelo Ministerio das Relações Exteriores da Italia no Anno de 1910. Amparo, 1911.

A provincia de São Paulo no Brazil, emigrante: lede este folheto antes de partir. São Paulo, 1886.

"Questões agrícolas." *Revista Agrícola de São Paulo* (1902): 130.

Ramos, Augusto F. *O café no Brasil e no estrangeiro.* Rio de Janeiro, 1923.

———. "Questões agricolas." *Revista Agrícola de São Paulo* (1902): 26–28.

Rangoni, Domenico. *Il lavoro collettivo degli italiani al Brasile.* São Paulo, 1902.

Revista do DNC 1, no. 6 (December 1933): 702–3.

Riccardi, Adelino. "Parnaíba, o pioneiro da imigração." *Revista do Arquivo Municipal* 44 (February 1938): 136–84.

Rios, José Arthur. *Aspectos políticos da assimilação do italiano no Brasil.* São Paulo, 1959.

Rocha, Joaquim da Silva. *História da colonisação do Brasil.* 3 vols. Rio de Janeiro, 1918–20.

Rodrigues, Duarte. *Discurso pronunciado no congresso dos lavradores paulistas reunido em Campinas a 26 de março de 1899.* São Paulo, 1899.

Rossi, Adolfo. "Attraverso le 'Fazendas' dello Stato di San Paolo (Brasile)." *Rivista d'Italia* (October 1902): 639–50.

———. "Condizioni dei coloni italiani nello stato di San Paolo (Brasile)." *Bollettino dell'Emigrazione*, no. 7 (1902): 3–88.

Saito, Hiroshi. *O japonês no Brasil*. São Paulo, 1961.

São Paulo, Commissão Geográphica e Geológica. *Exploração do rio Peixe*. 2d ed. São Paulo, 1913.

———. *Exploração dos rios Feio e Aguapehy*. São Paulo, 1906.

São Paulo, Departamento Estadual de Estatística. *Anuario Estatístico do Estado de São Paulo*. Annual, 1901–29.

———. *Ensaio de um quadro do desmembramento dos municípios*. 4th ed. São Paulo, 1947.

———. *Publicação, 1889–1939*. São Paulo, 1940.

———. *Recenseamento demográfico, escolar e agrícola-zootéchnico do Estado de São Paulo, 20 setembro 1934*. São Paulo, 1935.

São Paulo, Repartição de Estatística. *Relatório*. Annual, 1894–1900.

São Paulo, Secretaria de Agricultura. *Brevi notizie sulla colonizzazione e immigrazione nello stato di San Paolo*. São Paulo, n.d. [c. 1910].

———. *O café, estatísticas de produção e exportação*. Annual, irreg., 1914–38.

———. *Catálogo da bibliotheca*. São Paulo, 1931.

———. *Dados para a história da immigração e da colonização em São Paulo*. São Paulo, 1916.

———. *Estatística agrícola e zootéchnica, 1904–1905*. 5 vols. São Paulo, 1906–10.

———. *Estatística agrícola e zootéchnica*. Annual, 1930/31 to 1939/40, except for 1933/34, 1936/37, and 1938/39.

———. *Estatísticas de produção e commércio do café, 1921–1930*. São Paulo, 1931.

———. *A immigração e as condicões do trabalho em São Paulo*. São Paulo, 1915.

———. *Lavoura cafeeira paulista e sua distribuição por nacionalidade, 1932–33*. São Paulo, n.d.

———. *Recenseamento agrícola-zootéchnico realizado em 1934; estudo dos estabelecimentos agrícolas, segundo a nacionalidade dos proprietários e a extensão territorial*. São Paulo, 1936.

———. *Relatório*. Annual, 1892–1930.

———. *Lo stato di S. Paolo (Brasile) agli emigranti*. São Paulo, 1902.

São Paulo, Secretaria da Fazenda. *Relatório, 1909*. São Paulo, 1910.

Schmidt, Carlos Borges. "Systems of Land Tenure in São Paulo." *Rural Sociology* 8 (September 1943): 242–47.

Schmidt, Cornélio. "Diário de uma viagem pelo sertão de São Paulo realizada em 1904." *Anais do Museu Paulista* 15 (1961): 337–458.

"Lo sciopero dei coloni." *Rivista Coloniale* 4, no. 11 (May 1913): 12.

Seckler, Jorge, comp. *Almanach de Província de São Paulo*. São Paulo, 1888.

Segundo Congresso Agrícola do 2° Districto Agronômico do Estado de S. Paulo reunido na cidade de Campinas em dezembro de 1910. Campinas, 1911.

Setzer, Jorge. *Os solos do estado de São Paulo*. Rio de Janeiro, 1949.

Sexto Congresso Agrícola do Estado de São Paulo, reunido na cidade de Piracicaba, dezembro de 1912. Piracicaba, 1912.

Silva, Sérgio. *Expansão cafeeira e origens da indústria no Brasil.* São Paulo, 1976.

Simonsen, Roberto C. "Aspectos da história econômica do café." *Revista do Arquivo Municipal* 65 (March 1940): 149–226.

————. "Recursos econômicos e movimentos das populações." *Revista Brasileira de Estatística* 1, no. 2 (April–June 1940): 199–228.

Skidmore, Thomas E. *Politics in Brazil, 1930–1964.* New York, 1967.

Slenes, Robert. "The Demography and Economics of Brazilian Slavery: 1850–1888." Ph.D. dissertation, Stanford University, 1976.

Smith, T. Lynn. *Brazil: People and Institutions.* 4th ed. Baton Rouge, 1972.

Sociedade Paulista de Agricultura. *Relatório referente ao ano de 1908, apresentado á Assembléa Geral Ordinaria em 30 de março de 1909.* São Paulo, 1909.

————. *Relatório da directoria: exercicio de 1922.* São Paulo, 1923.

————. *Sétimo Congresso Agrícola realizado na cidade de Jahu, 1913.* São Paulo, 1913.

Società Geografica Italiana. "Indagini sulla emigrazione italiana all'estero fatte per cura della Società, 1888–1889." *Memorie della Società Geografica Italiana* 4 (1890): 1–336.

Sousa, Antonieta de Paula. "Expansão da propriedade rural paulista." *Anais do IX Congresso Brasileiro de Geografia* 3 (1944): 710–14.

Sousa, Everardo de. "Nucleos coloniaes." *O Fazendeiro* (1908): 143–45.

Stein, Stanley J. *Vassouras, A Brazilian Coffee County, 1850–1900.* Cambridge, Mass., 1957.

Stein, Stanley J., and Stein, Barbara H. *The Colonial Heritage of Latin America.* New York, 1970.

Stinchcombe, Arthur. "Agricultural Enterprise and Rural Class Relations." *American Journal of Sociology* 67 (1961–62): 165–76.

Taunay, Affonso de Escragnolle. *História do café no Brasil.* 15 vols. Rio de Janeiro, 1939–42.

Taylor, George Rogers, ed. *The Turner Thesis: Concerning the Role of the Frontier in American History.* 3d ed. Lexington, Mass., 1972.

Teles, Antonio de Queiroz. "Lavoura e Imigração." *Revista da Sociedade Rural Brasileira*, no. 102 (November 1928): 331–34.

"Tipos de trabalhadores rurais no Brasil." *Conjuntura Econômica* 10, no. 12 (December 1956): 71–77.

Tomasi, S. M., ed. *Perspectives on Italian Immigration and Ethnicity.* New York, 1977.

Toplin, Robert Brent. *The Abolition of Slavery in Brazil.* New York, 1972.

"O trabalho agrícola." *O Fazendeiro* (1916): 231.

Ugolotti, Filippo. *Italia e italiani in Brasile; note e appunti.* São Paulo, 1897.

"Um bom exemplo de colonização." *O Fazendeiro* (1909): 148–49.

United States Bureau of Census. *Historical Statistics of the United States, Colonial Times to 1957.* Washington, D.C., 1960.

Varro Neto. "O nomadismo dos colonos." *Revista da Sociedade Rural Brasileira,* no. 107 (April 1929): 126.

Veiga Filho, João Pedro da. *Estudo econômico e financeiro sobre o Estado de S. Paulo.* São Paulo, 1896.

Velloso, José Ferreira. "Colheita do café." *Revista do DNC* 2, no. 21 (March 1935): 401–3.

Vergueiro, José. *Memorial acêrca de colonisação e cultivo de café.* Campinas, 1874.

Vert, Germano. "O café barato." *Revista Agrícola de São Paulo* (1902): 125–28.

Vianna, Francisco Jose Oliveira. "O povo brasileiro e a sua evolução." In Brazil, Directoria Geral de Estatística, *Recenseamento do Brazil realizado em 1 de setembro de 1920,* vol. 1, pp. 279–400.

Vidal, Gil. "A politica: ainda a lavoura." *Correio de Manhã* [newspaper, Rio de Janeiro], 18 January 1903, p. 1.

Waibel, Leo. "The Tropical Plantation System." *Scientific Monthly* 52 (February 1941): 156–60.

Walle, Paul. *Au pays de l'or rouge.* Paris, 1921.

Wallerstein, Immanuel. *The Modern World–System: Capitalist Agriculture and the Origins of the European World-Economy in the Sixteenth Century.* New York, 1974.

————. "The Rise and Future Demise of the World Capitalist System: Concepts for Comparative Analysis." *Comparative Studies in Society and History* 16, no. 4 (September 1974): 387–415.

Ward, Robert DeCourcy. "A Visit to the Brazilian Coffee Country." *National Geographic* 22 (October 1911): 908–32.

Werneck, Santos. "Despeza e receita do café." *Revista Agrícola de São Paulo* (1899): 1–7.

Wickizer, Vernon Dale. *The World Coffee Economy, with Special Reference to Control Schemes.* Stanford, 1943.

Winter, Nevin O. *Brazil and Her People of Today.* Boston, 1910.

Wolf, Eric, and Mintz, Sidney. "Haciendas and Plantations in Middle America and the Antilles." *Social and Economic Studies* 6 (September 1957): 380–412.

Wright, Marie R. *The New Brazil.* Philadelphia, 1907.

Zettiry, Arrigo de. "I coloni italiani dello stato di S. Paulo." *Rassegna Nazionale* 70 (1 March 1893): 59–96.

INDEX